MORE PRAISE FOR

GiRL GANGS, ZiNES, AND POWERSLIDES

"A take-everywhere-and-read-it book that is an accomplished and accessible piece of research. Each chapter — which showcases the personal reflections, anecdotes, and backstories of remarkable women — is a banger. All thriller, no filler. Natalie Porter shreds through the grip-taped ceiling, which has often held back or obscured women's contributions in skateboarding."
— Dr. Indigo Willing, sociologist and lead researcher of Skate, Create, Educate and Regenerate and co-author of *Skateboarding, Power and Change*

"With sharp research and a keen eye for the overlooked change-maker, Natalie Porter masterfully presents stories that document the fact that women have always been skateboarding, despite being routinely left out of the narrative. *Girl Gangs, Zines, and Powerslides* entertains and enlightens — a must read."
— Betsy Gordon, curator of *Ramp It Up: Skateboarding Culture in Native America* and co-author of *Four Wheels and a Board: The Smithsonian History of Skateboarding*

"Reading *Girl Gangs, Zines, and Powerslides* grounded me in a history I never knew I was part of. Natalie Porter has revealed just how many women came before me who built scenes, shaped culture, and pushed boundaries. This book reclaims a legacy that was always there but had been buried or erased. Thank you, Natalie, for giving us back our past and lighting the way forward."
— Annie Guglia, Olympic skateboarder

"Flowing with intelligent research and gritty determination, Porter is a rock 'n' rogue historian of subversive proportions."
— Amy Mattes, author of *Late September*

"In *Girl Gangs, Zines, and Powerslides*, Natalie Porter embarks on a deeply personal quest to archive the marginalized history of skateboarding's women and non-binary figures. Porter documents a thriving DIY subculture with tenderness and obvious admiration, and it's thrilling to watch the early caution of her research yield to an obsessiveness and determination that are characteristic of her subjects. A monumentally inspiring book."

— Kyle Beachy, author of *The Most Fun Thing:*
Dispatches from a Skateboard Life

"*Girl Gangs, Zines and Powerslides* pulls together a vast and moving history of badass women and non-traditional skateboarders. Natalie Porter uses her librarian's eye, skater's resolve, and a scrappy DIY ethos to painstakingly gather and share the untold stories of these sporting icons, who span generations and continents, and are foundational to skateboarding as we know it. This book is a testament to the power of community and connection, and it shows us just how much meaning can be packed into a few sheets of Xeroxed paper."

— Cole Nowicki, author of *Right, Down + Circle*,
Laser Quit Smoking Massage, and the newsletter *Simple Magic*

NATALIE PORTER

GIRL GANGS, ZINES, AND POWERSLIDES

A HISTORY OF BADASS WOMEN SKATEBOARDERS

Copyright © Natalie Porter, 2025

Published by ECW Press
665 Gerrard Street East
Toronto, Ontario, Canada M4M 1Y2
416-694-3348 / info@ecwpress.com

All rights reserved. No part of this publication may be reproduced, stored in a retrieval system, or transmitted in any form by any process — electronic, mechanical, photocopying, recording, or otherwise — without the prior written permission of the copyright owners and ECW Press. The scanning, uploading, and distribution of this book via the internet or via any other means without the permission of the publisher is illegal and punishable by law. This book may not be used for text and data mining, AI training, and similar technologies. Please purchase only authorized electronic editions, and do not participate in or encourage electronic piracy of copyrighted materials. Your support of the author's rights is appreciated.

Editor for the Press: Jen Sookfong Lee
Copy editor: Crissy Boylan
Cover design: Caroline Suzuki
Front cover photograph of Anita Tessensohn courtesy Martin Willners

LIBRARY AND ARCHIVES CANADA CATALOGUING IN PUBLICATION

Title: Girl gangs, zines, and powerslides : a history of badass women skateboarders / Natalie Porter.

Names: Porter, Natalie (Founder of Womxn skateboard history), author.

Description: Includes bibliographical references and index.

Identifiers: Canadiana (print) 20250214741 | Canadiana (ebook) 2025021475X

ISBN 978-1-77041-792-2 (softcover)
ISBN 978-1-77852-476-9 (ePub)
ISBN 978-1-77852-477-6 (PDF)

Subjects: LCSH: Skateboarding—History. | LCSH: Women skateboarders—Biography. | LCSH: Skateboarders—Biography. | LCSH: Minorities in sports—History. | LCSH: Sexual minorities and sports—History. | LCGFT: Biographies.

Classification: LCC GV859.812 .P67 2025 | DDC 796.22092/2—dc23

This book is funded in part by the Government of Canada. *Ce livre est financé en partie par le gouvernement du Canada.* We also acknowledge the support of the Government of Ontario through the Ontario Book Publishing Tax Credit, and through Ontario Creates.

PRINTED AND BOUND IN CANADA   PRINTING: MARQUIS   5 4 3 2 1

Purchase the print edition and receive the ebook free.
For details, go to ecwpress.com/ebook.

For the skater nerds

CONTENTS

INTRODUCTION	(Liz Bevington)	1
CHAPTER ONE	On Barriers (KZ Zapata)	13
	Kristy McNichol	28
	Diane Desiderio	30
	Kathy Sierra	32
CHAPTER TWO	Director's Cut (Lisa Jak Wietzke)	43
	Lisa Whitaker	52
	Skate Witches	57
	SK8HERS	59
CHAPTER THREE	Origin Stories (Laurie Turner)	71
	Linda Benson	78
	Patti McGee	79
	Le Skate-Bord	81

CHAPTER FOUR	Platforms (Lauri Kuulei Wong)	95
	Gunk	103
	Villa Villa Cola	106
	Check It Out	110
CHAPTER FIVE	On Accessibility (Georgina Matthews)	123
	Mary Mills	130
	Stephanie Person	132
	Crystal Solomon	135
CHAPTER SIX	Whistleblowers (Bonnie Blouin)	143
	Cindy Berryman	156
	Leslie Jo Ritzma	159
	Vicki Vickers	161
CHAPTER SEVEN	Better Together (Lynn Kramer)	169
	La Femme	178
	The Hags	180
	Rookie	183
CHAPTER EIGHT	Infiltrators (Sue Hazel)	193
	Kate the Skate	200
	National Skateboard Review	202
	"Girls Who Skate"	204

CHAPTER NINE	Rebels (JoAnn Gillespie)	219
	Terry Lawrence	232
	Kim Adrian	235
	Cyndy Pendergast	238
CHAPTER TEN	Matriarchs (Beth Fishman)	249
	Judi Oyama	254
	Jean Rusen	257
	Amy Bradshaw	260
CHAPTER ELEVEN	Accountability (Jana Payne)	273
	Barb Odanaka	279
	Skate Like a Girl	283
	Consent is Rad	285
CONCLUSION	(Pam Judge)	297
ACKNOWLEDGMENTS		319
NOTES		321
INDEX		345

Liz Bevington protesting a potential ban on Venice roller sports in the *LA Herald Examiner* (May 31, 1989)

INTRODUCTION
(LIZ BEVINGTON)

It was not the post about an X Games vert champion or someone catapulting themselves down multiple sets of stairs on a skateboard that received immediate support from followers on my Instagram account. The post featured Liz Bevington (RIP) — a German-born, Venice Beach misfit who learned to skateboard at age fifty-two in 1976.[1] She wasn't content to sit around and watch her son have all the fun, and when Liz was eventually widowed, skateboarding became her core social outlet.

The history of women in skateboarding is the focus of my account, and the popular post included photos of Liz rocking her pink high-top shoes, wearing a tasseled "Skateboard Mama" beach T-shirt, and riding her custom skateboard with a windsurfer sail all the way into her eighties. The post also contained retro footage of Liz in vibrant spandex grooving to a disco beat on her skateboard, weaving through a street party, surrounded by lithe young men on roller skates.[2] Liz looks like she's having a blast, completely in the zone. Over forty-five years later, the online response to Liz's lifestyle was pure stoke.

"Oh my goodness she is GOALS! 😍"

"What an inspiration 😍 😍 😍"

"I love her so much!!! 🔥 🔥 🔥"

"This is my favorite skater on this account so far."

"Legend 👏👏"

"Wow she was so awesome. 👏👏 You dig up the best stories!"

"Thanks for sharing and creating this page 🖐 . . . RIP Liz aka Skateboard Mama love you and will never forget you."

Liz experienced being in the limelight to some extent during her heyday, making a cameo in a Coors Light commercial in 1984 and then a Pepsi ad in 1990, even receiving sponsorship from the clothing brand B.U.M. Equipment. The *Los Angeles Times* presented Liz in an article when she protested a proposed ban on roller sports in Venice, followed by a photo shoot of Liz skateboarding the Santa Monica pier.

As for historical accounts of Liz in skateboarding media, there's a tiny photo of her in the September 1984 issue of *Thrasher*. Liz is shown cheering on the competitors in a flatland freestyle contest at the Venice Beach pavilion, which included Diane Veerman (now Desiderio) and April Hoffman successfully competing against the guys. And yet Liz was never acknowledged as a contributor to the scene with the same status as a sponsored skater in their youthful prime. She was always described as a novelty act and a bit of an outsider. But Liz wasn't in it for the glory.

Liz loved the carnival scene of Venice Beach, interacting with eccentric people and posing for photos with tourists, and she loved skateboarding. When asked what her adult sons thought of her obsession during a PBS television show called *The 90's*, Liz said, "They are used to it now. They know that that's what I do."[3] And if she bailed on her skateboard, she would just "get up and go again!" Liz didn't see the point in babying her aches and pains because everybody has them. "Just go out and do something . . . I'm getting high on it."[4]

Liz had an aura of positive vibes, and at age eighty she made an appearance at the inaugural Mighty Mama Skate-O-Rama Mother's Day event in 2004 hosted by skateboarding author Barb Odanaka; Liz cruised through the skatepark, busting out her *Saturday Night Fever* moves. Four years later, she was still at it, wind-skating for a piece in the *Santa Monica Daily*, extolling the benefits of regular exercise and a mug of beer in the sunshine at Big Dean's Ocean Front Café.

I'm convinced that because Liz radiated authenticity, not necessarily as a "cool" skateboarder but as a person who knew herself and what brought her joy, people were drawn to her story. Liz didn't need anyone's permission. She cultivated her own style and wasn't swayed by popular thinking about age-appropriate behavior or attire.

I never had the chance to meet Liz — she died in 2020 at age ninety-six — but I've done my best to gather content about her in my online archive, Womxn Skateboard History. When I watched her interview from *The 90's*, I felt an immediate sense of admiration and awe for Liz, and this experience repeated itself multiple times with other skateboarders. I've foraged information on women in skateboarding for over twenty years, and the process of uncovering and validating individuals, especially older women who have been ignored or forgotten, has brought me great fulfillment. It's both the thrill of discovery and the accumulation of proof of women's participation in skateboarding that drives me. With every additional bio, I'm able to weave different stories together to create a bigger picture.

I've only met in person a tiny percentage of the people I feature, let alone the account's followers on Instagram, but over time many of these people have become friends. You might guess that my target audience is teenaged female skateboarders, but from a quick scroll I can see that folks are diverse in gender, age, and background, and sometimes their connection to skateboarding is unclear. There's even a handful of old-school dudes — collectors of skateboarding memorabilia — who have alerted me to vintage zines and photos, hauling out cardboard boxes squirreled away in their basements or garages. Their involvement has been critical.

I launched the Womxn Skateboard History archive and Instagram account on International Women's Day in March 2022, after several false starts. It's been a life-altering experience. I'm a nerdy, middle-aged skater librarian and would never describe myself as an extrovert, but this project has transformed me and continues to push me out of my comfort zone. Today I ask myself, *Why did it take me so long to go public? And what was I afraid of?*

I just want to drop in already.

At age forty-three, I was poised at the top of a quarter-pipe at my local skatepark in the Pacific Northwest, surrounded by forest, ferns, and blackberry bushes, with my skateboard balanced and waiting to drop in. After leaving Vancouver for a more affordable town further north with easy access to backcountry trails, lakes, and oceanfront in the traditional territory of the Tla'amin Nation, I found myself enticed to skateboard again. The park features a snake-run shaped like a concrete Celtic knot, a dilapidated bowl that resembled a giant bathtub, and a street section with handrails, banks, stairs, and a pyramid-shaped obstacle. Except for a variety of crude penis-shaped graffiti in the bowl, the setting was idyllic, but I was starting to lose my shit.

I was grateful that my muscle memory retained a smattering of basic skateboarding skills, but after a pause of more than a decade, I was in for a shock regarding the mobs of scooter kids swarming the park like locusts. I didn't want to be some nasty, weird woman yelling at kids having fun, but my patience had its limits, and that included abandoned scooters in my direct path and little boys staring at me like deer in headlights. I needed a break.

I noticed one other adult skateboarding the mellow flat-ground section of the park. A dad in his late thirties was practicing tricks while encouraging his two daughters to try skateboarding. *What a refreshing scene*, I thought. We made small talk about the challenges of returning to skateboarding in middle-age, the need to stretch more and wear wrist guards, et cetera. And then things got awkward. To my face, he said, "You know, there were no girls when

I started skateboarding." I was confused because I could have sworn that I had just told him that I started skating in the 1990s with a crew of young women not far from his hometown.

This skate dad announced that he "discovered" female skateboarders a few years ago by following the Berrics on Instagram. The Berrics is a renowned skatepark whose owners initiated a contest series in 2008 called Battle at the Berrics; in 2019, the organizers announced the first Women's Battle at the Berrics, pitting the top female street skaters against each other and broadcasting the recorded results online. The way Skate Dad described the event, it sounded like women in skateboarding hadn't existed prior to this contest, at least women he regarded as "real" skateboarders, capable of performing the same tricks or more advanced tricks than him.

I calmly told Skate Dad that there was a rich history of women in skateboarding spanning sixty years prior to the Berrics. But that's all I had in me. When someone is mansplaining away my precious time at a skatepark, the conversation only makes me resentful because it's not really a conversation, it's an uninvited lecture. I'm a classic librarian in the sense that I'm trained in de-escalation and dislike confrontation, and I don't believe that going into combat mode aids the learning process. But I still get triggered by odd encounters like this one with Skate Dad. I was left feeling rejected and disheartened, and I was unwillingly transported back to my teenaged years in the 1990s when female skaters were often unwelcome at skateparks and labeled imposters.

While it's not a malicious statement, I get tired of "There were no girls who skated when I was a kid" sneaking into articles and interviews with prominent skateboarders in the industry, and then it's regurgitated by random bros at the skatepark. Similarly, the declaration "I was the *only* female skateboarder" is also problematic. This narrative is common because it often really felt like we were the only girls in our respective communities. A better statement might be "I didn't know of any other girls who skated in my town." When we offer context, it allows for the possibility that someone in a neighboring suburb or distant country was forging away solo on a tennis court, hoping for a friend. It's fun to feel special, and when there's been limited airtime, funding, and affirmation for women, it can be hard to let go of stories about our identity that showcase us as unique. But there's space for everyone, including the skateboarders we haven't been exposed to or befriended yet.

As a constructive response to feeling frustrated, research and writing became my refuge and outlet. And the archive is now one beast of a website filled with hundreds of skaters' bios plus photos, videos, interviews, references, and zines. My hope is that it will be a gateway for exploration that eliminates any debate about women's participation. I call this quiet, obsessive approach "the Wrath of a Skater Librarian." Skate Dad reminded me that there was still a disconnect among skaters' understanding of the past, and I have the skill set as a librarian to help restore the imbalance.

Most people, if they choose to listen, can grasp the idea that female and non-binary skaters have always participated, and that a beginner or less talented rider is still a bona fide skateboarder. It's not a mental stretch to realize that skateboarding and its media outlets have imitated mainstream behaviors. For example, the coverage of women in sports has been notoriously inconsistent. Sportscasters and sponsors struggled to consider women's athletic accomplishments worth celebrating, let alone to imagine a lucrative market for women's sports (an attitude that now seems laughable). When the skateboarding industry witnessed mainstream advertisers push the predictable "sex sells" approach, they adopted it for financial gain, catering to prepubescent straight cis boys by objectifying women, while ignoring the efforts of female participants.

It's easy to dismiss past failings as a reflection of the times or to point our fingers at countries and cultures abroad that still harbor extreme patriarchal attitudes, but it is glaringly obvious that access to freedom, education, and opportunity for girls, women, and non-binary people is constantly threatened everywhere. I'm reminded of the documentary *No Comply* (2020), directed by Bibbi

Abruzzini; it features skateboarders in Morocco whose parents believe that their daughters' safety lies in getting married young and conforming to tradition rather than pushing boundaries. And then I watch the documentary by Kristin Kobes Du Mez called *For Our Daughters: Stories of Abuse, Betrayal, and Resistance in the Evangelical Church* (2024) on the impact of Christian nationalism in North America and know that any advance we make toward equity can be clawed back in an instant. The battle continues.

While I don't enjoy being a faultfinder, I believe that when historians avoid acknowledging some of the more disdainful activities and behaviors in our shared history, there's a risk of idealizing eras like the 1980s or 1990s as the "glory days" of skateboarding without asking, *For whom?* It's important to recognize our privilege, pursue balanced and accessible representation, celebrate progress, and encourage change, which are the intentions of this book.

In the late fall of 2007, I was on the picket line at Vancouver's Central Library — it was our seventy-fourth day on strike. Our union was bargaining with management and had us rallying for gender equity and equal pay, and the exciting news at our pep talk that morning was that award-winning author Naomi Klein and her personal researcher, a trained librarian, Debra Ann Levy, were joining us.

It would turn out to be a critical day for me.

There's a YouTube video of the presentation, posted by our union. I can see the picketers clustered together, seated along the amphitheater facing Robson Street, waiting in anticipation. Almost everyone wears a protest placard like an apron, looped around our necks with string. The sun is shining, but I know we must have been cold now that we'd stopped lapping the library's perimeter.

I spot myself seated at ground level. I'm bundled up for the weather wearing a black beanie and brown leather jacket, likely having just taken advantage of the donated coffee and donuts. Being born and raised in small-town Ontario meant practically living at a Tim Hortons during my teenaged years; it was our default youth center, along with the concrete footprint of a demolished factory, which we used as a makeshift skatepark.

The year before the strike, after a summer working as a youth intern at an anarchist bookstore called Spartacus, I landed a job as a library assistant thanks to the encouragement of a friend. It felt like a good match, so I applied to become a full-fledged librarian, studying at the University of British Columbia. And months later, I was in the odd predicament of protesting the institution that had launched my career.

Klein had just released her book *The Shock Doctrine: The Rise of Disaster Capitalism*, which she explained was about the war on the public sphere, where governments exploit and fabricate crises to manipulate people, and her belief that there are areas in life, like free access to information, where the profit motive should not apply. She said,

> In these simple acts of helping people access informa-
> tion . . . you are embodying this spirit that there are
> some things that are too important, too fundamental
> to our democracy to allow the profit motive to govern
> those transactions. And you're fighting for that. And
> people treat librarians like mousy figures, but mice
> roar at times, and this work is far too often taken for
> granted. Part of the reason it's taken for granted is
> because it's so squarely in the public. It is in the area
> of life where things are freely given and freely taken,
> not bought and sold. A different spirit governs.[5]

Klein's words landed with her audience, and then she hammered it home. Klein admitted that her book was priced out of reach for many people.

INTRODUCTION (LIZ BEVINGTON)

> I wrote this book so that it would be read by whoever wants to read it, and your work allows that to be the case, and I'm counting on you to protect this space. I also want to say that my research assistant, the woman who is responsible for the seventy pages of footnotes in *The Shock Doctrine*, Debra Levy over there is a trained librarian. Debra has educated me on so much; we used the hell out of libraries to produce this book. We could not have produced this book without the public library system.[6]

The crowd erupted into applause at mention of Levy's contributions, and not only was I inspired by Klein's speech, I was also blown away by the thought of how cool Levy's job must be. Having the opportunity to merge one's expertise as a librarian with a passion project in a slightly anonymous but meaningful role sounded incredible. A seed was planted.

Librarians are a mysterious coven. While usually operating in the shadows, serving an organization or a neighborhood, we sometimes go rogue when faced with book bans or threats to access to information. It's honorable work. We often have unexpected secret identities and get a kick out of the look of surprise and even disapproval when we reveal what really gets us going. For me, it's been skateboarding, joining girl gangs, and researching women skateboarders. But I've tended to avoid being present in my write-ups for the archive and in social media posts because it's a level of exposure I'm only beginning to get comfortable with.

There's safety in distancing oneself from the debate, but here I am on paper, writing transparently because my connections with women's stories and the individuals themselves have impacted me. I struggle to be an invisible curator when I'm prompted to reflect upon and synthesize history along the way. The timing is right because ten or even five years ago, I would've been afraid that this book would seem like a vanity project, an act of egotism to see my name in print. Or worse, a response to pangs of envy at other people's literary success. Thankfully, with age, it's easier to recognize that one's sense of value comes from accepting a belief that you are loved and you are enough, regardless of whether your tagline reads "published author" or "sponsored skater" or neither.

I am proud of what I've accumulated in the archive, but what I have yet to deliver — and what I hope to articulate in this book — is the backstory of how uncovering and sharing this history has been a worthwhile journey even if it means being vulnerable to criticism. The process has inspired in me a new confidence, and it's also helped me reconcile past hurts. I know that my early experiences as a 1990s female skater with the skateboarding industry and society at large, which often felt like an enemy, shaped me. I think anger was a valid response at the time, but I'm so relieved that this negative dynamic no longer defines skateboarding for me.

It's been over four years since I interacted with Skate Dad; in that short while, I believe that skateboarding, though still creative and chaotic, has entered a stage of maturity in terms of inclusion. In this era of social media, the perspectives of skaters within collectives and community groups have more impact compared to in the past when exclusively male pro skaters, company owners, and magazine editors had significant influence over trends, beliefs, and behaviors. This change is a good thing. Skateboarding is not a utopia, but it is evolving. Just as I'm learning to offer more grace to individuals I might have once labeled my nemeses (aka contributors to *Big Brother* magazine), I'm hopeful that this book will be welcomed with open arms.

I've chosen not to write a traditional timeline. Whenever I start to "write from the beginning," I become bogged down with mundane facts like contest wins and sponsorships, which may be important and require acknowledgment but often lack vibrancy when reported. And forgive me if I revert to a voice that mimics Wikipedia. I began this archival project by pumping out bios with a vengeance. I wanted to produce evidence that women have relentlessly skateboarded through every high in popularity and industry low.

The people featured in this book, like Liz Bevington, are not always "the best" skateboarders of their era. It is easier to gather content when someone has an abundance of competition results, interviews, and photographs in magazines, but there are equally inspiring skaters creating community from the sidelines. As a skateboarder with limited talent myself, I want to show that skateboarding needs people of varied abilities, especially those who fostered solidarity by organizing workshops and events, documented the scene, and created zines. I've emphasized the interactions that have given me courage to keep going. I've also extended my appreciation to those skaters who are non-binary, whose pronouns have changed; with their permission, I have included them in this history.

I'm aware that I sometimes drop names of people and companies familiar to most skateboarders that are not universally known and that there's skateboarding lingo ingrained in my speech that some readers may need to pull up Google to understand. I apologize in advance and will do my best to clarify helpful details. I hope that this book appeals to a wide range of people, beyond the skateboarding scene. You don't have to be a skateboarder to appreciate that drive to feel part of something, of a group that gives you a sense of belonging and identity, or that need for a role model to look up to and who makes you feel less alone.

If at any point a name appears in this book that piques your curiosity or does *not* appear and you wonder if their story has been explored, head over to the Womxn Skateboard History website, and there you can witness my obsession. You might even find yourself listed in the "mystery" section. If so, please reach out because this historical restoration doesn't end here — we are only just beginning.

KZ Zapata grinds a parking barrier in 1986, published in a "Time Machine" feature in *Thrasher* (March 1999)

CHAPTER ONE

ON BARRIERS (KZ ZAPATA)

To progress in skateboarding and take a familiar trick into a new realm of difficulty, there are multiple barriers a skateboarder must confront. There are physical barriers like sidewalk curbs, concrete parking lot dividers, city architecture and public art, even something as daunting as a three-hundred-foot mega ramp. And then there are mental barriers.

Overcoming a psychological hurdle when you're barreling toward a set of stairs slightly lengthier than the last or blasting up a ramp with more vertical than transition requires stamina. At any moment, if you're not in the right headspace, intrusive thoughts suggesting that you're incompetent and out of your league can creep in and throw you off course, literally. But skateboarders can be stubborn, and when they have a desire to improve, it's hard to deter them. That hopeful anticipation of relief and satisfaction once the trick is landed makes all those repetitive, painful attempts worth the effort.

Social barriers that have historically alienated groups of people, because of their gender, race, sexuality, and ability, have been replicated in the culture of skateboarding. Often, these barriers are based on falsehoods intended to rationalize poor behavior and are spread through opinions that get repeated unchecked, like a sentence I've heard multiple times: "The 1980s was too punk and too hardcore for girls." Don Bostick, who founded World Cup Skateboarding with his wife, Danielle, in 1994, explained that the attitude in the '80s was hostile toward women: "The guys heckled [female skaters] . . . A girl had to be pretty ballsy to drop into a pool. The guys sort of machoed them out of the way."[1] But did women quit or avoid skateboarding? Not necessarily, although it was certainly rare for a young girl to take up pool-skating as a beginner in the '80s because, according to legendary vert skater Cara-Beth Burnside, "Who wants to go skateboarding at 13 and get made fun of by guys?"[2] And when the media doesn't present you with a hero to emulate, and opportunities for a girl to thrive are nonexistent, the challenge of women's visibility and progression is compounded.

During an episode of the *WCRP on Skateboarding* podcast, hosted by pro skater Clyde Singleton (revered for his efforts in celebrating Black skaters[3]), Tony Hawk was asked to consider the situation of women skaters evaporating from magazines in the 1980s. Tony was aware that the population of skaters drastically declined after the collapse of the skateboarding industry in the late 1970s but was openly baffled about why the new iteration of skateboarding culture impacted women so profoundly. He said,

> Yeah, it's weird because when I first started skating [in the 1970s], you would see women in the magazines, especially freestyle, but also pool skaters . . . And Cara-Beth [Burnside], like I grew up skating against Cara-Beth at events. So, there was a faction of female skaters throughout those years, but it did seem like when skateboarding went underground [in the 1980s], there was less focus on them. I don't know if that was because of the lack of participants or because they were purposely not including them.[4]

I love that male leaders are contemplating these issues today because advocating for improved representation is a collaborative effort, and sometimes the answers aren't clear, names are forgotten, and stories are hidden in the pages of vintage zines. Thankfully, these grassroots publications, distributed via an underground network of female pen pals, reveal what it was like to be ignored or, alternatively, forced to compete against guys like Tony. It's been part of my mission to source these publications and reach out to anyone involved to celebrate their determination and acts of resistance. There was a near blackout of female skaters in mainstream magazines throughout the 1980s and 1990s, and these zines discredit any suggestion that it was because there were no women to promote.

If the term *zine* is unfamiliar, it refers to handmade, photocopied mini-magazines that have a do-it-yourself aesthetic because they tend to be cheaply made. While there have been "fanzines" since the 1960s, zines emerged in the 1970s and 1980s as clandestine newsletters created by queer communities and artists whose perspectives were heavily censored, especially during the HIV/AIDS crisis.[5] Zines became an alternative way to communicate and were adopted by different subcultures, like the punk music scene, to share ideologies, updates, and events, without the limitations of mainstream media (if the mainstream would have them, that is).

In the early 1980s, skateboarders found zines appealing because they showcased new tricks being performed in the streets or on backyard mini-ramps, highlighted local contests, and helped cultivate friendships. Zines were especially important for women because popular skateboard magazines published content almost exclusively about male professional skaters and the companies that sponsored them. Sometimes magazines included a token article or a smattering of photos featuring women as a benevolent gesture. Mostly, they didn't. You could fill a zine with the stories, drawings, rants, photos, and interviews of your choosing at a time when no one else was bothering to pay attention.

And yet there was an opportunity in the editorial section of skateboarding magazines for female skaters to have their voices acknowledged, even if it meant their letters were pitted against letters by people who despised them, as in a modern-day comments section online. Reading these letters, I can sense the girls' frustrations as they process loneliness and anger, demand recognition, request pen pals, condemn the system, and propose solutions. In January 1986, *Thrasher* printed a prime example of one such letter by "Jane Doe," which became a critical call-to-action.

> I never thought I would write into your mag . . . I am a girl and started skating last January. I thought I would get a lot of support from the locals, especially since I live in California where supposedly the raddest skaters roam the streets. What a joke. When they found out that I started skating all they did was tell me how much I sucked and what a poseur I was. If they are so "great" then why don't they teach me. Their favorite word to call me is loser, but we will just see who makes it . . .
>
> Sometimes I feel like quitting all together but I'm not that stupid. I love skating and think it's the best thing in the world, and I can understand why so many people are starting, but if I had known I was gonna get harassed instead of accepted as any normal human beings would have done, I would have stuck to my Big Wheel because no one deserves this type of emotional abuse . . . They think they're so hot because they are punk rebels.[6]

In pre-internet days, women often had little opportunity to connect with other female skaters who were a city, state, or province away. Letter-writing was vital because it signaled to others that you were out there, and when you found a like-minded friend to interact with these letters could be a lifeline to help maintain motivation and keep skating.

Jane Doe's letter is both a statement of defiance and a cry for affirmation, and I can guarantee that letters like hers did not go unnoticed by fellow female skaters. In fact, it was Bonnie Blouin (featured in Chapter Six) who came to Jane Doe's defense with a follow-up letter. Bonnie would eventually propel a women's skateboard network along with her pen pal, KZ Zapata, who was the drummer of an all-girl punk band called PMS and author of the skateboard zine *Push, Push, Then Go!*

KZ's intent as a zine writer was to create visibility for women and oppose an attitude that female skaters should be compared to men and subsequently dismissed by them as irrelevant and inauthentic when they performed differently. As a biracial person of Peruvian and Swedish heritage, KZ often felt like an outsider, but with skateboarding, they found freedom and had no interest in being limited by old-school gender roles.[7] I only learned about KZ's story because I took a risk and did something completely out of character — I clawed through Facebook like a creep and emailed them at their workplace.

Like most librarians, when a library patron requests my help, I become fixated on finding a satisfying answer. You want to know "who wrote the book with the blue cover"? I'm on it. You're wasted on a case of Budweiser beer and need to know the calorie content in a pinch, just call me at the library. Over the years I've received the strangest requests, but I'm rarely fazed by an inquiry.

When it came to my own interests in starting this project, the drive was still there to find answers, but I was initially less gentle with myself, compared to how I treat library patrons. I could be my own worst enemy. My brain would ask, *Who am I to pluck names buried in old magazines and seek them out? Who am I to consume someone's time when I have no media outlet, let alone a skill set as a journalist? What right do I have trying to upend and influence skateboarding history?*

Another barrier I had to overcome was the reality that often the only source of information on women's skateboard history is the individual skateboarder, and being an introvert, I would rather read an article or an interview than request the help of a stranger. An added challenge was that I live nowhere near Southern California, universally considered the birthplace of skateboarding with its historic ties to surfing culture, although residents of Florida and New York will debate this. I live close to mile zero of Highway 101 in Canada. It takes two ferries and a six-hour haul from Vancouver to access my town unless you want to splurge on a floatplane and experience flight inside a sardine can. I'm also in my forties, child-free, recently returned to skateboarding after a long hiatus, and likely considered a bit strange in my small community. My idea of a good time, especially on dark and rainy nights on the West Coast, is scouring skateboard mags for proof of women skaters' existence.

During one of these dismal evenings, I found a tiny photo of someone credited as "Karen Zapata" in the digitized July 1986 issue of *Thrasher*, and I was stoked. The photo was maybe three by one inches in black and white, although it was hard to tell without a physical copy. Zapata was described as the lone woman competing in the Sacto Streetstyle contest in Sacramento, California; in the photo, KZ was propelling themself over a concrete parking divider, performing a boneless with one hand gripping and one foot still firmly on board, the other foot planted on the obstacle, offering leverage and height.[8] A burned-out car covered in graffiti with smashed-in windows was behind KZ, along with a crowd of young men lining the perimeter of the parking lot.

The male spectators were in the hundreds, likely waiting to see Mark Gonzales, Steve Caballero, Natas Kaupas, Christian Hosoi, Jeff Grosso, and Tommy Guerrero, professional skateboarders still revered today. And yet the audience was forced to witness a bold act of independence when this young woman took ownership of the course. *Who the hell is she?* I wondered, which prompted my full-blown librarian beastmode to engage.

Zapata was acknowledged a few months later in a *Thrasher* article about the Vision Sims Street Attack contest: "Eighty amateur streetstylers were going at it in an attempt to gain top honors . . . A note of recognition should also go to Stephanie Person and . Karen Zapata. Karen managed a 16th place finish, which is no small feat in a field of 80 aggro skaters."[9] I searched for the name in Bonnie Blouin's pivotal article on female skateboarders, "Sugar and Spice . . ?"[10] from the April 1986 issue of *Thrasher*, and sure enough, Zapata was included. There was a caption that read "Karen Zapata, 19 years old and a student at UCSB, puts guys to shame when she rides" under a stylish photo of KZ kick-turning on a concrete bank.

While my first attempts at finding KZ on Facebook resulted in failure, the mention of UCSB prompted me to search for a connection between KZ and the university. After a series of ineffective queries, I finally Googled a magic sequence of words, reviewed the images, and struck social media gold. I landed on a university class reunion album that provided a tagged photo of a middle-aged KZ playing drums with PMS. I determined their profession, sourced a website with a staff directory, and then brazenly emailed them at a work address.

My curiosity forced me to connect directly with a skater who could possibly reject or ghost me. In my introductory email, I sound apologetic and embarrassed because my route to sourcing KZ's email address might have crossed a line in personal privacy. "Would you be remotely interested in being interviewed?" I asked. "I'm a librarian and hope my online sleuthing isn't creepy. I genuinely want to piece together skate history from a female perspective, and the '80s is sort of notorious for promoting a boys' club mentality." I alluded to an idea that the interview could be published in a skateboard zine, but this was not a guarantee; I just wanted to sound intentional. Early the next morning, there was a reply waiting for me in my inbox. I felt sick to my stomach, but I clicked the message and was instantly flooded with joy.

"YES!!!!! I would LOVE to be interviewed!! I actually had a girl's skate zine and was really interested in helping girls blossom in the world of skating."

I later learned that their name is KZ now, with a pronoun preference for she/they, and after a flurry of back-and-forth emails, we scheduled a time to chat. My first interview with a stranger.

In 2002, I interviewed my skateboarding friends for my master's thesis, and the process seemed easy. I had moved to Montréal the previous year with the help of my friend Louise Hénault-Ethier (whom I met competing at Vancouver's Slam City Jam contest). I was welcomed into a growing mob of female skateboarders, and we decided to call ourselves "The Skirtboarders." Today, skateboarding in flowing garments — from ribbon skirts to saris to polleras — has become a powerful movement, especially among Indigenous skaters, but back then our Montréal crew just thought it would be a funny name.[11]

In the winter months, we produced a series of zines called *Armpit*, our own videos, and a website to keep ourselves motivated thanks to the initiative of Erika Dubé and Mathilde Pigeon. I honored the DIY spirit of female skateboarders in my writing and the significance of taking over the city streets as a girl gang, celebrating our wounds, licking bloody hands for the camera. Our actions were in opposition to the young men interviewed in a dissertation called "The Subculture of Skateboarding,"[12] who believed that they weren't encountering girls at the skatepark because girls "don't want to have scars on their shins" and "they don't look good with bruises." It's not surprising that attitudes like these were prevalent when mainstream media in the 1990s was intent on portraying women as unblemished and docile.

My thesis was titled "Female Skateboarders and Their Negotiation of Space and Identity,"[13] which compared skateboarders' experiences with women athletes and female punks. In my writing, I was sensitive to the corporate "girl power" strategy that had co-opted the Riot Grrrls, profiting from bands that were traditionally feminine and inoffensive, like the Spice Girls and All Saints, as opposed to a radical, feminist, and queer band like Fifth Column who were often censored.[14] I was also immersed in hot feminist topics of the 1990s like the fear-based and punitive tactics men in the sports industry exerted over female athletes like tennis legend Billie Jean King,[15] which included the threat of being outed as lesbian and the lack of sponsorship for women who appeared "mannish" and therefore couldn't be commodified as objects of heterosexual desire. As feminist scholars Susan Birrell and Nancy Theberge put it, "By 'discrediting' all women in sports as lesbians, men can rest assured that their territory is not being invaded by 'real' women after all; by mobilizing social prejudices against homosexuality, they may be able to keep the number of women involved in sport to a safe minimum."[16]

The goal of my thesis was to contest traditional subcultural theory because it was a field of study established by mostly male academics who asserted that subcultures were a domain to explore masculinity and deviance, to the exclusion of women whose value was solely as a romantic partner or sidekick rather than a contributor to the scene.[17] My friends were living proof that female skateboarders were active cultural producers, and their stories helped bring meaning to my academic rants.

Interviewing my friends had been positive. I had an assignment, I was trusted, and everyone had something to offer. Cold-emailing and interviewing a stranger as a mature woman felt very different. I'll admit to feeling nervous, but the resulting conversation with KZ Zapata was a game changer. Thanks to the global adoption of Zoom during the COVID-19 pandemic, I conversed with them from the comfort of my home office in December 2021 and watched the recording afterward.

KZ was so cool, chilling in a black hoodie with a flower design that reminded me of a Japanese irezumi tattoo. They wore gold hoop earrings and matching reading glasses in an aviator style without the tinted lens. I wore a mustard-colored knit cardigan over a shredded flannel plaid shirt, channeling the nerdy librarian look with a hint of gritty skater. I awkwardly proposed that we "launch into this and travel down memory lane," and KZ agreed. They appeared relaxed and excited to dig up their old zines and share their stories.

KZ's skateboarding upbringing wasn't unusual as I would later discover after conducting more interviews, and I immediately felt aligned with them. KZ had older and younger brothers who started skating in the late 1970s, and they simply wanted to hang out with them and be part of their scene. "Why would I just sit there and watch?"[18] KZ questioned, and I couldn't agree more. Growing up with two big brothers myself, I remember not wanting to miss out on anything they were doing. I wanted to bask in their social orbit and trail them into every sport.

KZ received a plastic skateboard for Christmas, and recalled how the whole family would skate together, especially after they were allowed to build a half-pipe in their backyard in Albany. This was pivotal because the local skate sessions around Berkeley were hierarchical; access to someone else's ramp was based on who you knew and how good you were. KZ explained, "You would be standing there, calculating when you could get your turn, and I learned that I could not overthink why I was there. There was a voice in my head that was like, *What are you doing here? You're a girl, you don't belong here*, and so I learned to be like, *If I don't do this, I don't get heard*."

When KZ described this scene, I felt like I was there at the ramp, attempting to drop in without getting cut off. Punk music raged in the background, the energy and testosterone hung heavy in the air, and the air crackled with the anxiety of trying to find an opportunity to insert oneself into the session. And just like that, something clicked as KZ spoke. Why was I afraid of interviewing and validating another awesome human being? I needed to revert to that childlike state of confidence that allowed me to teeter on the edge, take a deep breath, and try anything at least once.

While mini-ramps were popular in high school for KZ, they still required a plot of land and cash for materials. As a result, there was a shift among skateboarders, who were not always from middle class or affluent families, onto the city streets by the time KZ entered University of California, Santa Barbara and lived in Isla Vista. KZ was soon launching off DIY kickers and grinding curbs in a form of skateboarding branded as "streetstyle."

> At the end of my first year, there was this contest in Isla Vista. I signed up and competed, and that's when I got sponsored. Skip Engblom, who owned Santa Monica Airlines, was there and asked me to skate for SMA, and suddenly I was a sponsored amateur! He sent this note, "Here's your first flow," with skateboards and stuff.
>
> Skip was very cool and experimental. He knew that girls were different, and he sponsored me not based on comparisons to a bunch of guys. That conversation was really important, and it's what I was most interested in talking to other girls about, asking how we can do this thing we love and not feel like we're being compared. That's when I started making this zine called *Push, Push, Then Go!*

I felt like Gollum from *The Lord of the Rings* in the vicinity of "my precious" when I asked if KZ still had copies of their zine. I desperately wanted access to this portal to the past. As a skater librarian, *Push, Push, Then Go!* was the kind of sacred, unfiltered evidence I sought to get a real sense of how female skaters thrived in the 1980s. I was so relieved when KZ immediately produced several issues, which we pored over together. I wished I had taken a puff of my inhaler before the interview; I needed a reminder to breathe.

The zine was not exclusively about female skaters, but KZ pointed out that from the very first issue, there was always an intentional "Girls' Scene" section that spoke to the barriers women faced. In issue one, KZ wrote,

> Every time I go skate I'm surprised by finding more and more girls who're skating and are really good. I couldn't believe that there were about 4 girls competing at the last C.A.S.L. [California Amateur Skateboard League] contest. I think it's high time things start happening for girls in skating. As a sponsored AM [amateur] I come in contact with a lot of girls who skate and want to compete but not against a bunch of guys who are highly competitive and better than they are. I think it's time C.A.S.L. and these organizations establish a GIRLS DIVISION . . . ALSO, I did the skate camp this summer and I improved so Fucking much there and if we could get a session or two to ourselves at next years camp it'd be a definite bonus.[19]

I eventually formed a good guess as to the four other girls at the California Amateur Skateboard League contest thanks to another zine, *Ladies Skateworld*, which shared KZ's perspective. Both publications organically evolved because the writers were attentive to rumors of fellow female skaters out in the wild. KZ said,

> I met four girls at a contest, I gave them my phone number, and we would insist on having our own division. I was like, "Let's organize!" And everyone was doing a zine, so I was like, "I should do a zine!" I'd go over to Kinko's in Berkeley, and literally everything is

taped on, cut and pasted, with a bunch of Wite-Out. I don't know how many copies I made, but I was always mailing them out.[20]

KZ decided to have a "tricks tips" section in the zine featuring photos of girls performing and describing their favorite moves. The photo from *Thrasher* of KZ performing a boneless was reproduced with this intention because they thought the reader might be more motivated to try the trick if they saw another female skater make a successful attempt. KZ noted that when male skateboarders and their abilities were established as the standard, it could lead to feelings of inadequacy, of not being "good enough" or not being a real skateboarder.

After getting sponsored by SMA, KZ took a year off school to skate with their friend Amy Paul and start networking with other female skaters. The goal was to support Bonnie Blouin's dream, as expressed in *Thrasher*, "to see through the formation of a nationwide, nonprofit girl's skate club, a directory of names and addresses, a video and a contest. We are out here. We are few and far between, but we are out here."[21] Bonnie even made the trek from Richmond, Virginia, to meet KZ out west, which she reported on in her "Skater's Edge" column in *Thrasher*.

One of Bonnie's contacts was Stephanie Person, who would become the first Black female professional skateboarder in 1988. (She is celebrated in Chapter Five.) KZ said,

> Stephanie was doing cool stuff and was going to be in the State of California antidrug commercial, but she injured herself and gave them my name. I was nineteen years old and had no idea what I was doing. They flew me out to Sacramento, I did an interview, and they offered me the job for five hundred dollars.
>
> So, I got flown out again and they introduce me to the "expert," who was a forty-year-old guy who

had skated in the 1960s. I was like, *Oh, shit!* The little ramp he built was awful — the transition was so tight. I felt like I looked really dumb, just dancing around, and then they combed my hair out. It really bugged me when they combed my hair, but I was too young to say, "Fuck this."

I asked KZ, who is Latinx with naturally curly hair, if they wanted to abandon the commercial, as it was obvious that messing with their hair texture was crossing a serious boundary. I also imagined that as someone who played in a punk band, they might have found the antidrug campaign uncomfortable. But KZ was determined to follow through because the flight was paid for and allowed them to compete in the Sacramento Street contest.

When the commercial came out, it was played in movie theaters, before the start of a movie. I was really embarrassed, but I was meeting people who said, "I saw that ad, and it inspired me." I felt seen as a girl or kind of a queer girl or someone that was tomboyish, so it had positive repercussions.

I checked out the "Right to Say No (To Drugs)" commercial thanks to YouTube, and it was exactly how KZ described. The ramp is practically a jarring wallride, which KZ manages, and the 1980s dance routine has hints of *Footloose* but doesn't quite deliver the same energy. The message is to "be an original" and refuse drugs, but KZ is literally the only thing original about the production, even with their hair straightened and feathered. Despite the spectacle, KZ found the silver lining by recognizing that there were girls in those movie theater seats taking notice of an alternative female skateboarder on screen, even if the performance was embedded in an uncool PSA.

TOP LEFT: Saecha Clarke boardslides a handrail during a skate mission with Ethan Fox in 1991

TOP RIGHT: Cover of the zine *Push, Push, Then Go!*, number 4 from 1988, by KZ Zapata

MIDDLE RIGHT: Diane and Primo Desiderio perform a freestyle routine, shared in *Equal Time* zine 1989

BOTTOM LEFT: KZ Zapata performing a boneless at the Sacto Streetstyle contest, which appeared in *Thrasher* (July 1986)

COOL / UNCOOL

Kristy McNichol
Actress best known as "Buddy" Lawrence in the TV show *Family* (1976–80)

Decades before Kristy McNichol revealed to *People* magazine that she was a lesbian and had been living with her partner since the early 1990s, she was a 1970s child star. Kristy's character Buddy in the TV show *Family* was a skateboarding tomboy, and she may very well have been the most beloved skateboarding character in television history. The role resulted in Kristy winning two Emmy Awards, and her performance in the episode "Jury Duty" — during which Buddy fends off an alleged child molester with her skateboard and wins a slalom race — was memorable.

In 1977, at age fourteen, Kristy agreed to be part of a CBS *Celebrity Challenge of the Sexes*, in which a number of stars competed in athletic events, men versus women. Kristy competed against Dan Haggerty of *Grizzly Adams* in a slalom skateboard contest. The course included a starting ramp for speed, a twelve-foot tunnel, and cones to dodge. A report in the *Wild World of Skateboarding* magazine said the actors were "head to head at the bottom of the ramp . . . but [Dan] did a beard plant at the tunnel entrance. Kristy floated through to win easily."[22] While more for entertainment than legitimate contests, the television special banked on the notoriety of the 1973 tennis matchup between Billie Jean King and Bobby Riggs, with King emerging victorious. Even if the skate contest was a playful gimmick, Kristy helped solidify the participation of women in skateboarding in popular culture, capitalizing on her status as a known celebrity.

CBS followed up the program with *Challenge of the Sexes*; one segment featured Ernie Martin, the Guinness World Record–holding skateboarder in high jump, and Robin Logan, the first female skater known to land kickflips, also skilled in freestyle and bowl riding.[23] The competition aired in January 1978 and was described as a modern Olympic decathlon: "The best overall performance was judged by the individual competitor's skill in each event . . . competitors competed, not only against each other, but also against themselves and world records."[24] Again, the female contestant proved to be cool and calm under pressure, and Robin won, leaping over barrels and riding a half-pipe with confidence.

The skateboarding role of Buddy was a natural fit for Kristy, and while the general public accepted the fictional portrayal of a tomboy child, attitudes began to shift as Kristy grew older. One magazine inquired, "Kristy McNichol — Is She Tired of Being a Tomboy?" and then proceeded to scrutinize her body and appearance; she was fifteen years old. Living under Hollywood's microscope, Kristy experienced several mental breakdowns in the 1980s.

There was always a core group of fans who revered Kristy, including members of the queer community. Kristy unknowingly became a queer punk icon in the DIY zine called *J.D.'s* (aka *Juvenile Delinquents*), written by G.B. Jones, Bruce LaBruce, and the New Lavender Panthers, printed in Toronto. Issue six from 1989 is flush with references to Buddy including images from the "Jury Duty" episode, which were photographed from a live TV viewing and collaged into the zine. The caption reads "Buddy uses her gnarly board as a weapon." The photos are positioned next to G.B. Jones's drawings of her super badass "Tom Girls," which were heavily stylized leather-dyke skateboarders.

It's highly unlikely that Kristy would be aware of her impact as a female skateboarder or that her Buddy character had a life of her own in an underground, banned publication. I have no idea if skateboarding continued to be an outlet for Kristy after *Family* ended, but I'm not surprised that she expressed being "overwhelmed with love and support" in 2012 when she publicly shared her sexuality to help combat the bullying of queer youth.[25]

Diane Desiderio
Professional freestyle skateboarder (1980s–present)

Diane Desiderio (née Veerman) embraced the 1980s in all its glory with big hair, big earrings, and neon workout gear with geometric designs. She was skateboarding's answer to Olivia Newton-John and secured sponsorships with Tracker Trucks and Madrid Skateboards. Diane was a natural performer and determined competitor, often the lone female professional in freestyle contests. She was a lead skater at San Diego SeaWorld's "City Streets" show, which included skateboarding, BMX riding, and dance. Her routines introduced skateboarding to the masses, but from the perspective of the dominant skateboarding culture, this was not cool, and it certainly wasn't punk.

In the June 1986 issue of *Thrasher*, an article was published about the death of skateboarding during the peak of its popularity in the 1980s.[26] The *Thrasher* writer known only as "Pete Pan" condemned the corporatization of skateboarding, the mass-produced *Back to the Future* skateboards, and the zines made by poseurs, which he regarded as toilet paper: "Skating should not be talked about. It should be done . . . I've seen posers [sic] come and go for 23 years. I will feast on the third death of skateboarding. It will clean the foul air of the fakers and phonies who pollute our pavements."[27]

For someone who insisted that skating shouldn't be talked about, the writer had a lot to say about his own status as an authentic skater. To prove his point, a two-page centerfold photo of Diane skating at SeaWorld, surrounded by gleeful dancers holding skateboards as props, accompanied the article. In juxtaposition to Pete Pan's rant, it was implied that Diane was a sellout for performing to a mainstream audience — the ultimate proof of the co-opting of skateboarding.

Diane and her husband, Primo, were offering six demos a day in the summer, and two a day in the winter, at SeaWorld.[28] She would have been the first female skateboarder that thousands of children witnessed with awe and wonder, rather than judgment, but to the *Thrasher* writer, this was blasphemy. Pete Pan despised mainstream popularity because it meant his own identity as a skateboarder was threatened, watered down, and lumped in with "all the little eunuchoid hairless soft-asses" and "phony dorkers" who "have never ridden anything but a skin flute" while he wanted to maintain a vision of skateboarding being "a sadistic way of crashing on pavement at high speeds."[29]

With so few photos in magazines of women skateboarding, it is suspect that Diane was chosen to accompany this article. *Thrasher* could have presented a mob of snotty-nosed kids with their flimsy plastic boards or included a photo of rich frat boys from Rhode Island with the expensive setups that Pete Pan was so upset about. My theory is that this photo was chosen partially because Diane was a freestyle skater. Freestyle skateboarding was being purged by the industry as an uncool discipline in the 1980s, replaced by street-style, which was purported to be grittier, more chaotic, aggressive, rebellious, and therefore masculine.

In the 1970s, the established disciplines of skateboarding were freestyle, slalom, and vertical performed in a pool or bowl. Freestyle was popular because the competitor could choose their own music and choreograph a routine that displayed balance, strength, control, dexterity, and grace. There was no sense of freestyle being inferior or gendered, and yet because women, often with backgrounds in gymnastics and dance, were so competent in freestyle, it started to gain a reputation of being the discipline of choice for women.

I'm convinced that because the skateboarding industry was trying to reinvent itself in the 1980s as an exclusively male activity, banned by the authorities and forced to thrive in the city streets, any association with a so-called feminine pursuit had to be shunned. Some companies and individuals went so far as to label freestyle "gay," the ultimate insult in the 1980s, to distinguish themselves as the opposite. For example, one skateboarder explained how, "There was a time back in the day when everyone used to bray with laughter at some weirdo called Rodney Mullen doing a 'gay' trick called a kickflip on his stupid little freestyle deck (as if that would ever catch on) while they trash-skated instead to Suicidal Tendencies, Black Flag and McRad."[30] In June 1992, Rodney's shoe sponsor Etnies acknowledged the shit-talking in an ad in *TransWorld* which had the tagline "Just another gay freestyler," during a time when Rodney was rebranding himself as a technical street skater.

Skateboarders in the 1980s had an immature habit of using references about sexual minorities in a thoughtless manner. There's an extensive thread on the SlapMagazine.com forum from May 2020 exploring how the organization Skate Like a Girl proposed reclaiming and changing skate trick names and terms like "tranny," "sex change," "gay twist," and "les twist" to resolve this. While the discussion was mixed, both defensive and supportive, the overriding consensus today is that we should use terms that are inclusive. It's unfortunate that it happened in the first place and that a conversation about its negative impact took so long to occur.

Meanwhile, in the 1980s, Diane persisted with her love of freestyle and acquired a signature skateboard in 1988, designed by her brother Max with an elegant purple peacock motif. Diane then had a full part in the groundbreaking video *SK8HERS* in 1992 (dir. Ethan Fox), which was the first all-women skateboard video. Over the years, Diane and Primo built their own backyard mini-ramp, received a Freestyle Hall of Fame award in 2008, and still have pro signature skateboards available from the company Sk8Kings. In my opinion, Diane's decision to ignore the trends of the mainstream skateboarding community and stick with freestyle was more authentic and badass than Mr. Pete Pan moaning about recreation centers building ramps for kids and "soft-bellied whiners."

Kathy Sierra
Freestyle skateboarder and game developer (1980s–present)

In a February 2015 issue of *Wired* magazine, an article by Kathy Sierra was published called "Silicon Valley Could Learn a Lot from

Skater Culture. Just Not How to Be a Meritocracy." This is the same Kathy Sierra who was featured in *The Verge* as "one of the most visible women in tech"[31] because of her cutting-edge blog — before she was ruthlessly targeted with death and rape threats. Kathy had enraged a group of men for suggesting that online comments be moderated. One hacker posted fake ads implying that Kathy was soliciting sex alongside her home address before distributing her Social Security number online.

It took great courage for Kathy to reemerge in the public sphere, and it's interesting that she drew parallels between her experiences in skateboarding and tech. Sierra explained how in the 1970s, she was a sponsored rider for Santa Cruz, preparing for international contests, until she suffered a serious knee injury. In 1983, when she had recuperated and wanted to rejoin the skateboard world, Kathy discovered that "freestyle had vanished, and so had most of the women. The world-class footwork and flat tricks I did were now mocked mercilessly . . . I was not a 'real' skater."[32] To fill the void, she found a new passion, which was programming and writing code. Eventually that experience was sabotaged, and she was pushed out of the tech industry by trolls.

Sierra asserted that in the 1970s, even though sexism was rampant, embedded in the culture and workplaces, skateboarding was a pursuit in which women could thrive. The expectation was that opportunities for women would continue to improve, but "in the '80s, skate culture devolved from a vibrant, reasonably gender-balanced community into an aggressively narrow demographic of teen boys."[33] She believed that while skateboarding and computer programming were purported to be places of refuge for society's outcasts, blind privilege and misogyny had been allowed to proliferate.

In the *Wired* article, Kathy's frustration was aimed at a TED Talk presented by her former skateboarding hero, Rodney Mullen, which featured a slide presentation focused on men's accomplishments. Knowing that Rodney had been harassed and targeted in the 1980s,

I have some empathy, but his lecture sounded beyond disappointing. Rodney's girlfriend in the 1980s was Canada's national champion, Sophie Bourgeois, who competed in slalom and freestyle and was on the Powell Peralta amateur team. Rodney would have been aware of this sphere of female skaters carving out space for themselves.

Sierra's opinions on skateboarding triggered significant debate online, including discussion of Hubba, a skateboard wheel company that consistently printed ads featuring heavily-endowed women in lingerie or naked, posing next to their products. In a debate on the *Skate and Annoy* blog, one woman was prompted to write how odd it was that after Title IX in 1972, which banned sex discrimination in federally funded programs and gave American women the right to equal opportunities in sports, "skate advertising and deck graphics seemed to become aggressively more sexist."[34] The same woman also observed that "the vitriolic hate-filled trolling that followed [the *Wired* article] was proof enough that meathead-ism is alive and well."[35]

While little has changed in terms of online trolls, Kathy Sierra concluded that if she were to present a PowerPoint on what skating can teach tech, she would make sure to include pioneers from the 1970s like Ellen Berryman, Edie Robertson, Ellen Oneal, Terry Brown, Desiree Von Essen, and many more. "Because if you think the male skaters are inspirational . . . you should get to know the women."[36] The *Wired* article ended on a hopeful note with a passage on Skateistan, the nonprofit skateboard society that was launched in Afghanistan in 2007 and expanded around the world with an emphasis on girls' participation and supporting street-entrenched youth to receive an education.

While Kristy McNichol, as a trained actress, appeared composed in a contest setting, KZ was a bundle of nerves before an event knowing that their presence wasn't welcomed by everyone. As they described the Sacto Streetstyle contest in 1986, KZ said, "There's a video of that contest, and I remember I was shaking. It happened every time I competed, but I actually really loved to compete because I loved to show that girls can skate. Maybe we don't have the same tricks [as the guys] but we're still doing it, and that contest was really big."[37] KZ was willing to risk it all, to appear foolish and be fodder for condemnation, if it meant even one other girl was inspired.

It's curious that less than a decade earlier female skateboarders and contest organizers had the opposite challenge. In 1978, skateboarding was so popular in California that there could be multiple contest divisions for boys and girls, broken down by age groups, such as the divisions at the California State Championships. As more companies were sponsoring skateboarders, a skater might compete in a sponsored amateur division with the hopes of gaining professional status and receiving a salary for their efforts, vying for prize money at events like the Oceanside Pro-Am Freestyle Contest. The only problem was that if you were a female professional, the prize money was significantly less. At the 1976 Free Former World Freestyle Championships, the top five men received cash prizes of two thousand, one thousand, seven hundred fifty, five hundred and two hundred fifty dollars respectively, while only the top three women were funded, with Ellen Berryman receiving six hundred dollars, Laura Thornhill three hundred and Ellen Oneal one hundred.[38]

The 1970s was still an era of liberation and progress, with milestones like the 1974 Equal Credit Opportunity Act that allowed women to have their own credit cards and apply for loans without a man's permission, but the female skaters who thrived in the 1970s were told that they were too old to skate upon reaching their late teens and early twenties. There was an expectation to "grow up," which meant abandoning their skateboard to pursue college or a career and ultimately start a family. Skateboard legend Cindy Whitehead explained that the first wave of 1970s female skaters were

> moving toward adulthood, with jobs, college, and dating filling their time. Skateboarding was left behind

and, in some cases, it wasn't because they wanted to leave but rather because they financially had to. Male skaters who were winning contests and had endorsement deals could make a decent living, but unfortunately for the women that was not an option.[39]

In 1980, Cindy competed as a pro in the Gold Cup series against Pattie Hoffman, Gale Webb, Denise Danielson, Leigh Parkin, and Kim Adrian, and while the talent was there, the funding for women was not. And it didn't help that the industry was tanking with the mass closure of skateparks across North America because of insurance claims.

Professor Iain Borden explained that despite the low injury-per-participant ratios at skateparks in the 1970s, "the inevitable accidents led to entanglement with the prevalent US liability culture. 'Every parent of a kid with a broken wrist,' recalled Big O's manager Gerry Hurtado, 'wanted to grab a lawyer and sue for the one-mil cash out.' As a result, by 1978 many skateparks found meaningful insurance difficult to obtain."[40] Borden also described how many ambitious skatepark designs were not financially viable: "Already in 1978 many US skateparks were insolvent after lavish costs had necessitated admission fees of between three and six dollars per two-hour session, and by 1980 most had closed."[41] Debbi Bennett, a skateboarding activist who wanted to legalize skateboarding in the streets and sidewalks of Los Angeles, said, "Not everyone can afford to go to a skatepark [and pay entrance fees] and not everyone lives close enough to one,"[42] and in 1978 she predicted that skateboarders would soon be considered "outlaws" in the city streets.

In an issue of *Skat'nNews* from January 1981, the editors celebrated amateur pool and bowl skaters Cara-Beth Burnside, Sue Smith, Lisa Forman, Shirley McClelland, Gale Springer, and Joanna Field. But they still wrote, "It's very possible that next season, they may have to compete with some of the boys, which at this point, it appears that they will do quite well."[43] That suspicion came true when the Association of Skatepark Owners (ASPO) stopped offering a separate category for girls in its contest series in the summer of 1981. Some individuals like Cara-Beth did take on the guys with success, as Tony Hawk noted. For example, she had a first-place finish against fourteen boys in the pool competition at the Whittier Skatepark that April. Most girls opted to avoid contests that pitted them against the boys.

The elimination of a girls' division was likely a temporary plan to weather the downturn in the skateboarding industry, but the legacy of ASPO's decision persisted well into the 1990s. It's disappointing to realize that when skateboarding reclaimed its status as a cool, money-making, youthful pursuit, the prevailing attitude was that girls should suck it up and prove themselves against the guys (or not skate at all); this was the era when KZ was involved. While there were always individual male skaters like Jim Thiebaud (KZ's teammate on SMA) who were sympathetic and stated, "Girls should have their own league to skate in, they should get everything guys are getting,"[44] change wouldn't occur until the Women's Skateboard Network formed and made its move as a collective (discussed in Chapter Seven).

If skateboarding had been a welcoming and inclusive community, mixed-gender contests organized well could have been revolutionary. The reality was that women were made to feel inferior, and contests became stages that glorified young men and sold their sponsors' products. All you have to do is Google the controversial name Mark "Gator" Rogowski, a professional rider for Vision skateboards, a top-selling brand in the 1980s, to see an extreme example. Gator was talented and hero-worshipped, but his career and personal trajectory are also a reflection of skateboarding at its ugliest.[45] After Rogowski was finally charged in March 1992 with the rape and murder of Jessica Bergsten, there was a predictable silence from the skateboarding industry. I don't know if anyone at that time considered the impact of misogynist culture, but the lack of response had harmful consequences.

From a purely graphic design standpoint, Gator's board is iconic, but when the owners of Vision reissued his signature board in 2009 to capitalize on his notoriety, it was a red flag that the community still had unresolved issues. A blog post from *Skate and Annoy* revealed that there was a range of opinions regarding Gator's actions and his sponsor. One person commented how it was "a truly sad day for skateboarding . . . shame on Vision," while another wished he had bought a collectible Gator T-shirt that read "lady killer," and someone else justified their purchase because "before this murder, [Gator] was a nice guy, and I assume OJ was as well." And finally, my favorite sentiment: "dear vision, go fuck yourselves. love, skateboarding."[46] Justifications for Gator's actions have continued in recent years, as recently as April 2022 during a podcast called *The Nine Club*, when a friend of Rogowski's was interviewed and tried to defend him, and later admitted that his own comments were ignorant and insensitive. This time, the predominant reaction by the general skateboarding community was disgust, articulated best by writer Anthony Pappalardo on his Substack who critiqued the narcissism and lack of accountability in certain podcast settings.[47]

In the 1990s, after Rogowski's incarceration, instead of an outpouring of love for female skaters, the industry made things worse. For example, in the March 1991 issue of *TransWorld* magazine, before his conviction, readers were blessed with photos of Lori Rigsbee skating ramp and Saecha Clarke boardsliding a handrail. After that, dead silence. It would be another two years before *TransWorld* published a single photo of a woman skateboarding — the August 1993 issue featuring Floridian vert skater Jodi McDonald.

To ditch women for twenty-nine issues is surely a media record in alienation, but what is so devastating is that this was a time when we needed an expression of support the most. All fourteen women from the *SK8HERS* video could have been interviewed. This avoidance of both Gator's crime and female skaters feels pivotal because it suggests that the industry was incapable of taking a stance against femicide and rape culture. And because the industry never explicitly condemned the violence, antiquated attitudes and rumors were left unchecked. Sadly, the 1990s unfolded with some of the most tedious "sex sells" marketing campaigns that deteriorated into extremely violent board graphics and advertisements.[48] Women were more likely to be seen fondling skateboard products like wheel bearings and griptape half-naked than actually skateboarding in a magazine. The message was that skateboarding was best suited for men to pour out their angst and aggression, and if women were alienated as a result, that's just the way it was.

A vert skater from Scotland, Michelle Ticktin, recalled going into her local skate shop around this time "where they had a photo wall. There was one of me skating up there and someone had scrawled on it, 'The man's thing' with an arrow pointing directly at me. I never found out who wrote it; no one owned up to it. Beyond it being an insult, I still don't really understand it. And the people behind the counter left it up there for all to see."[49] This experience was followed up with a guy at her skatepark declaring, "If I see you again, I'm going to kill you," when Michelle was just a teenager. She described the interaction as "a low point."

My response to stories like this is rage. Sifting through skateboard magazines for photos of my heroes and coming up empty while having to look at scantily clad models in cringeworthy advertisements only adds to it. The best thing I can do is be fueled by frustration and forge on. When I finally land upon a historic photo of someone like Jodi McDonald, who has a legacy of overcoming adversity since the 1980s and is now battling cancer, it's very satisfying, like finding an oasis in a desert wasteland or stomping a kickflip for the first time. I know the effort is worth it.

For a Latinx Heritage Month article in Berkeley High's school publication, KZ Zapata, now a high school teacher and adjunct professor, was interviewed. KZ said, "What I teach about is that there are lots of different ways we dehumanize one another and oppress one another . . . My goal in my classes is to connect stories we tell ourselves to justify the treatment or mistreatment of others."[50] KZ reminded me that it's important to question generalizations and question the past, because that process enables us to explore a range of possibilities, avoid archival silence, and unpack histories with greater intention.

When I hear statements from male pros like "The door pretty much closed for the girls" in the 1980s and that skateboarding "really wasn't a place for the girls,"[51] which were mentioned in the documentary *Skategirl* (2006, dir. Susanne Tabata), I know they aren't trying to be hurtful, but it prompts me to pause and ask what impact these comments have had. I feel that these assumptions have blocked curiosity about the past. Based on zines like *Push, Push, Then Go!*, I've realized that KZ, their skateboarding pen pals, and fellow zine writers who thrived in the 1980s despite the multiple barriers they faced, were too punk and too hardcore for the industry to accept, not the other way around. This story could also be about men's progress as they make space for others without feeling threatened, learn to listen, support inclusive and accountable community, and not impose standards of authenticity that serve to elevate men alone. Even better, when men recognize that they have privilege and use their platforms to be an ally, that's an indication of real change.

While concluding our interview, KZ explained that even though the skateboarding industry was problematic for them, the act of skateboarding still provided a space to explore their identity.

> Skateboarding freed me to live on the margins. I wasn't fitting into any box because I didn't fit any description, even racially, so I embraced it . . . If life doesn't work for you, there's a way outside, but it's not easy. If you're Black or Brown or have

complications of identity, just accept *you* — know the box and try to be outside it. You have to put a bit of effort in, especially in the 1980s, but you can find like-minded people. I tell my students all the time, "You gotta find your crew."[52]

If you've ever felt isolated as a skateboarder, finding friends with a similar outlook can be a game changer and impact your decision to persevere. With a group of peers, you can overcome barriers with greater ease. You're motivated to try a new trick, create your own zines, websites, videos, companies, and contests and to build community. I experienced this DIY mindset firsthand as a member of the Skirtboarders in my twenties, but as someone in their late forties, I was stumped thinking about finding *my crew* today, as KZ advised. Networking as a skateboarding adult in a small town would turn out to be a whole new barrier I hadn't anticipated, but skateboarding had a hold on me, and after thirty years it was obvious that it wouldn't let up, and I didn't want it to.

Lisa Jak Wietzke in the 1990s skating a ramp in Santa Cruz documented by Riot Grrrl, Kym Agresti

CHAPTER TWO

DIRECTOR'S CUT (LISA JAK WIETZKE)

I was sent a YouTube link for a grainy video filmed in 1990 with a title that gave me reason to pause. The B-grade movie was called *Grinding to Win,* and I assumed it was going to be a *Dirty Dancing* spin-off or some kind of joke. Fortunately, the sender clarified that he thought I would find the video interesting because I was Canadian and this movie had been filmed at West Vancouver Secondary School and the nearby skatepark, Seylynn Bowl. My expectations were low. And yet there were elements in the video that, once I realized how significant they were, caused me a moment of shock mixed with euphoria. *Grinding to Win* not only featured a female skateboarding protagonist and stunt double, but it was directed by a woman. OMG!

I'll repeat: *a female skateboarding stunt double in a film by a female director in 1990 about a girl who skateboards.*

You're asking, *What's the big deal?* With YouTube, Instagram, TikTok, and whatever's next on the market, skateboarders today have a plethora of opportunities to create and enjoy visual content. We can take this accessibility for granted. In the 1960s and 1970s, skateboarders had to study photographs in magazines and manuals to visualize the components of a new trick, many of which were recently invented. And if you weren't immersed in a dynamic scene in places like Southern California, where you could watch the local pros at a skatepark, those photographs were crucial. Skateboarding on film was even more impactful.

In the 1960s, there were a few films that celebrated skateboarding, like *Skaterdater* (1965, dir. Noel Black), but by the 1970s, the activity began to spark the imagination of directors, and women often had cameos. Child prodigy Jennifer Dimon (known today as slalom racer Jennifer Coppa), along with Andra Malczewski and Debi Eldredge of the Unity Skateboard Team and several other girls, appeared in a classroom film called *Skateboard Safety* (dir. John McDonald) from 1976. Debi also appeared in a dreamy slo-mo sequence in *The Magic Rolling Board* (dir. Jim Freeman and Greg MacGillivray) that same year, although the footage focuses more on showcasing her flowing blond hair than her skateboarding skill, apart from a proper hippie jump over a measuring stick.

Robin Alaway, Edie Robertson, and Dodie Hackemack scored background parts in the 1976 movie *Freewheelin'* (dir. Scott Dittrich), while *Skateboard: the movie* from 1978 (dir. George Gage) included Ellen Oneal in a key role as Jenny Bradshaw who offers a classic freestyle demonstration. Oneal followed that up with a gig as a stunt double for actress Cindy Eilbacher in TV's *Wonder Woman* alongside Lori Rarey, who doubled for Lynda Carter, in an episode called "Skateboard Wiz." In the 1978 documentary *Skateboard Kings* (dir. Horace Ové), Oneal was seen once again, cruising the hills of La Costa, while Kim Adrian performed her skills at the Skatopia skatepark. Adrian was documented in two scenes ripping around the snake-run and then working the half-pipe, representing her sponsor by wearing a *Sims* jersey.

In 1980, the after-school crowd was entertained with a thirty-minute TV special on CBS called *A Different Kind of Winning* with Skateboarding Hall of Fame inductees Cara-Beth Burnside and Edie Robertson playing the lead characters in a feel-good drama. The show was based on a delightful book with a cutting-edge plot called *Skateboard Scramble* by Barbara Douglass from 1979. The two girls were deemed the best skaters around, competing in mixed-gender contests, and it had nothing to do with beating the guys, but rather how they exhibited camaraderie toward each other. Besides Kristy McNichol as the skateboarding Buddy on *Family*, the concept of female skateboarding protagonists on television didn't catch on. We would have to wait forty years for that to happen with Crystal Moselle's HBO series *Betty* in 2020, which followed the success of her feature film *Skate Kitchen* (2018).

Vancouver skateboarder Lisa Jak Wietzke was unaware of this history of women's representation in skateboarding media. Her interest in skateboarding began in 1986 when she was dating a skater and decided that she didn't want to walk to the corner store. "I took his board, and I was barefoot in a hippie skirt and instantly loved how I felt to be free and to cruise along. I was hooked from that moment on."[1] After three months of using her skateboard to avoid walking, Lisa bumped into a friend skating downtown and was introduced to a crew of skaters who were exploring the city parking garages to practice tricks, which was a revelation for her. "I had no idea that there was a culture or that people skated together."

Lisa's interest would only grow stronger when popular culture marketed skateboarding as a trending activity for youth. The skateboard movie as a genre was officially established in the '80s with titles like *Thrashin'* from 1986 (dir. David Winters), featuring Josh Brolin as Corey Webster (looking like a waxy Ken doll in the promo poster) and *Gleaming the Cube* (1989, dir. Graeme Clifford) with Christian Slater projecting Billy Idol vibes as Brian Kelly. But these films never challenged the status quo. Women were still stuck playing passive girlfriends, not driving the plot in lead roles as skateboarders.

In *Thrashin'*, there's a scene where Corey and his love interest, Chrissy, are watching the Red Hot Chili Peppers serenade the skater punks before the couple heads out into an alley for a heart-to-heart. Corey offers his board to Chrissy, and after flicking off her high heels, she begins spinning 360s in her pink prom dress, and the camera zooms in on her bare feet. The stunt double was freestyle champion April Hoffman who informed me, "Those are my feet. Unfortunately, as was the culture back then, not only did I do it for free . . . but they didn't put my name in the stunt credits. I supposed that was because they didn't pay me."[2]

April brought her grandma, the beloved Jeanne Hoffman, who has been recognized in the Skateboard Hall of Fame for her tireless work organizing contests and being the co-owner of the Pipeline Skatepark in Upland, California, to the studio to shoot the scene. April filmed countless rotations for four hours in the middle of the night for nothing. Way to support the ladies, Hollywood! And yet even a glimpse of a girl like Chrissy skating barefoot sparked inspiration in a young woman's mind. Lisa Jak Wietzke took the plunge and began skateboarding as a means of transport, and that snowballed into something profound that altered her sense of identity, expanded her array of friends, and led to her own opportunity in film.

In the late 1980s and early '90s, skateboarders became early adopters of home video technology to capture their progress and document their scene. A talented skater might even recruit a friend to film them skateboarding so they could produce a "sponsor me" video to submit to companies, hoping to maybe score a few free boards if they were lucky. One's footage could also be sent to the producers of *411 Video Magazine* (*411VM*), a unique production that distributed quarterly videos on VHS (and eventually DVD) to subscribers' doors from 1993 to 2005. This video series helped alert skateboard companies to new talent, solidified new styles, and presented the latest action by professional skaters with greater frequency than the annual videos released by companies to promote their team of riders.

It took a certain level of confidence to believe that you deserved to be filmed and sponsored, and given the expectations that lingered from the 1980s, that confidence often eluded female skaters who felt that their tricks had to be on par with men to receive recognition. For example, Saecha Clarke, now inducted into the Skateboarding Hall of Fame, was reflecting on her experience skateboarding in the late 1980s and early 1990s and said,

> I really regret not filming and being part of the *Rubbish Heap* video. World [Industries] had asked me to film for it, and I remember being very shy and scared to film. I had always compared myself to all the guys on the team and thought that I wasn't good enough to be in a video with them. I think I was afraid that I would be judged and get hated on.[3]

Only exceptionally talented women in the 1990s, token members of a male-dominated team, were invited to contribute short clips and the occasional full part in a company video. These appearances were made by Cara-Beth Burnside in *Risk It* (1990) for the Santa Cruz Speed Wheels team, Lori Rigsbee in *Propaganda* (1990) for Powell Peralta, Elissa Steamer for the Toy Machine videos *Welcome to Hell* (1996) and *Jump Off a Building* (1998), followed by *All Systems Go!* (1998) for Pig wheels and *Baker Bootleg* (1999), Jaime Reyes in *Non Fiction* (1997) with Real Skateboards and Zoo York's video *Heads* (1999), and Perri Morgan for 5boro's *Fire It Up* (1999). These highlights were interspersed between lengthy features of dudes, but news travels fast when a female skater is included. The kickass part by Alexis Sablone in *P.J. Ladd's Wonderful, Horrible, Life* (2002) was a critical reminder to male skaters of that era that there was no shame in promoting your female friends.

All these women were killing it, and their video parts were game changers, but they were still scrutinized by the male majority who were unable to imagine a female market for skateboarding. Ed Templeton, owner of Toy Machine, provided an interesting example from 1998 when the company elevated Elissa Steamer to professional status. Toy Machine's website "got a tidal wave of response. Fifty percent of them were kids who were really pissed . . . They thought that they were just as good as her and that they were more worthy of being pro. They judged her purely on her tricks. The other 50 percent were writing in support of Steamer and coming to her defense."[4] In 2003, Templeton concluded that Toy Machine's experiment with Elissa proved that "women's skateboarding is not as marketable . . . For some reason, boys don't want to buy a board with a girl's name on it. Everyone respects the girl pros for doing what they do, but the big market, which is young boys, just doesn't buy it."[5]

In the 1990s, catering to an audience of female skaters seemed unimaginable. A prime example is the story of Jessica Krause who was sponsored at age thirteen by a leading board company called Think in 1996. At age fifteen, Jessica was filmed boardsliding the iconic Presidio rail in San Francisco, as well as nose-sliding a monster ledge known as the John Cardiel ledge, named after the male professional skater who first claimed this obstacle. And yet instead of promoting these massive achievements, Think never bothered to include the clips in its videos. Jessica wouldn't see her footage for twenty years, not until the person who'd filmed it posted it on Instagram and the online skateboard community expressed shock at her accomplishment. One person wrote, "Holy shit why isn't this talked about more." Unlike Toy Machine, Think treated Jessica like a gimmick in its ads even though she had the potential to be revered alongside Elissa Steamer.

I am grateful that Toy Machine took a financial risk by sponsoring Elissa, warming up other companies to the idea that female skaters should be supported. But I also feel disappointment knowing that women in the 1990s were only given crumbs, like the situation with Jessica Krause. After the Paris Olympics, there were exclamations of awe and surprise about women's seemingly rapid progress in skateboarding, and it is impressive, but the truth is, the potential was always there. If our participation and representation had been accepted and promoted decades ago, it wouldn't appear to be such a sudden onslaught today.

Even with its blurry quality and simple plot, I could relate to *Grinding to Win* and found pleasure in noticing certain details in the film that only a female skater could appreciate. The opening sequence began in darkness with just the sound of skateboard wheels crackling along rough pavement. It's a familiar sound that skateboarders are attuned to but might provoke curiosity from viewers unaware of what is approaching. There is a swell of electronic pop music, reminding me of the Go-Go's, and then the camera reveals a skateboard being propelled forward by someone wearing a pair of high-top Converse shoes and torn jeans. The camera tilts upward and pulls out, and there she is — Chris, the new girl heading to school.

The plot quickly unfolds with Chris entering the high school hallway where she immediately glances at a poster for a skateboard contest on the bulletin board. Chris is then approached by the popular gang of male skaters who assess her appearance and proclaim that she "probably sucks." The next day, Chris is interrogated by the skate rats who want to know what she's trying to prove because "girls don't' skate. Girls can't skate." Chris remains mute, but a female skateboarder could easily provide an inner monologue with a few expletives, especially when the next scene has Chris practicing outside her home with fierce determination. She's shown skateboarding on a makeshift ramp late at night, illuminated by a streetlight.

The film includes some accurate and timely details, like in Chris's bedroom. Her walls are plastered with skateboard stickers like one that declares "Skateboarding Is Not a Crime" and pages cut from magazines, including the iconic 1988 Powell Peralta ad with Anita Tessensohn and Leaf Treinen which states "Some Girls Play with Dolls: Real Women Skate." This ad was cherished by female skaters because you could tell that Anita and Leaf were badass: slouched against a brick wall holding their skateboards, wearing high-top shoes scuffed from hard use. Stacy Peralta, owner of Powell Peralta, noticed Anita and Leaf at the Willamette Dammit Skate contest in Eugene, Oregon, in 1987; that was where they lived and skated alongside a gang of ten girls.[6] When he took their photo, I wonder if Peralta intuitively understood that women represented the ultimate skateboarding outsider, more punk than punk. His decision to publish the photo in an ad was a surprise to all and a rare expression of industry approval for female skaters in the late 1980s.

Meanwhile, Chris finds friendship and support from other girls at school and encourages their interest in trying her skateboard. She is unfazed by the guys, keeps practicing, and continues to show up and skate. Her perseverance pays off, and when one of the skate rats is injured, she's called upon to fill his spot on the school team. Contest day arrives and Chris proves that she rips and the team wins. But the icing on the cake is when Chris snubs a guy who tries to flirt with her, and instead of him reacting with animosity, they ride off on their skateboards as friends.

After watching *Grinding to Win*, I immediately went on an internet search rampage trying to find out if the lead actress, Traci MacKillop, was an unknown skater waiting to be discovered. It was a total dead end — I needed more clues. This time I let the credits roll. I jotted down the director's name, Samantha Reynolds, and then a few more names caught my eye. Gordon and George Faulkner, identical twin skaters who had always been kind to me and my friends in our early days as a girl gang in Burnaby, British Columbia. Turns out they had been recruited to be part of the contest background scene, and conveniently, I was still in contact with them.

DIRECTOR'S CUT (LISA JAK WIETZKE)

It's early days writing this manuscript, and my first thought at breakfast is *No one wants to read about you*. The thought seems valid but also unfair. I've committed time and energy into writing about influential and forgotten female skateboarders, some of whom never entered a contest, let alone found their photo in a magazine or landed a part in a skateboard video. I can see *their* value but wonder if it's necessary to insert my own voice in the narrative.

There's another more reassuring whisper reminding me that if I go down a negative path, choosing to exclude myself, doubting my motives and the value of my story, then why write about anyone? If the skateboarders I'm celebrating ignored messages of condemnation, so can I.

When my friend Mathilde Pigeon in Montréal began filming our Skirtboarder gang at various street spots in 2002, it was tempting to shy away. I thought that my lowly heelflips and kickflips were a waste of her time, but Mathilde was persistent. Mathilde had seen her male friends working on a video to represent their team and imagined herself doing the same. "I was thinking, *If I get a camera maybe I could just film a little bit and make like a two-minute film*. Two minutes! That was like the biggest thing I was imagining. I just started filming and filming. I filmed the whole summer . . . I got all the girls, everyone who was skating this summer."[7]

When Mathilde launched our first video called *Boy* on VHS in 2003, which was an admirable fifteen minutes in length with ten skaters featured, we partied. I was included in the montage with my friends, and no one cared about the quality of filming or our skill level. Mathilde explained, "I'm making this video not to sell it, just so people can see it, be proud and see us doing it . . . This is something we all did together this summer to show that we're out there skating . . . This video is going to be the truth, some evidence. Everyone was like, 'Yeah sure, film it.' Shy at first, but you know we just made it all together."[8]

Being filmed while skateboarding means being vulnerable. You might be seen at your worst, swearing, bailing, impaling yourself on an obstacle, or stomping in frustration like a toddler. Or you might be portrayed at your best, landing something epic, celebrating with friends, kissing the concrete that almost destroyed you, in humility and thanks, while maybe regretting the over-the-top displays of emotion upon reflection. The only reason I allowed Mathilde to film me was because I trusted her, especially when she turned the camera on herself.

ROLL CAMERA

Lisa Whitaker
Skateboarder, videographer, photographer, webmaster, and owner of Meow Skateboards (1980s–present)

If I'm going to talk about trust, women, and skateboard filming, I can't not point to Lisa Whitaker. Lisa's name pops up repeatedly in this book because she has single-handedly filmed the most footage of female skaters ever, and that's come down to a combination of dedication, skill, perseverance, and trust. While an acknowledgment of Lisa's work is sometimes buried in film credits, her influence is profound.[9] In a feature video about Lisa's skateboard company, Meow Skateboards, which was founded in 2012, legendary pro skateboarder Vanessa Torres stated, "Lisa has always just been the catalyst for women skateboarding . . . She's committed and you can't help but feed off of that . . . I celebrate that human daily. She's been a part of so many pivotal moments in my life."[10]

Lisa began skateboarding in 1985 when her parents bought her a skateboard from a big-box store.

Then sometime around 1987 one of the older kids in the neighborhood built a launch ramp. As soon as I

DIRECTOR'S CUT (LISA JAK WIETZKE)

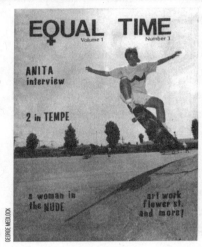

TOP: Mob of badass female skaters at the Powell SkateZone in 1991, documented by Ethan Fox

LEFT: Anita Tessensohn on the cover of *Equal Time* zine in 1989

RIGHT: VHS cover of *SK8HERS* film from 1992, directed by Ethan Fox, featuring Cara-Beth Burnside

saw it, I knew that is what I wanted to do. I talked my dad into getting me a Powell Peralta Lance Mountain board, discovered skate videos, magazines, and learned that it was possible to do tricks.[11]

Even though her favorite skaters were guys as a kid, "there was something way different about seeing other girls skate for some reason. Like, the little section in the Powell video [*Public Domain*] with Anita [Tessensohn] and Lori [Rigsbee]. That had such an impact on me."[12] In fact, seeing Anita land kickflips prompted Lisa to believe that she could do the same.

Skateboard companies in the 1980s, like Powell Peralta, started creating their own narratives in video form by featuring their sponsored riders. Women had to pay close attention if they wanted to witness their female peers in action. Thankfully, Powell Peralta offered glimmers of Anita Tessensohn skating street, Sophie Bourgeois performing freestyle, and Lori Rigsbee shredding her mini-ramp in *Public Domain* (1988). It's not hard to imagine that these clips were repeatedly rewound by young women like Lisa, desperate for inspiration.

Lisa's first experience filming was "a launch ramp session in front of my house with my dad's over-the-shoulder VHS camcorder . . . about 1989."[13] Around age fourteen, she began to film her friends as they improved, sending the footage to their sponsors, submitting content to *411 Video Magazine*, among other productions, and creating her own DIY videos including *What* (1990), *911* (1994), and *The Wonder Years* (1995).[14] One of her friends, Koji Harmon, was an amateur photographer and submitted a batch of photos to *Thrasher*, which happened to include Lisa. It was a surprise when the photos were printed in the "Photograffiti" section in June 1994 and then a year later in a two-page collage of female skaters called "More Girls Who Skate." Lisa recalled being stoked about the acknowledgment, even if her style had changed over the year, in particular her red Christmas socks.[15]

Lisa's skateboarding abilities were getting noticed, and in 1997, Rookie Skateboards recruited her for its team (discussed in Chapter Seven), which gave her the opportunity to travel, compete, meet more women, and be associated with a female-owned company. And yet it soon became apparent that in spite of the growing population of talented female riders, no one was bothering to document their progress, so Lisa stepped up and initiated change. "I realized that a lot of these girls didn't have any videos of themselves 'cause there was like no outlet for it. I'd been filming these girls for like two decades basically. I knew how hungry I was for that content . . . I know how it felt because I was one of those girls."[16] The footage needed a home and a way for female skateboarders to easily access it.

The internet was a new tool for communication in the late 1990s, and Lisa started out just wanting to learn the technology and decided to build a website.

> The content I had was all friends and the skating I had been filming, so I used that as a demo concept to build this site, never thinking that anyone would see it, but shortly after it went up, I started receiving emails from girls around the world. Stories like "I've always wanted to skateboard, but my parents told me it was only for boys. I found your site, showed them, they're giving me a skateboard now," or they were inspired to keep skating, seeing that there was others.[17]

In 2003, Lisa had called her website the Side Project, since that's all it was intended to be, but it began to get traction. Lisa saw its potential and became even more motivated, renaming the website the Girls Skate Network, which is still active. The site was soon filled with video blogs, women's contest results (which the popular magazines rarely included), interviews, and news updates.

Lisa's website normalized the documentation of female skaters, provided a hub for women, and through her "blog cam" concept — female skaters were shown having a blast during a day-to-day skate session — the women became relatable and recognizable, garnering fans.[18] Torres explained that in the mid-1990s, "there was no real destination for women's skateboarding. Nobody else was filming us . . . Girls Skate Network was a huge focal point, a destination for any young girl or young woman to see what was going on in the world of women's skateboarding."[19] Kristin Ebeling, director of the nonprofit organization Skate Like a Girl and pro skater for Meow Skateboards, was one of those young girls. She said, "To be completely honest, I would have quit skating if it wasn't for having access to that content, you know. Seeing videos of Vanessa Torres, Amy Caron, really felt like I was a part of something even though I didn't even know them personally."[20]

Lisa proved that women could circumvent the dominant media outlets that were ignoring female skaters and build a global community online. Lisa also contributed to *AKA: Girl Skater* (2003, dir. Mike Hill) featuring the Gallaz female pro team on a tour of Australia, had a major role in the Villa Villa Cola film production *Getting Nowhere Faster* (2004), and supported the hour-long documentary *Skategirl* with her footage from contests like the All Girl Skate Jam and Slam City Jam. And it's thanks to Lisa that this critical era of progress in the early 2000s is archived so thoroughly and accessible to all.

In the same way that Cara-Beth Burnside has been an anchor and mentor for female skaters over multiple decades, Lisa's actions, while often behind the scenes, have been monumental. Her footage and website filled a void and spawned comparable initiatives like MAHFIA.TV, founded by Kim Woozy in 2010, which backed the production of the female-focused film *Quit Your Day Job* (2016) by Erik Sandoval and Monique O'Toole, among others. So, if you ride a Meow Skateboard or wear their gear, you can feel confident that you're supporting an advocate and an incredible team of skaters. As Meow pro skater Amy Caron acknowledged, "Lisa is the mayor of girls skateboarding."[21]

Skate Witches
Short film directed by Danny Plotnick (1986)

The video *Skate Witches*, only two minutes in length, has become a cult classic. Filmed on Super 8 by Danny Plotnick in the summer of 1986 in Ann Arbor, Michigan, while he was attending the University of Michigan, it includes performances by Dana Mendelssohn, Jenny Parker, and Karen Kibler, and Plotnick's pet rats (Maggie and Mr. Ig Wig). The Skate Witches as a girl gang were fictional, but their defiant attitudes motivated a new generation of skaters.

"Skate and Destroy" by the Faction is the punk soundtrack for *Skate Witches*: it sets the stage for three female skaters who assert their manifesto while skating in a plaza. One member is wearing a black Misfits T-shirt emblazoned with a giant white skull, another sports a heavy leather jacket in the middle of summer, in contrast to her bleached blond hair, and they all have pet rats, which was a gang requirement. The Queen Witch would "only ride at midnight" and acted as a bouncer, terrorizing the guys and stealing their skateboards if they got in the way. The core message was: "We don't take no crap from no one."

It's not clear how or when the YouTube upload of this retro video reached its target market, but once it started circulating, *Skate Witches* was adopted as a symbol of women's experience in skateboarding. Kristin Ebeling, recognized previously for her role in Skate Like a Girl and sponsorship from Meow, remembered being shown the video in the early 2000s by a friend. Kristin said, "Because of that video I ended up getting a broom and skateboard 'Skate Witches' tattoo when I was 19."[22] And when Kristin and her friend Shari White needed a name for their team at a Seattle skateboard contest, it seemed obvious to reference Plotnick's film. Kristin and Shari then produced a hugely popular zine called *The Skate Witches* with a run of sixteen issues from 2014 to 2019, chockfull of female and non-binary skaters. "The main motive for the zine is to make non-traditional skaters feel badass and inspired to get out and skate . . . The Skate Witches is like our imaginary dream world where girl skaters run shit in skateboarding, dominating skateparks, blasting Beyoncé, and doing whatever we want."[23] The crew also created videos including *SRSLY* (2017), *THX* (2019), and Shari White's full-length film *Credits* (2020), celebrating a wealth of talent including Breana Geering, Fabiana Delfino, and Una Farrar, who all acquired professional status.

The all-girls skateboard collective in New York called the Brujas (Spanish for "witches") said that they chose to name their crew in honor of the 1980s video because "their main principle is sisterhood."[24] In a *New York Times* article, the Brujas cofounder Arianna Gil posed the question, "Skater bros all think they're rebels, but who are the real outsiders here?"[25] Another reference to the film came from Alicia van Zyl in Johannesburg, South Africa, in 2017; she was tired of being faced with hostility, threats, and even rape jokes from the local dudes when any attempt at a ladies' skate session was promoted. Alicia named her all-girls organization the No Comply Coven to strengthen their resolve, like a gathering of punk witches, acknowledging the impact of Plotnick's video.[26]

Danny Plotnick said that the motivation for the video came about after a conversation with Dana who wanted to retrieve her old skateboard from her family home, to be able to skate across campus with ease.

> However, she felt she would get hassled by all the boy skateboarders in town . . . Skate culture was obviously big in the 1980s, but the documentation and the lore of that era probably features little in the way of women skaters. And any woman skating probably did get grief . . . The film was born out of Dana's frustration around the likelihood of being given grief for something she wanted to do.[27]

This frustration still rings true with many young women decades later, and the rebellious message in *Skate Witches* has become a unifying theme, one that speaks to a shared experience of alienation and a desire for safe and inclusive opportunities. Even if we had no desire to tackle some cocky skater boy to the ground, we could live vicariously through Dana's character and forge on with our friends.

SK8HERS
All-girls skateboard video directed by Ethan Fox (1992)

During the early 1990s in Santa Barbara, where skateboarding was thriving in backyards on mini-ramps and at the Powell Skate Zone indoor park, a core group of women connected through the Women's Skateboarding Network, *Equal Time* zines, and word of mouth. In 1992, filmmaker Ethan Fox sought out these skateboarders and directed the first all-girls skateboard video called *SK8HERS*.

As an avid reader of *Skateboarder* magazine, Ethan was impressed with 1970s legends Ellen Berryman, Laura Thornhill, and Robin Logan, explaining, "Even back then, I knew that they were as talented as their male counterparts and infinitely more graceful, but due to chauvinism, they were likely under promoted."[28] This is an important observation because while Ethan's generation could still recollect a more equitable representation of female skaters in magazines in the 1970s, by the 1980s and 1990s, the majority of male skaters did not have any point of reference that skateboarding could be or once was more inclusive. Thankfully, as Ethan noted, the male skaters within the Santa Barbara community seemed supportive of the women, and he wanted to be an ally.

In 1991, Ethan approached Simitar Entertainment out of Minneapolis which approved the *SK8HERS* concept and would distribute it on VHS, but it was Ethan who funded the production. Once he had the support of skaters JoAnn Gillespie and Rhonda

Doyle, who helped track down Cara-Beth Burnside, the project was launched. Ethan was aware that some of the skaters seemed "reserved when approached by some random thirty-year-old with a camera, but once they realized I was harmless, they came around, even the relatively shy Saecha Clarke. You couldn't hold JoAnn back with a chain-link fence. She was very excited about the project." JoAnn joked in our interview that "Ethan just stalked us, found us, filmed us, put it together, put it on VHS,"[29] and she was flattered that he had thought to list her and Rhonda as associate producers for their efforts in recruiting their fellow skateboarders.

Cara-Beth has a strong presence throughout the video. Ethan explained, "Cara-Beth was *the one*. She had the air of excitement around her for sure." The pro vert skater was the first female to grace the cover of *Thrasher*, for its August 1989 issue, so she ended up taking a lead role in announcing the women's video parts, showcasing her own skill, and offering words of wisdom and encouragement to female viewers. Cara-Beth was a spokeswoman in multiple documentaries in the decades to come: *Live and Let Ride* (1999, dir. Tara Cooper), *Skategirl* (2006, dir. Susanne Tabata), *UNDEREXPOSED: A Women's Skateboarding Documentary* (2012, dir. Amelia Brodka), and *Skate Dreams* (2022, dir. Jessica Edwards).

Inside the local skateboard scene, there was enthusiasm for *SK8HERS* and Ethan didn't sense any negativity from the guys. There was even a launch party with a screening at Moose McGillycuddy's pub in Marina Del Rey, known for its massive outdoor patio right on the ocean, surrounded by palm trees and moored sailboats. "Lots of the girls were there, moms too. It was great." The girls and women featured (as listed in the video in alphabetical order) included: Cara-Beth Burnside, Saecha Clarke, Diane Desiderio, Rhonda Doyle, Heidi Fitzgerald, JoAnn Gillespie, Pattie Hoffman, Lynn Kramer, Jessica Lawing, Stephanie Massey, Julie Sack, Patty Segovia, Christy Smith, and Peggy Walden.

Thanks to Ethan's initiative and photography, there's a fantastic group photo of many of these women during a skate session at the Powell Skate Zone indoor park, which was published in the October 1992 issue of *Thrasher*. I'm not sure of the editor's rationale to place it in the "Trash" section of the magazine, or the weird caption with a quotation from Ivana Trump overlaid on the photo, which reads, "I no longer like the puffball look," but it's proof of women's existence in the early '90s scene. Sadly, I have yet to find any acknowledgment or review of *SK8HERS* in a mainstream skateboard magazine. Either the editors were unaware of it, or perhaps they deemed it inconsequential to their male-dominated readership and chose to ignore the film.

In our interview, Ethan said the industry today is "still kind of a good old boy network, so women in skateboarding are still taking a back seat,"[30] but he was adamant that female skateboarders were getting harder to ignore now that they had more control over their representation and more financial support from sponsors. He also advocated for women taking the lead when creating media about female skateboarders, such as the *Skate Dreams* documentary, directed by Jessica Edwards, which premiered at the annual Exposure Skate festival in Encinitas, California, in 2022. Exposure was a natural venue for the premiere because the contest was established in response to pro skater Amelia Brodka's documentary, *UNDEREXPOSED* (2012), which aimed to analyze "the media and marketing tactics of the skateboarding industry,"[31] increase opportunities for women, and prevent the elimination of women's vert and bowl contests.

By today's standards, the production level of *SK8HERS* is pure DIY; its "special effects" remind me of excessive strobe lights at a high school dance. But for the participants and the female skaters who were fortunate to have purchased it, the video would have been validating, and as a time capsule, it is priceless.

Vancouver was the city that beckoned me away from my small town in Ontario in the fall of 1996 when I was eighteen. The West

Coast was considered *the mecca* of Canadian board sports, including skateboarding, with its more temperate weather. I offered my parents the rationale that I was leaving home to pursue higher education, but I had ulterior motives.

There's a photo of me posing in front of my mom's silver Nissan hatchback, loading my earthly possessions into the car. I'm a string bean wearing my older brother's jeans, brand name Blind and held up by a belt because they were intentionally oversized. My brown T-shirt has a graphic of a low-rider bicycle, and my long hair is loose and parted like a hippie. My curated appearance is completed with a chain-wallet, although the wallet's contents were likely empty. I project confidence, but I remember I was barely holding it together. I was going to miss my golden Labrador who naively hopped into the car trunk thinking she was going for an adventure.

When I was forty-three, my mom apologized to me with reference to that photo. Apparently, she had reprimanded me just before it was taken for packing my skateboard with my luggage. She had felt that skateboarding was too juvenile for someone my age about to enter university. I had no memory of the conversation, but it gave me a good laugh as a middle-aged skater, and I have Skateistan to thank for my mom's breakthrough.

My mom had randomly watched the 2019 short film *Learning to Skateboard in a Warzone (If You're a Girl)* directed by Carol Dysinger. The film explores Skateistan's initiative to connect children in war-torn countries like Afghanistan with skateboarding, providing them with a fun activity without stigma or gendered expectations, while also providing opportunities for education. The film pays close attention to the experiences of girls, some of whom had been street-entrenched and expected to sell goods to contribute to their family's income rather than attend school. Upon reaching their teens, many would be hidden from society, their social contacts limited to their families and, eventually, husbands. I had spoken of Skateistan before with my mom because my best friends Rhianon Bader and Erika Kinast have been heavily involved with the NGO since 2010, but something about the film made my mom pause and reconsider her perspective on skateboarding.

When positioned against the dramatic footage of war and devastation, and the extreme restrictions that fundamentalists in power impose on girls, skateboarding ended up looking pretty good. The film has emotional resonance and depth, and it's not surprising that it received multiple awards including an Oscar and a BAFTA for best short film. These Afghan skater girls exemplified courage. Subsequently, my mom realized that skateboarding had more to offer than she had given it credit for. It could be used as a tool for meaningful connection among children, providing a sense of accomplishment and leading to further opportunities like an education.

I accepted my mom's apology, but even without it, I would skateboard whether it was deemed appropriate for my age or not. When I arrived on campus back in 1996, a skatepark was actually being built near my university in Burnaby called Confederation Park. A handful of young women including Michelle Pezel, who went on to become the owner of Antisocial Skateboard Shop in Vancouver, started meeting there in 1997.

Our crew expanded to over a dozen female skaters, and these relationships were unlike high school acquaintances — these friendships had longevity. A shared love of skateboarding meant you were different; you valued your independence and had an appreciation for something that was cool and alternative. I had finally found my people — like-minded girls who would practically live at the skatepark with me when I wasn't writing essays or cramming for an exam. I would spend the next four years attending university with my hands and elbows consistently encrusted with brown scabs from skating and bailing and living my best life.

Most of the guys I met in the 1990s at Confederation Park, like Gordon and George, were supportive of this rogue girl gang. And when I reached out to the brothers about *Grinding to Win*, they confirmed that the pixelated name for the stunt double who played Chris was Lisa Jak Wietzke, not some skateboarding dude wearing a wig, as I had feared. The Faulkner twins led me straight to Lisa, who was living on Vancouver Island and active on Facebook. And then LinkedIn provided a route to contact director Samantha Reynolds. Everyone was game to reminisce and share their story.

The feedback from Samantha and Lisa was full of surprises — both had chosen to write out their responses to my questions, taking time to reflect. Reynolds wrote that the idea for her film came from the fact that

> I had been an avid skateboarder since I was ten so I wanted to write a story that best described some of my experiences as, many times, the only female / girl skater amongst many males / boys. I did not personally experience any teasing or bullying from the male skaters . . . but the film needed some sort of conflict, so I added that in.[32]

Reynolds made the film for a school project at the University of British Columbia, and when she was scouting for talent at local skateparks, it was the guys who introduced her to Lisa Wietzke.

Lisa confirmed that the locals at Seylynn Bowl knew about her, and while all the skaters got along, she was an anomaly in the scene as a female skater. Lisa had a humble beginning as a skateboarder, using it simply as a form of transportation, but when she was shown footage of Cara-Beth Burnside, most likely her part in *Risk It* (1990), Lisa was inspired. She made it her destiny to emulate Cara-Beth and learn how to drop in and excel on the vert ramp, which averages from eleven to fourteen feet in height. Luckily, the ramp from Vancouver's Expo 86 TransWorld skateboarding contest had been moved to the Richmond Skate Ranch. With access to a vert ramp and encouragement to improve, Lisa's progress skyrocketed. She eventually found herself traveling to the United States and even got the opportunity to meet her hero, Cara-Beth, in 1992. Lisa skated a demo with her at the Los Angeles

County Fair, and Cara-Beth "made me sit with her signing posters for little girls at a booth. It was the coolest thing ever!"[33]

Lisa was aware that her presence at the Ranch skatepark was unexpected, especially her choice to pursue skating the vert ramp, but it gave her such a high. "I love speed and the thrill of being weightless and floating... Funny thing is the boys that didn't know me would think it was 'cute' that I was climbing the ladder up to the [vert ramp] platform. They would let me go... 'Oh, no, after you... Chuckle, chuckle...' Then I'd clean their clock and it was on. Girls can't skate!! Right?!" The issue was that as Lisa improved, the guys in her scene who had always treated her like a sister began changing their attitude.

> Over the years I realized that not all of them were stoked that I became better than them. But I never took it to heart. It would hurt until I realized why they stopped taking me to the ramps. I just started going on my own. I learned real fast that skateboarding is a man's world and I was intruding on their playground but, like anything that people are passionate about, if someone respects it and can "walk the talk" then gender slides away, I guess.

The script for *Grinding to Win* spoke to Lisa, and she was excited to participate. She loved witnessing the behind-the-scenes magic of moviemaking, but she never got to see the final production. *Grinding to Win* was screened at the university in a local festival and Reynolds won "Best Student Film in BC," but that's as far as it got. Reynolds wasn't aware of other short film festivals, and perhaps it never occurred to the local skateboarding community to host a premiere for a movie centered on a female skater.

While it was disappointing to learn that there had been a narrow audience for *Grinding to Win*, this information gave me motivation to spread the word. I decided that my findings were worthy of public acknowledgment, to help place Vancouver on the map for contributing to the history of women's skateboarding, even if the film was under the radar. I reached out to a local news outlet to pitch an article because I knew that the editor had a connection to skateboarding.

The response was strange and disheartening. I was told that because the editor had lived in California and had been embedded in the skateboard industry, he was an expert. And because he had never heard of the film, my claim to its existence and cultural importance was dismissed. An article would not be circulated by that publication. If I had dropped the name of a male pro skater who was also among the extras, I wonder if the response would've been different, but I had no interest in appealing to this person's biases.

The rejection to my article gave me a flashback. Years ago, I had tried to pitch an idea to a publisher for a coffee table book featuring historical photos of female skateboarders throughout the decades. I even had a skateboard photographer contact who had successfully produced his own book with this publisher. I waited months and then was informed that because they already had a book about skateboarding, there was no need to add another one to their roster, regardless of the different angle and audience.

I had felt discouraged then, and those same feelings emerged after reading this magazine editor's email, but this time something would change. I needed to find my audience, people who would recognize the value of what it meant for a female skateboarder to receive some recognition in a video. I would channel my DIY spirit from those days as a Skirtboarder and make shit happen. The obvious place to start was social media.

I joined Instagram in October 2020, a tad late to the party, but I was determined to be part of the mix once I got going. I had sworn myself off social media years ago, but along came the COVID-19 pandemic and global isolation, so I had found myself reconsidering my options. I tracked down a modest number of friends to follow, and then my virtual world completely opened, revealing the vast array of skateboarding meetups, workshops, and organizations for everyone under the sun, whether you were middle-aged, non-binary, a beginner, a single mom, anything.

We were still dealing with the virus, and I was living far from any city center that drew diverse skaters together, but it was evident that things had drastically changed in the years since I had stepped away from skateboarding. I never stopped watching skateboarding contests online, especially in the lead-up to the Tokyo Olympics, but to know that so many grassroots organizations were thriving around the world was inspiring.

What I loved most about social media was the level of autonomy that individual skateboarders had over their representation. Anyone with some initiative could collect a following of fans because people at all skill levels were looking for motivation and instruction. I liked how certain individuals, regardless of their age or filming ability, dismissed and challenged any hint of judgment that they weren't worthy of being documented. Consider the social media account featuring Aunty Skates, aka Oorbee Roy, a middle-aged mom, whose video of herself flowing through a concrete bowl wearing a gorgeous purple sari and matching helmet went viral in 2021. The bold act celebrating her age and Indian culture launched Oorbee's career as an influencer.[34]

And then a post caught my eye that felt like destiny. A woman-owned skateboarding magazine put a call out for someone to help them create a directory of all these dynamic Instagram accounts and monitor what companies were stepping up to support women, BIPOC, and/or LGBTQ2S+ skateboarders. The editor wanted a searchable structure and someone who was organized. Did you say organized? *Hello!* I signed myself up and put all my librarian skills to work on one beast of an Excel spreadsheet. Finally, I was merging my two worlds, and I was secretly hoping that if I proved myself valuable, that something positive would happen with my own mission of elevating female skaters in history.

Regrettably, after a month of intense work, the magazine folded. The editor apologized, explaining that skateboarding had lost some spark for her, and while she would pay me for my efforts, she was going to sell the directory I had created to another party. I felt defeated again. I had so much content hoarded away on my computer and no clear outlet for it. At least the interview with KZ Zapata was accepted for publication in a skateboard zine called *Double Down*, so I could justify our connection, but I wanted to do more, and I didn't want to be dependent on someone else's decisions or bias. I wanted to be the director of this passion project.

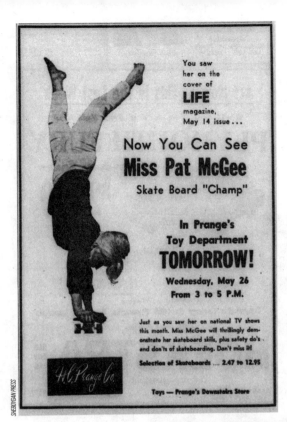

An ad for Patti McGee's demo at a department store, May 25, 1965, in the *Sheboygan Press*

Leigh Zaremba and Dee Jay Cobb ride a skateboard in tandem for the *Pasadena Independent* (May 29, 1959)

She's Winning a Scholarship

The Spokane Chronicle celebrates Laurie Turner's win at the International Skateboard Championships (May 24, 1965)

CHAPTER THREE

ORIGIN STORIES (LAURIE TURNER)

Skateboarders know that pain is inevitable and that it never lets up no matter how skilled you become. A freak injury can even happen while you're casually rolling down the street, Fleetwood Mac soothing all your sorrows. Out of nowhere, a pea-sized pebble decides to sabotage your vibe, causing your wheel to seize up. Your board screeches to a halt, and you get hurtled to the ground, plowed face-first into hard concrete.

This is called a lesson in humility and it occurs more than one would like. But skateboarders persist despite this risk of bodily harm. It can be difficult to justify the pursuit to an outside observer who prefers self-preservation over scabby shins, bruised heels, swollen ankles, broken bones, and open wounds. The safety gear argument then arises, but as I've discovered, even if you're willing to abandon all illusions of being cool by encasing yourself in wrist guards, shin guards, knee and elbow pads, you're never infallible. There are soft tissue injuries lurking in wait to immobilize you.

Every sport has its unexpected drama: a soccer player clutching their hamstrings mid-game because of some excruciating muscle spasm or a marathon runner collapsing at the straightaway with the finish line in sight. But I struggle to compare skateboarding and its self-inflicted pain with traditional sports. Is there something addictive about skateboarding that makes people pursue it obsessively, or is there something peculiar about the people who take up skateboarding and their relationship to pain, or both, or neither? There's no definitive answer, but skateboarding does seem to offer something deeper than athletic glory, and while it can be different for different people, usually it comes with a sense of belonging. And sometimes being accepted by a crew overrides the threat of personal injury.

Pain is strange. It can be devastating when a ligament is torn and requires surgery and lengthy recovery, but with skateboarding the proof of pain can also trigger feelings of pride, defiance, and celebration when it is overcome. I think everyone can agree that skateboarding is impressive to witness at a certain caliber, and if you're taking the plunge and committing to it, you'll know that the adrenaline rush of stomping your first kickflip or dropping in on a mini-ramp can consume and motivate you. It's part of our origin stories and rites of passage, and most skateboarders have a photo or two in their albums showing off their bloody elbows and oozing palms.

For female skateboarders, a bit of gore can also signify a rejection of conservative expectations to be passive and flawless and therefore dateable by a certain sector of predictable, heterosexual men. I've heard guys say they wouldn't date a girl who skates due to the likelihood of bruises or other unsightly scars, or they don't think girls should skate because they don't want to see them get hurt. Are those the same men passing out when their partner gives birth? While it might sound like an honorable comment, the rationale to deprive someone an experience for their own protection can feel condescending rather than supportive. A person's gender does not dictate their likelihood of pursuing skateboarding over more docile hobbies that avoid the threat of daily road rash.

I've found proof dating as far back as 1959 that women wanted a piece of skateboard action regardless of the consequences. I had been clawing through a newspaper database when I stumbled upon an article in the *Pasadena Independent* by Pete Gall from May 1959 announcing a new craze called a "surf skateboard." What caught my eye was a photo of two students from Pasadena High School named Leigh Zaremba and Dee Jay Cobb, cruising on a skateboard together in tandem. Leigh has a massive smile on her face and is wearing a starched white blouse and full poodle skirt with crinoline. This is the earliest photo of a woman on a skateboard I had ever seen outside of kids in New York from the 1940s and 1950s ripping around on modified fruit crates on wheels.

And when I came across Gall's statement that "the girls have been sneaking into the sport, too, braving the occasional scraped knee or skinned elbow to skim the cement with the guys,"[1] I gave the air a little fist pump because I was thinking, *Hell yes, of course they have!* Who could resist the fun of this weird new "sport"? For the youth in Pasadena,

> the idea came from surfing movies seen by some of the seniors during Easter weekend, where they saw 24-hour surf enthusiasts using a modified skateboard to ride the cement ramps at La Jolla. In less than a week, the new "dry land surfboards" were developed for Pasadena use by seniors Ed MacKenzie, Dennis Smith, Bill Welsh and Steve Ondeck.[2]

It was obvious that skateboarding, also called "sidewalk surfing" or "skurfing" if you lived in Canada,[3] was catching on, even if it was deemed a passing fad on par with Hula-Hoops. Skateboards were branded a toy for any child to use, so the sport was relatively equitable in the 1950s and 1960s.

Unfortunately, a week after Gall's first article, he produced a follow-up report on the dangers of skateboards in an article titled

"Scraped Skin and Broken Bones: Skateboard Casualties Mount."[4] The Pasadena Emergency Hospital had reported four injuries from the previous two weeks and had issued a warning.

I will never know if Leigh Zaremba continued to skate after that photo shoot, but as skateboarding became increasingly popular in the 1960s, it was evident that it wasn't just one thing for one type of person. A skateboarder could be a child, an athlete, an ambassador, an entrepreneur, and in the case of Laurie Turner from Berkeley, California, skateboarding could help deflect being labeled by social stigma and shame.

Laurie started skateboarding because "my neighborhood guy friends and I and one of my girlfriends were all into surfing . . . Skateboarding developed out of wanting to do something similar when the waves were down and you couldn't go surfing. I took a two-by-four, and I split my metal roller skate and made my own skateboard."[5] Laurie described going on "skateboarding safaris" with her friends to explore the neighborhoods, finding "cool concrete structures" that might serve as a playground for fun and innovation. Laurie would also spend afternoons taking the bus to the top of a hill, then bombing down it to improve her skills and get a rush of adrenaline. For Laurie and her friends, skateboarding represented freedom.

Some of Laurie's male friends were sponsored by a team called the Topsiders, and six of them attended the Sports and Boat Show at the Cow Palace in San Francisco in 1964. An agent for Hobie Skateboards and Vita-Pakt Juice was in the crowd, and even though they already sponsored a Southern California team, they were looking to expand by developing a Northern California team. When the agent inquired if the boys knew of any female skaters, Laurie was vetted for sponsorship.

The new team was nicknamed the Super Surfers, and the kids had all their equipment supplied. Laurie remembered, "They gave us jackets with the embroidered logo on the back. They would take us to shopping malls and places to get kids to come out and watch us do tricks to encourage the sale of skateboards."[6] Laurie was living the dream, except for the fact that her home life was in upheaval, which had the potential to disrupt her social status among her peers.

While many sidewalk surfers in the 1960s discovered skateboarding via their association with surfing, my gateway sport was snowboarding. Thanks to my brothers who imported snowboards from western Canada to our small town in Ontario as a side hustle, I was introduced to snowboarding at age eleven. In 1988, I was riding a baby-sized Burton on the toboggan hill at the local ski resort once they permitted snowboarders to purchase lift tickets. I eventually made snowboarding friends who chose to skateboard during the offseason, when the four feet of snow had finally melted. The offseason quickly reversed, and skateboarding became the leading love in my life, more affordable and accessible for a student.

I was susceptible to an activity like skateboarding, which emphasized social interaction over a strict regimen, because during my teen years my attitude toward competitive sport shifted. At age fourteen, after several years of success in long-distance running, I started experiencing insomnia and anxiety over my upcoming races. The weight of expectation to always be performing at my peak meant that running no longer felt fun. I wanted to be cool and independent like my brothers, and I wanted to feel special. I no longer liked being known as "the runner," because I learned the hard way that flat-chested long-distance athletes were not considered attractive, at least by the guys that I lapped at the school track meet in the 3000-meter event.

Even my coach thought my physical appearance was a joke, yelling at me to "stick out your chest" during our team photo at a track championship in front of friends and family, and announcing to a teammate that my nickname would be "Boobs." I was certainly a lanky runner, but at fourteen years old I wasn't immune to ridicule. I wrote about these experiences in my diaries, how devastated and humiliated I felt. Journals from one's teenaged years are almost always tragic and illuminating, but it's fair to say that I didn't like the way insecurity was starting to eat away at my sense of worth.

Like most teenagers, I wanted to figure out and assert my identity, so in the summer of 1994, after my second eldest brother left home, I dug out his old Rob Roskopp Santa Cruz skateboard with Independent trucks and Slime Balls wheels from his bedroom closet. The setup was a heavy barge from the '80s but would serve its purpose. I was about to turn seventeen when I began the slow process of learning how to ride and fall without any mentors or videos. I was lucky to know one other skater girl at high school named Kate, and we would practice in the back parking lot where all the smokers and "bad kids" hung out. For an academic achiever, I was excited by the prospect of expanding my worldview as a skateboarder, but I could never fully abandon my nerdy inclinations. In a journal entry from 1995, I explained how important skateboarding was becoming to me:

> Since I last wrote I have mainly been busy with school and skateboarding. This is the last week for the skateboard park to be open, so I went for a session with my buddies last night . . . The other day our Principal banned boarding from school and so I wrote a really thoughtful letter. He is quite reasonable to talk to and we organized a large meeting to discuss the problems.

There's no further reference to the meeting or the "problems," and maybe they disappeared because the snow came early that year, but I was ready to represent my newfound crew and take their concerns seriously.

The other motivating factor was this sense that I had something to prove as a girl. As a snowboarder, I was always pushing myself to blast big air just like the guys, and because skateboarding was even more male-dominated, I sought out the challenge with feminist purpose. I would no longer be a gangly jock with acne and a double set of braces and retainers, bound to a training schedule for track and field. I was a skateboarder, and my anthem was "She rips, when she skates, 'cause she never hesitates!" — a slight modification of a Suicidal Tendencies song.

What I hoped for was that my new skateboarding identity would shroud me in coolness, like the way I perceived my brothers, and protect me from verbal assault, but that wasn't the case. In high school, there was a hallway where hockey players would lounge, sitting on a long stretch of radiators. It was known as "Perv Hall," and it had a distinct odor, like a sweaty locker room, and the heat from the radiators at full blast in winter made the deadliest stench. Even the teachers would avoid the hall, but sometimes it was the shortest route to class.

It made no difference if I was a skateboarder or an athlete, the hockey players heckled me for being a "carpenter's dream" and my friend with a large chest was deemed a "slut" for simply existing. There was no escaping the toxic banter, and when a couple of douche bags in a pickup truck winged beer cans at me while skateboarding, I figured I was officially in the outcast skater club.

The first time I rolled and sprained my ankle on a skateboard was right before a cross-country running event. I knew that if I told my coach how I'd sustained the injury, I would get lectured, so I entered the race, finished it, and then claimed that my swollen ankle was a result of twisting it on the rugged course. That was the beginning of the end of my high school running career. Skateboarding was now my number one.

SURF SKATE

Linda Benson
Surf and skateboard pioneer (1959-69)

Linda Benson holds a massive list of firsts as a champion surfer, which made her the perfect representative for selling skateboards — an exciting new toy on wheels which she easily learned how to ride. In 1959, at age fifteen after only four years of surfing, she won the first national contest in the U.S. at Huntington Beach, followed by the international surfing contest at Mākaha as its youngest competitor; she is also credited with being the first woman to surf the big waves of Waimea Bay.[7]

From 1959 to 1969, Linda won over twenty first-place surfing titles and was recruited to act as a surfing stunt double for Annette Funicello in the *Beach Party* films and then for Deborah Walley in *Gidget Goes Hawaiian* in 1961. She was included in the first *Surfer Magazine* in 1960 and was the first woman to be photographed for the cover of a surfing magazine, *Surf Guide* in 1963.[8]

As a household name in California, Benson was recruited to showcase skateboarding. Linda recalled, "I think the year was 1962 . . . Don Hansen decided to make a Linda Benson and an L.J. Richards model, shaped like a surfboard with our names stenciled on the tail block."[9] Instantly, Linda became the first female with what we now call a pro model or a signature board, a board branded by a company with an individual's name knowing that they have cachet. The rationale is that because people are aware of the skater's accomplishments, or surfing skills in Linda's case, they might want to be associated with the name and buy the board.

Linda then went on a road trip up the coast to Santa Monica with her sponsor, performing demos at hardware shops, because there were no sporting goods stores at the time, selling Hansen skateboards one by one. The trip even involved a performance in Hollywood for a popular daytime variety show called *Art Linkletter's*

House Party in the CBS parking lot. Linda was proud of her skateboard: "The wheels were the best made at the time, a roller-rink type that we screwed on by hand in the back room of Hansen Surfboards' old shop in Cardiff."[10]

Surfing was Linda's first love, but her role in promoting skateboarding as a brand ambassador ensured its early status as a fun activity for all children, regardless of gender. Her stamp of approval established skateboarding as equitable and cool.

Patti McGee
Skateboard pioneer (1962–66, 2002–24)

Patti McGee's fame was sealed when she appeared on the cover of the May 1965 issue of *Life* magazine at age nineteen performing a rolling handstand, her signature trick, photographed by Bill Eppridge. Patti wore an outfit that I imagine a college girl of the era might wear — white slacks and a red letterman sweater. She also encapsulated a vision of California by skating barefoot like a surfer, her blonde hair secured in a beehive, still intact even though she's upside down. It was a fabulous photo, but Patti said, "Keep in mind this was during the Vietnam war, and I was on the cover of a major news magazine! The cover and article about skateboarding was most likely run as a feel-good piece to help readers take their minds off the war."[11]

Like Linda Benson, Patti was also an avid surfer. She first witnessed skateboarding in 1962 at the Hollywood Teen-Age Fair, which was located at Pacific Ocean Park during her Easter vacation. Skateboarding seemed like a great option to Patti for when the waves were too flat for surfing.[12] Her brother Jackie made a skateboard in woodshop, using clay roller skate wheels, and she was soon bombing hills and inventing new tricks.[13]

In 1964, Patti and her brother were invited to join the Bun Buster skateboard team, and she got a taste of the good life as a sponsored skater while performing a demo at a premiere for the Walt Disney movie *The Moon-Spinners*.[14] On December 4, 1964, Patti won the girls' division at the National Skateboard Championship at Santa Monica Park, placing ahead of Giola Siciliano, Colleen Jones, Valerie Perez, and Gail Yarbrough, and it was this event that kickstarted her legacy.[15]

Patti promptly took her trophy and some glossy photos over to the Hobie Surf Shop in Dana Point at the same moment the owner, Hobart "Hobie" Alter, was rushing out the door. "He said, 'I haven't got time for this.' I said, 'But look! I'm the women's national skateboard champion and I want to be on your team!' He said, 'Can you babysit?'"[16] Fortunately, Patti met Hobie's family and asserted herself as a skateboarder and things worked out in her favor, but at that time, the Hobie team only included young boys. In the short video *Skaterdater* (1965), the girls are on the sidelines, a distraction for the boys who are having all the fun, which was not the reality of what was happening on the streets.

Patti was persuasive and found herself being paid 250 dollars a month to teach skateboarding safety and travel the country, all the way to New York where she scored her cover for *Life*. This iconic image led to a commercial for Bell Telephone and appearances on *What's My Line?* and *The Mike Douglas Show*. Patti even skated at the Dick Clark Young World's Fair in Chicago in front of forty-five thousand youth in 1966. She is also credited for being the first female skater on the cover of a skateboarding magazine, which was the October 1965 issue of *Skateboarder*, along with a four-page profile called "The Lady Is a Champ" by Susan Adams.

Patti stated, "Well, some people say girl skateboarders are just a novelty. I myself think that skateboarding is 100 percent just as much for girls as it is for boys."[17] And at that time, the skateboarding community seemed to agree. To raise awareness of Patti's history after she returned to skateboarding in 2002 at age fifty-five, her daughter, Hailey Villa, created the board companies The Original Betty Skate Company and Silly Girl Skateboards, while sponsoring talented riders.

In 2010, Patti was an obvious inductee for the Skateboarding Hall of Fame, and she often made appearances at the annual Mighty Mama Skate-O-Rama on Mother's Day with Hailey.

In October 2024, Patti sadly passed away due to a stroke, and the skateboarding community mourned her and celebrated her legacy. There was a special memorial at the Exposure contest, which is exclusive to girls, women, and non-traditional skaters: Olympian Bryce Wettstein shared her memories of Patti and performed a song, and many of the young skaters performed a rolling handstand as a tribute. Rest in peace, Patti.

Le Skate-Bord
French skateboarders (1960s–70s)

In French surfing communities on the Atlantic coast, in towns like Biarritz and Hossegor, news traveled fast about "roll surf" or "le skate-bord" as a form of dry-land surfing back in the early 1960s. In 1964, Jim Fitzpatrick, a legendary American surfer and skateboarder for the Makaha skateboard team, brought a dozen skateboards to France on a promotional tour, according to French historian Claude Queyrel.[18] The activity was embraced, and just like their Californian peers, French women took up skateboarding with enthusiasm equal to men's.

The first French skateboarding championships were hosted in Hossegor in 1965, described in an article from *Sud-Ouest de Landes* newspaper. The names Jackie Arquie and Isolde Gérard are listed as competing neck and neck in the ondines category, with Jackie taking the win.[19] The two women are considered skateboarding pioneers in France. The following year in 1966, Marie-Pierre Bianco became the new champion. Marie-Pierre, also a surfer, was the spitting image of Kathy Kohner, the surfer who inspired the Gidget book and films, with her short dark bob. Marie-Pierre still has her skateboarding trophy, which she proudly displayed on social media.

A decade later, thanks to a young woman named Laurence Lannes, a whole new generation of skateboarders in France emerged. Laurence had a family home in Biarritz where she learned to surf and received an introduction to skateboarding. She then brought Nicole Boronat on board, literally, and formed a crew with Naomi Harris and Corinne Dupin. The skaters frequented Place du Trocadéro, in view of the Eiffel Tower, and Béton Hurlant skatepark with many other young women. The Parisian friends were featured in a four-page article called "Le Skate au Feminin,"[20] in 1978, and Nicole received significant attention after winning the 1978 French championships in Marseille.

Decades later, when an interviewer suggested that the hardcore "skate and destroy" attitude in the 1980s eliminated women from skateboarding, Nicole didn't bite the bait but simply replied, "Les filles sont souvent minoritaires, mais celles qui se jettent dans une 'aventure,' ou une 'expérience' sont souvent incroyables. Il n'y a pas d'époque ou de domaine."[21] In translation, Nicole said that in every generation and area of life, there would always be women embracing adventure even if they are in the minority, and they tend to be incredible. I would wager that Nicole was not surprised to see skateboarding in the Olympic Games, let alone the high standard of women's abilities exhibited in Paris in 2024.

When the first skateboarding magazine, *The Quarterly Skateboarder*, was launched in the winter of 1964, the editor wrote, "Today's skateboarders are founders in this sport — they're pioneers — they are the first. There is no history in skateboarding — it's being made now — by you."[22] Laurie Turner submitted three photos to this debut issue, and she became both the first female skater included inside a skateboard magazine and the first female photographer to have her skateboarding photos published.

Laurie received fifteen dollars for her photos taken at the Whittier school grounds in Berkeley. Two pictures are of her friends "Bootsey" McGhee and Danny Escalante, and one of them is of Laurie holding a surf position called a Quasimodo. The pose required Laurie to squat down low with her arms outstretched, and her head is tucked down between her knees.

The following spring, in May 1965, Laurie's team, the Super Surfers, were selected to travel and compete at the International Skateboard Championships at Anaheim's La Palma Stadium against some serious competition. The event was televised by ABC's *Wide World of Sports*, and the black-and-white footage shows stadium stands full of spectators — polished men wearing suits and ties or casual sporting attire like polo shirts tucked into khakis, the women with coiffed hair and cat-eye glasses. Most of the competitors wore oversized helmets with chin guards, likely designed for football, and skated barefoot, performing handstands, nose wheelies, 360 spins, acrobatic tricks, and footwork that mimicked longboard surfing.

At the age of fifteen, Laurie won the title of overall female champion after taking first in a figure eight contest, second in slalom, and then performing a handstand and several smooth 720 spins to win the tricks contest. It was explained that "Laurie, showing a dazzling form and complete mastery of her board, nosed out Colleen [Boyd] by an eyelash."[23] Many of these skaters, including Laurie, are now recognized in the Skateboarding Hall of Fame like Wendy Bearer, sponsored by the Makaha Skateboard Club, and Colleen Boyd, skating for the Palisades Skateboard Team.

For her grand prize, Laurie received a team dinner at the Disneyland Hotel, a custom surfboard from Hobie, and a five-hundred-dollar college scholarship. When I read the contest report in *Skateboarder*,[24] it took me a moment to realize that Laurie's prize was identical to the boys' award. How was it possible that the organizers of a contest in the 1960s had the audacity to consider the girls as deserving as the boys, an attitude that was not shared thirty and forty years later? I was stunned.

In 1998, the organizers of Vancouver's monumental skateboard contest Slam City Jam (the North American Skateboard Championships that ran from 1994 to 2006) finally offered a girls' street-skating division. Megan Kelleher described being part of a group of girls who "heckled the judges to give us a female street run if we got all of us to sign up."[25] Megan was motivated because "I grew up being told I wasn't allowed to skate since it was for boys. So, once I learned [to skate], I could never stomach us being left out. It felt wrong and dismissive."[26] Megan had just convinced her local skate shop, Brotherhood in Santa Rosa, to support a female crew, aptly named the Sisterhood, and when the Slam City Jam contest organizers told her to pull together a list of thirty female skaters willing to compete, she followed through.

The local girls in Vancouver also had a tactic. At the 1997 edition of Slam City Jam, my friends and I noticed professional skateboarder Ed Templeton alone outside BC Place Stadium. We were fans of Ed's company Toy Machine but felt disappointed that he wasn't accompanied by his teammate and our hero, Elissa Steamer. We decided to corner him and told him that he wasn't welcome back to Vancouver the following year unless he brought Elissa. It wasn't a real threat, and we might have requested his autograph all the same, but I remember feeling delighted when I heard Ed joke about the pseudo-near-death experience of being cornered by Elissa's Canadian fans in some long-buried interview.

Ed understood the mission because Elissa arrived at the contest in 1998. She had had a groundbreaking video part in *Welcome to Hell* (1996), and coupled with the pressure from Kelleher's list of female skaters, the organizers had to allow us to compete. The girls' event was scheduled early on the Sunday morning before most of the spectators were due to arrive at the Pacific Coliseum, likely sleeping off their hangovers. The timing was a bit of a slight, but at least entering the girls' contest for a mere twenty dollars (according to my diary) was cheaper than paying for a three-day pass, so it was a no-brainer to compete. If you were looking to make some cash for a win, that was another story. Lisa Whitaker, skateboarder, filmmaker, and owner of Meow Skateboards, recalled placing fourth in the 2000 street contest and receiving a check for forty dollars, which bounced and put her in the hole.[27] Meanwhile, the top male skater that year received seven thousand dollars, and this amount multiplied in the years to follow. The girls' prizes remained stagnant.

The 1998 girls' street contest had revealed that there was serious interest in competitions, attracting a pool of talented, sponsored skaters who traveled to the event in subsequent years. And to their credit, the organizers of Slam City Jam hosted a women's vert ramp contest starting in 1999; it was the only World Cup event to do so for several years. ESPN's X Games permitted women's vert and street-skateboarding as demonstration sports from 1998 to 2002, until Cara-Beth Burnside, Jen O'Brien, and Mimi Knoop sought out "ESPN to tell X Games executives how they felt about the absence of women in the biggest televised skateboarding competition in the world."[28]

The following year, a report on EXPN mentioned that it was a last-minute decision to change the women's demo into a contest with medals and prizes: "The only downside of the last-second demo-to-contest switcharoo was scheduling did not allow for practice time. So the girls had to get right down to business without much of a warm-up,"[29] and their presence was not televised. There were eight women invited to skate the street course and only five included in vert, with no clarity on how they qualified. A surprise entrant in the street contest, twelve-year-old Karen Feitosa of Brazil was quoted as saying, "The women's competition should have started at the first X Games . . . There should be more opportunity for women amateurs like me."[30]

In 2005, the X Games competitors discovered that the top male vert skater would receive fifty thousand dollars in contrast to two thousand for the top female, the same amount for the last place man, and the women felt burned.[31] That year, Knoop and Burnside along with Drew Mearns, a former sports agent, founded the Action Sports Alliance, which became the Women's Skateboarding Alliance.[32] Leading skateboarders Jen O'Brien, Elissa Steamer, Vanessa Torres, Amy Caron, and many others joined the group and waged an all-out strike, demanding some semblance of equal prize money and acknowledgment.[33] A temporary agreement was made, and the women competed with a promise of a meeting with X Games management.

The skateboarders "got nothing for months, and eventually contacted someone at the *New York Times.*"[34] The front-page story in the Sports section triggered some action. Chris Stiepock, the general manager of the X Games, justified not televising the women's events in anticipation of a ratings decline. He said, "There's only room for so many sports . . . Our ultimate responsibility is to our viewer, and our viewer is a male teen."[35] The Alliance persevered, and in 2007 for X Games XIII, women's events were televised live with Lyn-Z Adams Hawkins taking gold in vert and Marisa Dal Santo gold in street. Lisa Whitaker recorded the action for the Side Project website, and in her footage, you can see the skaters annihilate handrails, clear massive sets of stairs, and stomp flip tricks over obstacles in rapid succession.[36] Finally, in 2008 there were equal prize purses at the Winter X Games, which solidified a new standard moving forward.

Or should I say, an old standard was revived. In the 1960s, when skateboarding and competitive sport for children were new, the sponsors of the Anaheim International Skateboard Championships perhaps didn't think to alienate the girls. They automatically put up matching prizes for the winners regardless of gender, and the televised content on ABC was balanced.

When Laurie was inducted into the Skateboarding Hall of Fame in 2014, she said, "Skateboarding was a godsend for me . . . My family was going through hard times; my parents were divorced; my dad wasn't around. Back then that was the exception, not the rule . . . That positive label of champion got me through lots of difficult times."[37] Laurie's story reveals that skateboarding can be a refuge for misfits, offering a fun outlet away from family drama at home; it gave her an identity as a champion rather than being stigmatized as a child of divorce. She was a kickass skater, full stop.

Skateboarding will mean something different for every individual skater, especially as it has evolved throughout the decades. This diversity of perspectives became apparent at the 2016 Olympics in Rio de Janeiro when the International Olympic Committee announced the inclusion of street and park skateboarding, the two most popular forms, at the 2020 Olympics in Japan.

If this had been the 1960s, Olympic approval would signify validation. Even the editor of the first issue of *The Quarterly Skateboarder* wrote in 1964, "We predict a real future for the sport — a future that could go as far as the Olympics. It's a much more 'measurable' sport than surfing and therefore lends itself more to competition."[38] In this context, someone like Laurie Turner could strive for Olympic gold in slalom, freestyle, and high jump, which reflected more traditional Olympic sports.

Similarly, in the 1970s, those who were intent on competition viewed the Olympics as a positive opportunity and logical progression. For example, in the April 1977 issue of the *National Skateboard Review*, it was reported that the United States Skateboard Association was collaborating with skatepark owners and local organizations in "an effort to standardize contests and scoring methods which would set the stage for 1979 competitions to select a team"[39] for the 1980 Moscow Olympic Games. It was hoped that skateboarding would be a demonstration sport, although anything beyond being an exhibition seemed unlikely because "it is doubtful that the old fashioned and staid leadership of the International Olympic Committee will accept skateboarding as an event for medalist competition by 1980."[40]

When asked about skateboarding as an Olympic sport in the October 1977 issue of *Skateboard!* magazine, world champion Laura Thornhill said, "No doubt about it, they'll have freestyle, compulsories, slalom, cross-country and bank-riding."[41] She also felt that it was important to have coaching, "especially for the Olympics. Entrants will have to train and be coached intensively. Here's looking forward to it." In April 1978, a skateboard contest at the Magic Mountain amusement park in Los Angeles was dubbed the "Hang Ten Olympics" as a nod to aspirations of future Olympic glory. Some of the competitors, like Jana Payne who placed second in the junior women category (for ages thirteen to seventeen), even held off on turning professional since the Olympic Games was only for amateur athletes.

The Moscow Olympics ended up being boycotted, but there was a contingent of hopeful skateboarders in 1984, when the Summer Games arrived in Los Angeles. The National Skateboard Association organized its own mini summer Olympics series with freestyle and streetstyle events, but unlike the real Olympics, the organizers had the women competing against the guys. The results of April Hoffman, Michelle Sanderson, and Leslie Anne Miller, the top freestyle amateurs, were buried and unacknowledged.

The Olympic dream was then thoroughly squashed in the 1980s and 1990s, as skateboarding became rejected, rebranded, and embraced as rebellious, in opposition to mainstream sports and institutions. Many skateboarders prefer this gritty, punk representation of skateboarding. As a result, the introduction of skateboarding as an Olympic sport in Tokyo 2020 was not universally embraced as positive news, and a lively debate ensued.

On any given day, I could appreciate the arguments for and against Olympic inclusion with one exception. The against side was the most entertaining. There were creative initiatives like the T-shirt and bumper sticker design that proclaimed "Skateboarding *Is* a Crime. Not an Olympic Sport," referencing the movement in the 1980s by skaters who were tired of being ticketed and harassed by police. This argument was a defiant refusal to be judged by outsiders. *Thrasher* entertained its readers with the notion that competitors would have to wear skintight Lycra uniforms and came up with some unique alternative designs.[42] And in *Vice* magazine, one skateboarder suggested that "95 percent of them won't be able to compete. I think it's going to be quite hard [for skaters] to get clean for the Olympics"[43] and pass drug tests. I'm not going to question skateboarders' appreciation of weed, but the pothead skater stereotype isn't universally true.

Another camp was more focused on how skateboarding encompassed individuality and creativity, and the Olympics was viewed as a threat, imposing its rules, judging standards, and regulations. This perspective was articulated in the form of an online petition, "No Skateboarding in the Olympics!" The petition racked up over 7,500 supporters who declared that skateboarders had nothing in common with the typical Olympic athlete. The funniest part was that some signatures came from people who despised skateboarders, describing them as degenerates who would disgrace the Olympic Games. I guess that's the miracle of the Olympics, bringing eclectic people together with seemingly disparate viewpoints.

The petition was critiqued in an article for *Inside the Games* that suggested a broader, more global view be considered. Skateboarders living in countries outside the U.S. would receive funding to compete, and it was likely that Olympic exposure would result in skatepark development around the world, which would be a huge benefit.[44] Similarly, some women viewed the Olympics as an opportunity for bringing international awareness to their presence and

GIRL GANGS, ZINES, AND POWERSLIDES

talent. Pro skater Nora Vasconcellos, who never pursued Olympic glory herself, summed up these sentiments:

> I don't care because skateboarding will always be skateboarding to me. If anything, it's good because as women skaters we now have more contests to go to and travel opportunities. It totally changed snowboarding for the women. Once snowboarding was in the Olympics, women snowboarders were really able to just live off putting out video parts. The more girls who are making a living skateboarding, the more diversity there can be.[45]

This quote was part of a *Thrasher* article, "Skating in the Olympics: The Skaters' Perspective," which had recognizable skaters share a range of opinions including skepticism, ambivalence, suspicion, and enthusiasm.

Both sides had valid points, even the message that there "will always be a whole world of skateboarding that is completely removed from all that competitive jock shit."[46] The problem was that in the media, contest skaters were being pitted against "core skaters," as though you automatically voided your authenticity by being competitive. Contest skaters were characterized as corporate sellout jocks, and core skaters were the real deal, incapable of conformity. But isn't prescribing to the rebellious skateboarder identity, the kind that sneaks into abandoned pools while being shunned by jocks and cool kids, just another style of conformity?

I understand why skateboarding gets celebrated as hardcore: concrete is unforgiving and sometimes you need a burly punk soundtrack to get the adrenaline pumping. But if this definition is used as a measuring stick of who is authentic and who is not, and to assert some vague sense of exclusivity by self-proclaimed experts, I'm not buying the rationale. Even if you think skateboarding must always be balls-out, coma-inducing performances of bravado, that doesn't make it countercultural.

It's only when skateboard magazines use your gender, race, or sexuality as a punchline, as something to be ashamed of, or when you've got fellow skaters cutting you off, throwing your board in a dumpster and chasing you, that you've tasted what it is to be an outsider. These are just a smattering of lived experiences relayed to me by my Skirtboarder friends back in 2002 and in DIY zines from the 1990s.[47] If you're a historically privileged, white, heterosexual man, you're the last person who gets to define skateboarding's true identity because it doesn't actually exist. There are simply common experiences that we all share as skateboarders, and many more that we don't.

When the Olympics finally happened in 2021, the debut of skateboarding felt explosive and anticlimactic at the same time, partially due to the lack of spectators thanks to COVID-19 health measures. I would argue that the best aspect of the Olympics was that it provoked discussion about personal identity. The Netflix documentary *Stay on Board: The Leo Baker Story* is the perfect example. It begins with pro skater Leo Baker striving to qualify for the Olympics and then choosing to focus on his trans identity and embrace his authentic self rather than compete.[48] In 2019, when Tony Hawk said, "I feel like [the Olympics] need us, our cool sports image, more than we need their validation,"[49] his words resonated because skateboarding doesn't need the Olympics to justify its existence. But I also believe that the Games need skateboarders to question, prod, and challenge its values. The IOC wanted some youthful engagement, and it got it.

I think back to Leigh Zaremba from Pasadena in that 1959 newspaper, proudly cruising on a skateboard, embracing the possibility of ruining her prim outfit and scraping an elbow. In Leigh's time, the Olympics was extremely imbalanced with 2,938 men competing at the Summer Games in Melbourne, and a mere 376 women were permitted to participate in select events, certainly not cycling, basketball, weightlifting, let alone boxing or wrestling. Shifting the attitudes of the rule makers, whether they are ESPN executives, Olympic officials, or stubborn, old-school skateboarders, takes time, but change is inevitable.

With all this buzz, celebration, and debate around the Tokyo Olympics, I was surprised to discover that what I couldn't find online was a focused effort to explore the history of skateboarding from a female perspective. Occasionally a skateboard collector or photographer would stumble on a photo of a female legend from the 1970s and post it, or perhaps an organization would offer a throwback Thursday feature on Instagram and highlight a hero. But I thought there should be more.

When Laurie Turner was honored at the Skateboarding Hall of Fame, her daughter was inspired: "This is such a cool thing for women and my little girl [Laurie's granddaughter] to see . . . I'm excited this is finally happening. She's awesome. Sometimes you don't think of your parents having a life before you. It's cool for me to know she has such a super-cool backstory."[50] I realized that I wanted to bring these hidden stories to the forefront because with the success of the Olympics, there's a new generation of skaters who may be totally unaware of who paved the way for these opportunities to exist. And they need to know that the journey wasn't always easy.

Instagram's algorithm didn't approve of my approach. My first attempt at launching a women's skateboard history account was locked down after a few weeks, and I found myself banned before I even started. It was surreal to wake up one morning and be denied access to something I had begun to feel a sense of pride and ownership in, even if it was just a virtual curation of images and tags. I went through all the steps of appealing the decision, even taking a forlorn selfie holding a piece of paper with my handwritten name and the designated code to prove that I wasn't malicious.

I thought my dismissal was because I had been targeted or spammed, but then it dawned on me. Being an efficient librarian, I had systematically gone through the Excel database that I had created for the defunct skateboarding magazine and started following every account that was relevant. I remember being annoyed that there was a quota of how many profiles I could add each day, but I kept going and going. I wasn't spammed — I was penalized for behaving like a bot. I sabotaged my own Instagram origin story, but I had seen enough to stay connected and try again.

The interior of issue number 2 of Lauri Kuulei Wong's zine from 1986 called *Ladies Skateworld* with an announcement for the launch of the Women's Skateboarding Club

CHAPTER FOUR

PLATFORMS (LAURI KUULEI WONG)

Before Gloria Steinem became known as a feminist icon, cofounding the magazine *Ms.* in 1972, she wrote an article in 1965 called "The Ins and Outs of Pop Culture" for *Life* magazine, which addressed youth subcultures and trendsetting.[1] The article is interspersed with campy posed photos of Steinem, including one where she is barefoot, balancing on a stationary skateboard. Gloria looks more like a figure skater with her leg and arms extended, pretending to be mid-push. She's wearing cuffed jeans and an oversized sweatshirt with a 007 logo because Steinem considered skateboarding "dangerous enough for James Bond."[2]

The inclusion of skateboarding in Steinem's article made sense because she understood that "when money ceased to be a prerequisite for mainstream cool, it was possible for cool to come up from the bottom instead."[3] Steinem listed African American culture, British culture, and teenage culture, like skateboarding, as sources of "cool." In the 1960s, skateboarding was just emerging as a grassroots subculture established by youth from all walks of life, requiring only a two-by-four and a set of roller skate wheels. Steinem recognized the marketing potential of this pursuit and predicted the future. She wrote, "Teen-agers have buying power and they know what they want. Many businessmen insist they've found the key to the teen market, but the most successful ones are those who take the pulse and don't dictate."[4]

Within a decade, skateboarding would become a booming industry with companies outside the scene taking notice. For example, female skaters in the 1970s appeared in commercials for Pepsi, Coke, RC Cola, 7-Up, Mattel, Starburst, JC Penny, Nikon, Skippy Peanut Butter, Fruit of the Loom, and Astraltune; even companies in Japan reached out for cameo appearances. Unfortunately, by posing on a skateboard, Steinem also predicted an advertising practice that skateboarders would come to dread, which is when a company with zero association to the culture attempts to sell its product by including models awkwardly holding or standing on pristine skateboards.

These tacky ads and commercials are triggering for skateboarders and fodder for satire as seen on blogs like *Skate and Annoy*, which crushed the attempts by Levi's, Motorola, Mitsubishi, Kohl's, Axe deodorant, Claritin, Tampax, Crest, Doritos, and a barrage of fashion magazines, to name a few, that have co-opted skateboarding. Campaigns involving a pseudo-skateboarder seemed to run rampant in the late 1990s and early 2000s when everything was labeled "Xtreme," as epitomized by the No Fear clothing brand initiated in 1989, which has since branched out into energy drinks. And while it could be entertaining pointing out how flawed and staged these adverts were, it was irritating to realize that some of the campaigns must have been successful, at least with people who wouldn't know better. While marketers saw the opportunity in using the cool skateboard image, skateboarders themselves were left feeling resentful that their identity was being poached with little benefit to their day-to-day experience, especially when city bylaws and fines still targeted skateboarders.

The best part about being poorly co-opted by "the man" is that it gives you something to position yourself against. It results in underground activity with DIY zines and punk music as your platform. With every new generation of skater, there's a kind of ebb and flow of corporatization and resistance, but sometimes it's all a bit hazy. Nowadays, most companies have clued in to the fact that they need to feature well-known professional skateboarders if they want to be considered remotely legitimate, and it appears that there is more tolerance today for brand ambassadors and product placements. Why shouldn't a pro skater make a living?

The person who has been most successful at using his skateboarding identity for financial gain is Tony Hawk. But Tony isn't immune to criticism because when you align yourself with big corporations, the division of skateboarders who deem themselves the hardcore police cry "sellout." The term *sellout* tends to be flung at highly skilled skaters who have crossed a nebulous line into popular culture. I don't fault Tony for becoming a skateboarding spokesperson or even for his more unusual partnerships like with Bagel Bites and Gap. The advertisers can't get enough of the Hawk. My concern lies in how we've come to depend on Tony's endorsement and his perspective of skateboarding history.

Tony has always been an ally for female skateboarders, but for him to have an omniscient awareness of all the subtle activities in an underground scene like women's skateboarding is practically impossible. I know this because when I figured out the identity of an amazing skater with Chinese-Hawaiian heritage, who may have written the very first skateboarding zine for and by women skateboarders, and learned about her personal connection to Tony, I got pretty riled up that I had never heard of her. I felt like Tony had deprived me of a hero and my knee-jerk reaction was to feel slighted.

Even though I had barely made a dent in posting on my inaugural skateboarding Instagram account before it was shut down and needed a reboot, I didn't mess around mining the virtual content up for grabs. Early on, I started following an account of a punk zine collector who posted full scans of old skateboarding zines, including one called *Ladies Skateworld* that was published in April 1986. I felt like I was Indiana Jones finding the lost Ark of the Covenant when I swiped through the text and images. It was everything I had hoped for.

There had been zines in the 1980s made by female skateboarders that highlighted a local scene with mixed genders, like *True Devotion* by Bonnie Blouin and Gigi Gits, which celebrated skateboarders around Richmond, Virginia, and KZ's publication *Push, Push, Then Go!*, which focused on Isla Vista. But *Ladies Skateworld* was the first zine that appeared to be exclusively about women skateboarders; it focused on the Del Mar Skate Ranch in California, which was one of the few skateparks built in the 1970s that survived the early 1980s demolition blitz, lasting until 1987.

I needed to find the author of *Ladies Skateworld* because the content was altering my preconceived timeline of women's involvement in skateboarding. A skater named Lauri wrote an editorial that began

> SALUTATIONS! and welcome to the first issue of LADIES SKATEWORLD ZINE. It was pretty hard trying to get everything put together but I finally got it finished . . . Every issue will have an interview with a new female skater . . . I hope to have it out every month, but money prevailing will tell. This issue is full of typo's so don't mind it, Reason being is I only have the wee hours of the morning to work on this because I drive back and forth from Del Mar to Long Beach almost everyday and when I usually get home is one o'clock in the morning so by the time I finish working on the zine it's 3:00 AM!!![5]

I scrutinized the zine for Lauri's full name, and while I was stoked to see an interview with Lori Rigsbee when she was a precocious fourteen-year-old, before she came to fame with sponsorship from

Powell Peralta, Independent Trucks, and Airwalk, I wasn't having any luck figuring out who this Lauri person was.

I was about to give up when I took a closer look at a California Amateur Skateboard League contest report printed in the zine. CASL was an organization cofounded in 1982 by Tony Hawk's father, Frank Hawk, along with parents of skaters Sonja Catalano and Jeanne Hoffman. By 1986, its contest series wasn't offering a separate category for girls, so female competitors were often hidden in the results. Lauri wrote her own contest report in *Ladies Skateworld* to highlight the women's participation. Rigsbee, as a remarkable talent, had taken second place against the boys aged thirteen to fourteen, Rhonda Watson was "no placing" in the seventeen and over category, and Stephanie Person was "no placing" among the sponsored riders. And then there was a Lauri Wong listed, also no placing for seventeen and over, and thanks to the unique spelling of *Lauri*, I knew this was my critical lead.

Meanwhile, the content of *Ladies Skateworld* was offering me a steady supply of dopamine. Lauri was not satisfied with going through contest results, plucking out the names of female skaters hidden in a long list of dudes, to offer them a crumb of recognition. Lauri wanted an exclusive girls' division at CASL contests, so that they could be seen and recognized and inspire other women. She decided to use *Ladies Skateworld* as a networking tool and to advertise the efforts of another skateboarder named Lora Medlock to unite female skaters and create a Women's Skateboarding Club.

In the first *Ladies Skateworld* issue, an ad stated (minus the twenty exclamation marks), "ATTENTION GIRL SKATERS! ANYONE INTERESTED IN FORMING A GIRLS SKATING TEAM OR ASSOCIATION HERE IS AN ADDRESS AND PHONE NUMBER TO CONTACT. THE LADY IS A SKATER FROM WAY BACK AND A GOOD ONE AT THAT."[6] Lora's name was followed by a postal box, which was for the Breakers Surf Shop in San Diego. In the second zine, there were two similar announcements:

We need 7 or more female skaters to enter in our division for the C.A.S.L. series. We would be skating against each other. Sounds like fun? If so please contact . . . Lora Medlock . . . WE MUST BE ABLE TO PRESENT A LIST TO CASL ONE CONTEST PRIOR TO OUR ENTERING THE FOLLOWING CONTEST SO HURRY NOW.[7]

ATTENTION ANY AND EVERY FEMALE SKATER. AN ASSOCIATION HAS ALREADY BEEN STARTED FOR THE WOMEN SKATERS OF AMERICA. IT'S ABOUT TIME. THE ASSOCIATION IS PRESENTLY CALLED "WOMENS SKATEBOARDING CLUB" AND IS BASED IN SAN DIEGO . . . THE CLUB IS OPEN TO ALL FEMALE SKATERS, EVERY AGE, EVERY SKATE LEVEL . . . WE HAVE SKATERS FROM EVERY PART OF THE U.S.A. SO IT DOESNT MATTER WHERE YOU LIVE . . . DONT WAIT SIGN UP TODAY.[8]

Lauri and Lora were successful in creating their club, which would be renamed the Women's Skateboarding Network (WSN) in 1989. And by promising to bring their female members to contests, they convinced a smattering of contest organizers to create a separate division. They knew that being measured against the guys was not elevating skateboarding as a competitive option for the average girl but preventing them from getting involved, apart from the most talented and confident skaters.

I had always wanted to know how the WSN formed ever since I read a book in 2007 called *Skater Girl: A Girls' Guide to Skateboarding* by Patty Segovia and Rebecca Heller. The book provided many helpful details that were new and exciting to me, but there was information that I could never verify, for example, the statement that one "Laura Medlock" had created the Women's Skateboarding

Network in 1989. I had tried to find this woman for almost fifteen years but never had any luck. And now, thanks to *Ladies Skateworld*, a mystery was solved.

Staring at me on my screen was the proof I needed from this 1986 zine. According to *Ladies Skateworld*, the individual I sought spelled her name *Lora*, and I would eventually learn that she now went by Lora Lyons. These situations of misspelled names, nicknames, names altered in marriage, and names and pronouns changed due to affirmed gender became an expected part of my research. I became attuned to the possibilities of all kinds of variations.

After experiencing success finding KZ Zapata on Facebook, I had a feeling this was the platform of choice for a certain generation, so I looked for Lauri there, and a profile for one Lauri Kuulei Wong immediately popped up. My hunch was confirmed when I saw that in issue two of *Ladies Skateworld* she signed off as "L.K.W." I had thought her middle name sounded Hawaiian, and Lauri ended her editorials with "Aloha" and always included a Hawaiian word of the month, like holo pahe'e, meaning "to skate," or ho'okala, meaning "to grind." It all made sense.

I tried messaging Lauri directly on Facebook to no avail, so I took the creepier route and started digging online. I learned that she was running an award-winning charity called Future First Responders of America based out of Snowflake, Arizona, offering life-saving training for youth. The organization combined her work advocating for abused and neglected children in the foster care system with her role as the former president and captain of the Sheriff's Auxiliary Volunteers in Navajo County. I composed my letter and emailed the generic address I found on the site.

Dear Lauri,

First off, I wanted to congratulate you on your recent Governor's Award, and the awesome work you do with and for children, and in your community.

Reading up on your story I'm pretty sure I have the right person.

This will seem totally out of left field, but I'm a public librarian and also a skateboarder, and I run a website and Instagram account that pieces together and showcases the history of women skateboarders from the 1960s to the present. You may not know, but two issues of a zine called "Ladies Skateworld" from 1986, which I believe was written by you, were scanned by a zine collector on Instagram . . .

And then I saw some of your skateboarding, motorcycling and NASCAR photos and I just thought you looked so cool and likely have some amazing stories to tell! Would you be remotely interested in answering some questions about your skateboarding history? I can email them or we can chat over Zoom?

Lauri Kuulei Wong did not disappoint. "Good afternoon, Miss Natalie. WOW! How on earth did you find me!? Yes, that is me. Would you like me to call you?" she wrote, switching over to a personal email address. Turns out that Lauri was in the middle of campaigning for her town council but loved the bio I had written about her based on her zines and Facebook memories.

I then got to work trying to find Lora, who had submitted the skateboard club announcements. Thanks to Lora's daughter, who'd posted her mother's 1979 Big O Skatepark membership card on a Facebook page exclusive to fans of the Big O Skatepark in Orange, California, I had a breakthrough. I reached out to her daughter to see if she could arrange a conversation, and it resulted in an email exchange.

Lora shared that she was from Edinburgh, Pennsylvania, and began skateboarding after she graduated high school in the late 1970s when her boyfriend "bought a crappy plastic board and told me to come over after work. So, the first time I got on a board I was wearing a skirt and pantyhose, no shoes! I thought it was great fun though and we both were hooked after that."[9] Lora and George were married when they moved out west, and one of the skateparks they frequently visited was Del Mar Skate Ranch, where they met Lauri Wong.

Lora was then badly injured in an accident outside of skateboarding and was informed that irreparable damage meant physical activity like skateboarding was suddenly over. "That was really hard. I loved the freedom of being able to skate wherever there was pavement. A little part of my brain still tells me I can just take a board down the street, and it will be okay, but I think my knee replacement would beg to differ!"[10]

Lora confirmed that the *Ladies Skateworld* ads for a women's contest division were partially successful. She did end up going to the next CASL contest with Wong and a group of female skaters in the 1980s, competing in their own division, but she never knew how the initiative for the Women's Skateboard Club evolved. For personal reasons, Lora had to leave San Diego and resume her maiden name around this time. And while Lora had always hoped that progress was made for female skateboarders, there were other factors at play when she disconnected from the scene.

My conversation with Lora was a good reminder that our lives are complex, and while my agenda to piece together this skateboarding history is at the forefront, I need to respect individuals and the reality that not everyone will have a straightforward, celebratory story. I can do my best to glean information that's freely offered, especially through zines, but delivering a seamless and transparent history is next to impossible. I was still grateful that we had connected, knowing that I could now correctly acknowledge a person who had made a real difference.

CRITICAL ZINES

Gunk
Riot Grrrl band and zine by Ramdasha Bikceem (1990–95)

Ramdasha Bikceem received their first skateboard around age twelve, and while they didn't consider their choice to skate extraordinary, it would prove to be an important decision. Ramdasha said, "When I turned fourteen years old, my two best girlfriends also started to skate . . . But every time we'd skate with other boys we started to feel intimidated cuz we didn't know all the latest tricks or the 'cool' skate lingo."[11] Ramdasha and their friends weren't deterred, and they sought out creative ways to express themselves and motivate each other.

In 1990, when Ramdasha was fifteen, their group of friends formed an all-girl punk band called Gunk in Basking Ridge, New Jersey. Ramdasha was a self-taught guitarist, and the band's early shows were held in the basement of a friend's parents' place. Around this time, the Riot Grrrl movement was emerging in the Pacific Northwest as a feminist response to the sexist attitudes and violent behaviors that had prevailed in the punk music scene. Gunk was aligned with the movement and even performed at the 1992 Riot Grrrl conference in Washington, D.C., which was featured in the documentary *Don't Need You: The Herstory of Riot Grrrl* (dir. Kerri Koch, 2005). In that film, Ramdasha spoke about their frustration with often being the lone person of color at punk concerts and not feeling supported, even among the Riot Grrrls.[12]

Ramdasha wanted to advocate for the girls sitting on the sidewalk who were too uncomfortable to take part in skateboarding when male skaters opted to condemn rather than encourage them. "I remember reading in some skate magazine how one pro skater said he was annoyed when girls started skating because it was too 'distracting.' He went on to say that our only function was to sit back and shut up and watch boys skate and be their little fuckpigs after a hard day of skating."[13]

In the November 1991 issue of *Thrasher*, Ramdasha's letter to the editor was printed. Ramdasha wrote,

> The only time you see females in your mag is when they're standing there in some skimpy-ass outfit swooning over some skater guy . . . Anyway, I still love your mag, but I've decided not to wait around for you to include females in it. I'm going to start my own mag. So, all you skater chicks, send me pictures of yourself skating. (You don't have to be good, it's not a competition).[14]

It appeared that *Thrasher*'s editors didn't take Ramdasha seriously because they chose to juxtapose an ad featuring a woman in lace underwear directly beside the letter. But Ramdasha was true to their word and along came *Gunk* — the zine.

In the first issue, Ramdasha exclaimed, "We are girls!!! We are sk8ers. We are musicians. But most importantly, we are teenagers! We want to be heard! We strive to be free thinkers."[15] The same issue included a photo collage of Ramdasha and their gang, a skateboarding comic in which girl skaters were mocking the boys in a role reversal, zine reviews, an inspirational quote from Kim Gordon of Sonic Youth, advice from skaters, and Ramdasha's genuine excitement over discovering three sponsored skateboarders: Saecha Clarke, Cara-Beth Burnside, and Lori Rigsbee. To Ramdasha, the existence of these female skaters seemed miraculous, and they vowed to pursue more information about them by writing to the riders' sponsors for details.

Gunk lasted five issues from 1991 to 1995 and was a great outlet for Ramdasha and their bandmates to share frustrations, hash out lyrics for their songs, and make connections with other skaters like

Renee "Ne" Tantillo and Kym Agresti, who were included in the zine. Tantillo was later presented in the documentary *Not Bad for a Girl* (dir. Lisa Rose Apramian, 1995) riding her motorcycle to the Riot Grrrl convention in Washington, D.C., and performing some skate tricks. And Agresti was both a skater and a fellow zine writer, publishing *Hectic Times* from 1990 to 1995 in Santa Cruz.

At age eighteen, Ramdasha was interviewed for a book called *Girl Power* and explained how their outlook and confidence as a skateboarder had evolved. They no longer cared about pursuing the latest skate trick or appealing to the men who dictated industry trends. Ramdasha wanted to focus on having fun and being around positive people.

> I'm tired of wasting my time with these misguided young men. I see where they've taken skateboarding and frankly it disgusts me. I've seen what the majority of their companies think of me and the rest of us girls in their sexist ads . . . I don't need or want their validation anymore. I'm gonna do my own thing and hopefully with the help of other intelligent boys and girl skaters we will redefine what used to be (and still is most of the time) a fun sport.[16]

Ramdasha admitted that it was still frustrating to see girls "sitting on the sidewalk swooning over these macho shitheads"[17] but hoped that their presence skating the streets would cause these girls to question what they were doing on the sidelines and join in.

Villa Villa Cola
Skateboard zine and collective formed in 1996

In 1996 in San Diego, California, skateboarding twins Tiffany and Nicole Morgan decided to creatively use a college fund their parents had set aside for education to promote female skaters and build their community. The Morgans launched a skateboarding collective with their friends called Villa Villa Cola (VVC) and were undeterred when skate shop owners informed them that "there are no girls who skate around here."[18] The name was a tip of the hat to Villa Villekulla, the fictional home of wild child Pippi Longstocking concocted by Swedish author Astrid Lindgren. VVC published their own adventures in a series of original zines, and thanks to their friendships with skateboarders in Vancouver, these zines made their way to Canada and were the first that I ever encountered, when the concept of do-it-yourself was a revelation to me.

Lori Damiano, an artist, skateboarder, and VVC member, said,

> We didn't see ourselves reflected in the media of our skateboarding community so together we made zines and skate videos featuring the girls and women we knew that skated. Other frequent collaborators in the early days were Van Nguyen, Faye Jaime, Lisa Whitaker, Michelle Pezel, Jaime Sinift, Andria Lessler, and Rebecca Burnquist.[19]

The *Villa Villa Cola* zines were full of photos, stories, rants, drawings, recipes, and hilarity. Memorable features included a series of photos of Faye attempting to skate a ledge with a handbag, then taking out her wrath on her skateboard for "getting in the way of my purse"; reports on the All Girl Skate Jam contest series; road trips to Canada and overseas to Australia; touring with an oversized Barbie doll; and horoscopes that predicted "sex with an alien." Tiffany said, "We wanted to inspire more girls to skateboard by example. We set out to find girls who were already absorbed in it and also the ones who had never been introduced to our friend, the skateboard."[20]

VVC increased their efforts, producing skateboarding films like *Striking Fear into the Hearts of Teenage Girls* (1998), Lori's school project *Defeating Projections* (1999), and the groundbreaking video *Getting Nowhere Faster* (2004), sponsored by Element Skateboards and *411 Video Magazine*. During a VVC reunion in 2003 at Lisa Whitaker's house, Lisa pulled out some of the footage she had been accumulating, which included Alex White.

> Not only was White an absolutely amazing skater, but Whitaker had managed to get an excellent shot of a security guard pinning White to the ground, wrenching her arm behind her back, and threatening to beat her up if she tried to run. This was the kind of thing you saw in the guys' videos. It was priceless. The Villa Villa Cola girls were mesmerized.[21]

This footage, which would eventually make it into *Getting Nowhere Faster*, was just as important to Alex herself. "I remember when I was like fifteen I wrote to the Villa Villa Cola 'zine and got the video *Striking Fear*, and I was like, 'Wow!' I was so stoked on it. It was one of the reasons I got really into skating. I had this dream that I could be in a video."[22]

Originally, *Getting Nowhere Faster* was just going to be a bonus feature in an issue of *411VM*. Fortunately, when Whitaker dropped off the footage to Josh Friedberg, producer of *411VM*. Lisa said, "Johnny Schillereff, the owner of Element, was there when he watched it and they were completely blown away. They had no idea that there were that many girls skating or at that level. They were like 'forget the DVD bonus, we'll help you make a full video.'"[23]

Lisa shared that the VVC crew "had worked on videos together in the past and it seemed like we all had the same views on the need for a video which will expose these girls to the rest of the world and make something they can be proud of."[24] The film premiered in October 2004 at a theatre in the Emily Carr Art Institute (now called the Emily Carr Univeristy of Art and Design) in Vancouver alongside a VVC art exhibit and party at the Antisocial Skateboard Shop gallery, thanks to co-owner Michelle Pezel. Tiffany said that the video was produced during "a pivotal time before social media. VVC and GNF [*Getting Nowhere Faster*] were the way we connected to each other in a world of virtually zero representation and hardly any means to find each other. Epic, fun times with just the weirdest group of friends making the magic."[25] The film would go on tour throughout the Pacific Northwest, California, and New York in 2005, and was often given away during skateboard clinics with the Ocean Pacific Girls Learn to Ride program.

VVC members knew that they had to create visibility themselves, their own way. For example, *TransWorld* skateboarding magazine briefly allowed them to publish two pages of female-centric content buried inside a half dozen issues starting in October 2004. But the coverage was short-lived. Lori Damiano said their feature was canceled "because the magazine said it needed to sell the 2 pages for ads."[26] At the time, *TransWorld* issues were over three hundred pages, which is significant for a skateboarding magazine. I struggle to see how excluding VVC was related to business. It was a poor excuse, and the lack of any dedicated pages to female skateboarders was glaringly obvious.

I would wager that if you ask any woman who pursued skateboarding in the late 1990s and early 2000s, they will reference *Getting Nowhere Faster* as the single most inspiring and influential video for our generation. There was nothing else on the market with this kind of distribution or breadth of skateboarding skill. Plus, the video brought to life our heroes Vanessa Torres and Amy Caron, and it included a laundry list of talented and creative skaters, motivating us to rally our like-minded friends in our own communities and skate with joy and determination. We have the Villa Villa Cola crew to thank for this evolution — and those skate shop owners who informed Tiffany and Nicole that female skaters didn't exist.

GIRL GANGS, ZINES, AND POWERSLIDES

Check It Out: Sk84Girls
Zine turned magazine (1995–2007)

In Brazil, women began skateboarding the moment it emerged as a popular activity in the 1970s. Women like Maria Elaigne Ferreira who started skating in 1972 and was interviewed for the documentary *Into the Mirror: Fragmentos* (2022) by Emilie "Pipa" Souza. In the film, Souza celebrates the strong history of Brazilian female skateboarders, providing context for a contemporary movement. Today, there is a fierce contingent of talented female skaters competing out of Brazil all vying to be the next Leticia Bufoni or Rayssa Leal, two of the most dominant street skaters, with Rayssa racking up 9.1 million followers on Instagram and always a podium threat at contests.

In the mid-1990s, a group of Brazilian girls, who would have a profound effect on women skaters internationally, came to fruition. Liza Araujo from São Paulo was working in the mailroom for the Brazilian skateboarding magazine *Tribo* in 1995. "I got to read a lot of letters from girls complaining about the lack of support and discrimination every time they got to a skatepark or spot, or even buying a board at the shop, always a sexist joke," she explained in *Jenkem* magazine. "They wanted to skate and have fun with their friends, but they had to be tough to tolerate the jokes, and that would limit their progress. A platform for their voices had to be created."[27]

Instead of waiting around for *Tribo* magazine to be that outlet for girls, Liza knew she had to make change happen herself. Liza launched a zine called *Check It Out: Sk84Girls* in 1995, and to celebrate the publication, she "organized an all girl's contest at ZN [Zilda Natel] Skate Park in São Paulo, which at the time was one of the first Brazilian skate contests to include women."[28] She chose that skatepark specifically because "girls were getting beat up at the skatepark. They would get their boards taken, they would get cursed out, they would be discriminated as groupies, as lesbians. No respect at all."[29] If a mob of women showed up together at this notorious skatepark, it would send a message that female skateboarders weren't going away and had a right to occupy this public space.

And then Liza joined forces with photographers Luciana Toledo, who also had a zine, and Ana Paula Negrão. Vert skating pioneer Monica Polistchuk recalled meeting the *Check It Out* crew at the São Bernardo do Campo skatepark in 1998 while walking her baby in a stroller. Polistchuk had dominated the Brazilian championships throughout the 1980s, appearing on the cover of Brazil's *Hardskate* punk zine, but had taken a break to have three kids and raise her family. She just happened to be processing a divorce and needed a positive outlet to call her own when the skatepark encounter occurred.[30] Polistchuk was delighted by this powerful women's network, returned to skateboarding, and was given the cover of *Check It Out* issue four in the spring of 2000, performing a frontside 5-0 grind along the lip of a pool.

Check It Out steadily evolved, and thanks to the talented female skaters it portrayed, the publication got noticed abroad. The zine went from being a black-and-white photocopied newsletter with articles in Portuguese to a glossy magazine translated into English due to the demand from subscribers in the United States and Canada. Patty Segovia, organizer of the All Girl Skate Jam, used her network to help expand the magazine's distribution, and the editorial team moved to Encinitas to be closer to all the major contests and up-and-coming skaters clustered in California.[31]

During its lifetime, *Check It Out* celebrated the top women skaters like Alexis Sablone, Lyn-Z Adams Hawkins, Vanessa Torres, Amy Caron, Leticia Bufoni, Marisa Dal Santo, Jaime Reyes, and Elissa Steamer, but always with the intention of "uplifting and promoting young girls, even those who weren't sponsored . . . We wanted to feature girls with all abilities, because that's how we can push ourselves to the next level, when we feel supported,"[32] said Luciana.

Professional skateboarder and sports announcer Alex White, who appeared on the cover of *Check It Out* issue fifteen in 2003 launching off a twelve-set of stairs, interviewed the editors and explained how the magazine was a form of activism. The women demanded the attention of major advertisers, insisted on sponsorship for female riders who were unappreciated, and often forked out their own money to keep things afloat. However, the eighteenth issue in 2007 was their last. Liza concluded her final article by writing, "Back in the day we just wanted to be able to skate the park without being discriminated, bullied, and attacked by boys ... Big advertisers took a long time to pay attention to women's skateboarding, but the evolution brought this revolution and I'm glad we contributed."[33]

Every issue of *Check It Out* would be announced on the Girls Skate Network website, and I know that I couldn't wait to receive my copy. There was no other magazine, besides the brief run of *Push* magazine (2002–03) in Canada by Denise Williams, solely dedicated to women skaters published at such a high caliber. I'm eternally grateful for this publication; scans of *Check It Out* have formed the foundation for many of the biographies I have written on female skaters from the early 2000s for the Womxn Skateboard History archive, skaters I may not have found otherwise because so many of them were ignored by mainstream skateboard magazines.

Check It Out was also one of the only venues for female skateboard photographers to have their work published in magazines. The skateboard industry had created a system of male gatekeepers that determined not only who was represented in the media, but who was in charge of cultural production, such as editors, photographers, filmmakers, video producers, distributors, and company owners. *Check It Out* included photos by Magdalena Wosinska, Patty Segovia, and Erika Dubé as contributing photographers, alongside Ana Paula Negrão and Luciana Toledo. Wosinska, who immigrated to the United States from Poland in 1991, was mocked for being a girl who skated but found confidence from behind the lens and a means to gain acceptance in a male-dominated community. After three decades, Wosinska finally had one of her pictures printed on the cover of a skateboarding magazine (issue 49 of *SOLO* in March 2023) and published a book called *Fulfill the Dream* (2024), which features her early work from the 1990s.

Men still oversee the bulk of skateboarding media production today, but female and non-binary photographers like Elise Crigar, Hannah Bailey, Jenny Sampson, Jess Sung, Nam-Chi Van, Norma Ibarra, Olga Aguilar, Raisa Abal, Sarah Huston, and Zorah Olivia, among others, are disrupting this boys' club and there is now a growing selection of alternative skateboarding magazines receptive to their work, not unlike *Check It Out*.

Ibarra has even made it her mission to acquire a press pass for the 2028 Los Angeles Olympics because she was denied the opportunity at the Paris Olympics; she was forced to document the action from the spectator stands with Bailey and Abal, while their male peers occupied the coveted ground level positions.[34] This predicament was explored by Hannah Bailey in an article called "We Mind the Gap." She noted that the pool of accredited photographers was only 20 percent women at the Tokyo 2020 Summer Games, and at the Beijing 2022 Winter Games, it was a mere 12 percent. She wrote, "As a sports photographer specialising in skateboarding for over 15 years, I've witnessed this imbalance firsthand . . . The underrepresentation of female skate photographers at the skatepark reflects broader issues in sports photography at the Games and beyond."[35]

Ladies Skateworld zine spread the word about the Women's Skateboard Club and encouraged female skaters to demand a prominent place in contests. When I began to learn more about its creator, Lauri Wong, things took an unexpected turn. Firstly, I found out that Lauri had been the lead singer in a punk band called Death Roster, referenced in punk zines like *Flipside* and *Fight for Freedom* in the early '80s. This news wasn't entirely unexpected because the two subcultures — skate and punk — were so entwined in terms of ethos and style. Even her preferred mode of transportation — motorcycles — made sense.

In the comments section of Lauri's Facebook photos, she explained that while living with her dad in Long Beach, she was so determined to skate that she took a job working at the Del Mar Skate Ranch, which required a two-hour commute. Lauri's dad had taught her how to ride motorcycles at a young age, and this was her vehicle of choice to get to work, although occasionally she had some close calls for speeding. Lauri was pulled over by the cops while dodging backed-up cars in rush hour traffic on the 405, but her ticket was dismissed when the cop realized she was a rad female biker.[36]

Of course, Lauri was a punk musician, skateboarder, and ripping motorcycle rider. But what I didn't anticipate was Lauri's influential friendships at Del Mar Skate Ranch, especially her friendship with Tony Hawk. To shorten the commute to her job in Del Mar and avoid speeding tickets, Lauri wrote that she rented a room from Hawk in the first house he purchased. OMG! The author of the first female skateboarding zine, who elevated the voices of women in skateboarding and prompted a crusade for female contest divisions, had a personal connection to Tony.

Why was I only learning about this now? Why had Tony never mentioned that his former tenant was such an influential badass? Did he even know about her zine and efforts with the women's skateboard club? Was she just rent money to him? And why didn't he step up for his roommate and tell his dad, Frank, and everyone at the California Amateur Skateboard League to offer a category for girls, something Lauri had been advocating for? Or maybe he did? Was I missing something here and jumping to conclusions?

Tony has made use of many media appearances to elevate women in skateboarding. In 2021, he hosted a MasterClass on skateboarding, which includes a chapter called "Girl Skaters Rise: A Brief History of Women's Skateboarding." I'll admit, Tony is the obvious candidate for a MasterClass; the platform hosts the leading expert in a field to share advice, technique, and history. And when I looked at other sports-related MasterClasses, I didn't see Wayne Gretzky give a shoutout to women hockey players. I just wish Tony could've taken things a step further and suggested a female icon take the reins for that chapter, someone like Cara-Beth Burnside. Another great option would have been 1970s legend Cindy Whitehead who founded the Girl Is NOT a 4 Letter Word organization to empower young skaters, which led to a TEDxYouth lecture about her photobook, *It's Not About Pretty: A Book About Radical Female Skaters* (2017). At least vert and pool skater Lizzie Armanto was given ample screen time in the lesson, being the first woman to propel herself upside down and through a fourteen-foot-tall 360 loop; she was also the first, and only, woman celebrated on the cover of *TransWorld* magazine in their thirty-six-year run, in November 2016.

It was tempting to be irritated with Tony, but it didn't sound like Lauri Wong was holding a grudge, so I took a moment to assess. Lauri simply stated that there was a

> period of time when I was renting a room from #TonyHawk. It was his very first house. I was working and skating at Del Mar Skate Ranch. A legendary place where famous skateboarders were. I remember so many cool skaters and got to travel to tournaments. It was an exciting time . . . I'm not sure my children or anyone else for that matter believed me when I would tell the story.[37]

I decided that if ever I had the opportunity to be in Tony Hawk's vicinity, I would ask him if he remembered Lauri and those intrepid female skaters that she featured in *Ladies Skateworld*.

An opportunity came sooner than I thought when my presentation proposal was accepted for the Stoke Sessions: An International Conference on the Culture, History and Politics of Surfing and

Skateboarding at the San Diego State University in April 2023. In fact, the main reason I even applied was because I saw that Tony was the keynote speaker. Did I mention that librarians can be obsessive? As a conference presenter, I was allowed to submit questions to Tony in advance, and I knew this was it — I would likely never have this chance again to connect so directly and publicly with the Birdman. The day arrived, and I was sitting in a dim auditorium packed with students, professors, and presenters, and behold, there was Tony and his brother, Steve, seated on stage bantering about their passion for surfing and skateboarding. The question period finally arrived. The host was taking his sweet time delivering each question, and it was killing me, but I had my phone at the ready to press record.

At long last I heard, "Tony, as a skateboarding historian, I would be so grateful for your reflection on the scene at Del Mar in the mid-1980s, in particular, if you would remember the small yet vibrant crew of female skateboarders who worked and skated at Del Mar. Apparently, Lauri Wong —" and here the host paused, glancing at Tony for signs of recognition. Tony's voice expressed surprise. "Oh, Lauri, Lauri Wong — yes." The host continued: "— rented a room from you at your first house, and she was the author of the zine *Ladies Skateworld* . . . Any chance you remember her? Thanks."

I wriggled in my seat like a worm, my heart beating rapidly. I looked around at the audience nervously wondering if there was any interest or excitement about my question. *Am I the only person who is losing their shit right now?* And to my relief, Tony's response was gracious. He seemed genuinely interested in addressing the topic. Tony acknowledged that there was a small contingent of female skaters from his high school at Del Mar, and while they were a minority, they were welcomed to the space.

> And Lauri was . . . Well, I bought my first house while I was still in high school, and I needed roommates to help pay the mortgage and so Lauri was one

of my roommates. But yes, females skateboarding was definitely unappreciated and underserved for a long time, and I feel like it's finally had its comeuppance in the last, maybe, five years. So, equal prize money . . . and the future is bright.[38]

And the audience erupted with applause! I squealed like a guinea pig into my recording because the energy in the room felt tangible and I was pumped. Tony likely wouldn't recall this moment, but for me it was essential. I wish he had shared a bit more detail about Lauri, but at least I had my proof that she was on Tony's radar, even if he never had a chance to bask in the glory of *Ladies Skateworld* zine or fully grasp its importance. In that moment, I bought into the hype and have the selfie with Tony Hawk to prove it.

Tony Hawk doesn't owe women skaters anything — he's just a person with incredible talent and business savvy, and I'm trying to accept that. Although, I still want to print a T-shirt that reads "Tony Hawk was my landlord and all I got was this lousy T-shirt" for Lauri, just for fun. Lauri is important to me. She did something special through her zine: she recognized not only the talented riders like Lori Rigsbee, but she made space for beginners like her friends Ericka and Rhonda Watson to be seen and celebrated.

On a sidenote, it was thanks to Ericka Watson's mother that I felt at peace regarding my attitude toward Tony Hawk. I had written a website post on the archive based on scans from *Ladies Skateworld* featuring Ericka and Rhonda, and four months later while browsing for content on the Del Mar Skate Ranch Facebook page, I read that Ericka had passed away. Her mom wrote that Del Mar was Ericka's first job and that she had worked there until it closed: "She spoke often of her friendship with Tony Hawk, and he was a comfort to her when her little brother Jesse Moon died riding his skateboard in January of 1986, he was 9 years old . . . I am hoping perhaps someone on this FB page might remember Ericka."[39] Thanks to Lauri Wong's zine and this project, I reached out to Ericka's mom with the bio I had written about the Watson sisters, including photos from *Ladies Skateworld* that she never knew existed. And all this effort was instantly justified.

From an early age, I knew that advertising and the printed word had power. I remember presenting a real estate ad to my mom when I was eight or nine years old, from a magazine like *Time* or *Maclean's*, that I considered offensive. The ad displayed a nuclear family carved into chess pieces on a chessboard. The father figure was prominent and holding a briefcase, while the diminutive mother figure was in the background hovering over her two children and family dog. The headline said something like, "For those who make the important family decisions, choose XY company." I was upset because the ad implied that a woman was not a decision-maker. My mom suggested I write a letter explaining my irritation and mail it in, which we did together.

Not long after, but before I started skateboarding, I experienced an epiphany when I read in a snowboard magazine that a young rider named Janna Meyen had obliterated all the boys in a half-pipe competition down in Southern California. I was ecstatic. There was no photo of Janna, just a sentence or two about her triumph, but it was enough to ignite my imagination: it was possible for a girl to be a total ruler in a board sport. Janna would go on to win the women's half-pipe event at the U.S. Open Snowboarding Championships in 1991 as a thirteen-year-old amateur.

That sense of hope that someone like me was out there, pursuing their dreams and ignoring the male majority, proved useful when I would eventually delve into the world of skateboarding. It was also a good indication that to find information about heroes like Janna, I would have to seek it out with intention and retain the evidence. I knew I wasn't seeing the whole picture.

When activities like snowboarding and skateboarding become

marketable after starting out as youth subcultures, there is an element of loss that occurs as corporations attempt to mold and manipulate their audience. But sometimes there is unexpected gain. I remember on my eighteenth birthday, my brother gave me the October 1995 issue of *TransWorld Snowboarding* magazine. Unlike its skateboarding counterpart, I was overjoyed to discover an article entirely about female snowboarders called "No Man's Land." In an old journal, I found a typed copy of a letter I wrote to the editors; further proof of what a nerd I've always been, as well as a demonstration of my lifelong obsession. I wrote,

> Reading this article just before a skateboarding session motivated me to ride with more determination . . . In my seven years of snowboarding I have never subscribed to a snowboarding magazine due to the minimal coverage of female riders, but this may now change. I actually bought a second copy of the issue just so I could cut out the pictures of my heroines for my bedrooms walls and still have the article intact.

It wasn't criticism, but the compliment was thinly veiled. I was essentially saying, "Hello *TransWorld*, you're capable of getting your shit together in snowboarding, so step it up with skateboarding already, you bunch of idiots." I figured if the snowboarding industry was about to embrace women as a viable market, there was hope for skateboarding; it would just take a bit longer.

Before I established the history archive online and Instagram account, I had no clear rationale for why I was investing so much time and effort into uncovering these skateboarders' stories. And yet the connections I was making with interesting women energized me. I decided that if I wanted to publish the backlog of content on my computer, I would have to do it my own way and create my own platform rather than wait around for a newspaper or magazine editor to step up and promote my efforts.

My husband had been nudging me for some time to create a website, but I was too stubborn to listen right away. And then it dawned on me that a website could be dynamic. It could be updated and edited as new information came to light, like the name of a photographer, a lost interview unearthed, or when someone changed their pronouns. I could have agency and autonomy and make my own deadlines. Even if my graphic design skills were nonexistent, I was sick of feeling paralyzed. I needed a positive outlet and a way to spread the news. The Womxn Skateboard History archive was it — a basic WordPress website that felt manageable. I went public just in time for International Women's Day and gave Instagram another attempt simultaneously.

As a librarian, it initially pained me to deviate from a printed format and my longstanding dream of publishing a glossy coffee table book on female skaters, but I had to admit that the problem with solidifying history into print is that it freezes content in one moment for good and bad. It's ironic that I'm typing this while drafting a manuscript for print publication, but as this day evolves and I review the weighty foundation of research I've presented online (which can and will be updated and edited), I am content with this decision. And the more I connected the dots in history like a journalist, posing questions to Tony Hawk and reaching out to strangers, who in turn became mentors, the more my confidence grew. Who was this bold and intrepid skater librarian?

ABOVE: This photo of Stephanie Person by Mörizen Föche was included in the article by Bonnie Blouin called "Sugar and Spice..?" in the April 1986 issue of *Thrasher*

LEFT: The DVD cover for *AKA: Girl Skater* from 2003 featuring the Gallaz pros

BELOW: Cheryl Thornton competing against the boys in Fort Worth, TX, in 1977. The photo was taken by Rodger Mallison and published in the *Fort Worth Star*

Georgina Matthews in 2001 at the Arataki skatepark in Aotearoa with some massive air

CHAPTER FIVE

ON ACCESSIBILITY
(GEORGINA MATTHEWS)

While I'm delighted that skateboarding had a relatively equitable origin story in the 1960s in terms of gender, it has been more challenging to ensure a balanced representation of BIPOC female skaters. I'm mindful that male BIPOC skaters have faced their own battles and cultivated their own heroes, as described in the September 2020 issue of *Thrasher*, focused solely on skaters of color. But for BIPOC women, the obstacles have been multi-layered. And yet I would never suggest that women of color were not present in those formative years of skateboarding, especially with so many zine writers, like KZ Zapata, Lauri Kuulei Wong, and Ramdasha Bikceem, smashing barriers in the 1980s and 1990s.

When I sourced the 1959 photo of Leigh Zaremba in the *Pasadena Independent*, the earliest image of a woman on a skateboard, I was pleased, but what gave me even greater satisfaction was locating a news story about a skateboard contest in Fort Worth, Texas, in May 1977. The contest was organized by Willie Fulton on a basketball court at the Como Community Center, which was built in 1970 and still serves the city today. A large crowd of spectators were in attendance, cheering on the participants, and as far as I could see, everyone was Black.

A photographer named Rodger Mallison for the *Fort Worth Star-Telegram* photographed Cheryl Thornton, age twelve, competing against the boys and placing second in freestyle. Cheryl performed a handstand on her board, just like Patti McGee on the cover of *Life* magazine ten years earlier, and received a trophy for her efforts.[1] Cheryl was the first credited Black female skateboarder, competing in a skate contest, documented with a photo that I had found to date. And now that I was on Instagram, I could quickly tag a variety of accounts dedicated to celebrating skaters of color, including @black_girls_skate, to encourage them to check out the feature. It felt good being able to justify my obsessive digging and share the news.

One thing I won't do with my skate history website is turn it into a side hustle with a paywall for subscribers-only content that contains exclusive interviews and never-seen-before photos. The thought of preventing someone from discovering these rad skaters for an odd dollar makes me want to throw up, and that's the librarian in me. Who isn't sick of pop-ups demanding payment for monthly subscriptions and hierarchical tiers that alienate people? I understand that newspapers and journals need to pay their writers, but I am disheartened when certain publications won't even permit access through a library database, let alone a fee model that offers equity pricing. Everyone deserves access to quality reporting and entertainment, and public libraries were often able to help balance this privilege. Today, it's becoming increasingly difficult to maintain accessibility for all with streaming-only services and individual memberships for online publications.

When I'm faced with a barrier like an institution that tries to block my access to content, especially a kickass skateboarder, all I see is red. I will operate covertly and relentlessly to obtain the information I need. And I think my skater-librarian combo means that I'm especially stubborn. While it's a bit of a stereotype, skateboarders' commitment to enjoying public and private property in seemingly destructive fashion has resulted in a distaste for top-down authority. I just happen to channel that irritation to other fields like access to information. For example, when I received a three-page hate letter at the library demanding we purge a list of books by queer authors, I methodically bought the ones we didn't own, some of them in duplicate. Only an idiot gives a public librarian a book list for censorship purposes.

My stubbornness prevailed while working on a feature about Māori skater Georgina Matthews from Aotearoa (New Zealand). After making several Instagram posts featuring the 1970s, I wanted to offer some balance with a more inclusive and contemporary story. Everything was going smoothly until I learned of the existence of a show called *Aotearoa Skate* from the Māori television channel, which included episodes about Georgina. I wanted access to this footage immediately.

Georgina was born in 1987, raised in Tauranga, and was described as a wahine toa (a heroine) by the producers of *Aotearoa Skate* in the promotion for her 2004 interview. As a kid, Georgina had always pursued action sports, "but one day my brother brought home a skateboard and that's when the love of skateboarding all started for me."[2] In 1999, Georgina received her own board for Christmas from her parents, and she teamed up with two boys who lived on her cul-de-sac. They would skateboard together after school and on weekends, hitting up the 17th Avenue skatepark, motivating each other, building ramps and obstacles. Georgina then began competing. "There were no categories for girls so it'd just be me and 15 other boys . . . But in saying that, I'd always be in the top five and most of the time in the top three."[3]

At age thirteen, Georgina won the New Zealand national championships ahead of six other women, which was the first time she had seen another female skater since her skate journey began fifteen months prior. One of those women was Stace "The Ace" Roper, who had been skateboarding since the 1970s and throughout the '80s and was still active in the scene. Stacey became a kind of coach, looking out for the young Kiwi after noticing that Georgina was as consumed with skateboarding as she was. "I never thought about it being a mentor to others, but with Georgie, I could live vicariously through her to some degree . . . It was so rad watching her and others improve."[4] Georgina reciprocated the kind words in an interview for the New Zealand magazine *Manual*:

> Stacey and I have been great friends. Stacey travelled with me when we competed in the All Girl Skate Jams, Canadian World Cup, Globe World Cups, and all around the States and Australia. She is a big inspiration of mine, and she was one of the first competitive female skaters in New Zealand. Stace would tell me stories of growing up skateboarding in the '70s and '80s. She's even taught me a few old school tricks.[5]

Georgina's win at the nationals meant that she was flown to the Australian Girls' Street Skate Jam in Melbourne in June 2000. Traveling to Australia meant meeting other high-caliber female skaters from Down Under like Alicia Saye, Esther Godoy, Hilary Pearce, Jo Harrison, Monica Shaw, Sally Affleck, Sal Clark, and Sophie Allen, many of whom formed a crew called the Skullz, with an online forum that appealed to female skaters internationally.[6] Georgina proved herself on a big contest stage, and the *New Zeland Herald* reported, "Georgina fought her way to second place in the overall competition and won the best single trick title . . . But the highlight of the trip was sharing the limelight with [Jaime] Reyes, including interviews with Australia's Extreme TV crew, and picking up a sponsorship deal with Gallaz."[7]

While the *New Zeland Herald* acknowledged that Jaime Reyes was Georgina's hero, it didn't mention that Reyes was also a skateboarder of color, originally from Hawaii. Reyes had formidable skill as a street skater and became the second woman after Cara-Beth Burnside to claim the cover of *Thrasher*; in April 1994 she was pictured during a 360 flip at 'A'ala Park in O'ahu thanks to photographer Scott Starr (RIP). No wonder Georgina was starstruck. "I'd read heaps about her in magazines . . . I got to see all her moves and how she does things and I'm going to try some of them out."[8] Jaime was sponsored by Gallaz footwear, which had now recruited Georgina, and was a cutting-edge brand operated by the Australian shoe company Globe, catering to female skateboarders (and their smaller feet).

To promote its team and footwear, Gallaz produced a video in 2003 called *AKA: Girl Skater* with action footage by Lisa Whitaker. The video focused solely on the Gallaz pro skaters during their 2002 road trip through Australia. It was presented in a more documentary style and featured Jaime Reyes and rising stars Vanessa Torres and Amy Caron, as well as a local Australian skater, Monica Shaw, bonus footage with Georgina, and trick advice by Lauren Mollica, a street skater based out of New Jersey.

My copy of the video had long disappeared, but I still owned the issue of *Big Brother* magazine from June 2002, which contained a sixteen-page article by Dave Carnie about the road trip.[9] While it sounds odd for some random dude to be accompanying young skater girls overseas, Carnie had himself assigned to the task as a writer for *Big Brother*. Carnie declared himself the official "foster mom" for the team and was evidently enamored by his badass daughters.

Big Brother was mired in contradictions. The publication was founded by Steve Rocco in 1992 and purchased by Larry Flynt in 1997, which resulted in a surprising reduction of nudity but maintenance of vulgarity, according to Wikipedia. Rocco and his company World Industries were said to have started *Big Brother* in opposition to *TransWorld* and its conservative, clean-cut representation of skateboarding. It was a rogue magazine intentionally trying to provoke authority figures, and it became a magnet for companies that targeted teenage boys at their most base, jerk-off level. The articles were loaded with sarcasm, such as their stance on girl skaters — "they all suck."[10] Describing female skateboarders as smelly, ugly, pathetic failures and easy targets for sexual predators in the first issue was absurd, but even if the editorials were written in jest, their readership likely didn't have the intellectual bandwidth to make the distinction. They were there for the porn, crude banter, and *Jackass* antics.

There was limited acknowledgment of women in skateboarding in either *TransWorld* or *Big Brother*, so I guess that was one thing they had in common. But Carnie's article was an exception to the rule, so I purchased that issue. (The only other issue I purchased was August 1997 when Elissa Steamer was interviewed.) I was moderately surprised, even impressed by Carnie's coverage. Carnie explained how fascinating and refreshing he found the Gallaz skaters in opposition to mainstream skateboarding, which was being poisoned by grandeur. He wrote, "They're a weird group. You don't really know anything about them. They're such a weird little subclass. Kind of like how skateboarding used to be, you know, like the punks . . . How often do you see this little clique of girl skaters? They're just fucking skaters, that's all there is to it. Pirates at that."[11]

In 2002, after reading Carnie's article, I was prompted to write a letter to *TransWorld* magazine and even sang *Big Brother's* praise.

> I am disappointed with *TransWorld* for being so mediocre and apathetic. In the September issue you posed a question regarding the apparent lack of female skaters. I responded because I felt that it was an opportunity to share my opinion. I suggested that the problem had a lot to do with the lack of visibility of female skaters in magazines and videos . . .
>
> I am not upset that my letter wasn't printed, instead I am frustrated with the "anonymous" letters that were since they perpetuated stereotypes that I had hoped we were all well beyond. But, maybe I shouldn't be surprised because it seems like *Transworld* has failed to really challenge any of these attitudes by not promoting skaters like Vanessa Torres, Alexis Sablone, Amy Caron, Elissa Steamer,

Jaime Reyes, Jessie Van [Roechoudt], Cara-Beth Burnside...

I am not asking for a special all-girls edition, but simply some consistent recognition and support, like a female check-out each month. (Even *Big Brother* has featured more girl skaters, like the Gallaz team tour article and several interviews). If you truly loved skateboarding and want everyone else who loves it to feel included, you would realize that female skaters deserve to be recognized as valid participants.

My *TransWorld* letter was deprived the light of day, again, but I was still riding high on the Gallaz tour coverage. The *Big Brother* article was irreverent and engaging, the video felt world-shattering, the accompanying Gallaz website was a source for inspiration, and I would like to believe that Gallaz did well financially by catering to women — we were certainly grateful for their advertisements, product, and contest series for girls.

AKA: Girl Skater was easy enough to find on YouTube, but what I wanted was the bonus footage of Georgina to enhance the bio I was writing. I figured out that *Aotearoa Skate* had included this content and highlights of the Gallaz tour on one of its two TV episodes that celebrated Georgina's skateboarding. I started mining library catalogs and was so excited that a university in New Zealand listed the show as part of their digital archive — until I realized that they were holding the footage hostage. I know this sounds extreme, but that's where my mind went when I discovered that the public wasn't permitted to view the show. I decided not to give up. I would work some librarian magic to get the footage released. The process would turn into a whole new saga, testing my patience.

UNSUNG SINGING

Mary Mills
Surfer and skateboarder (1980s–present)

A photo of Mary Mills from 1984 wearing a striped Baja hoodie and high-top Converse shoes, while power-sliding her Santa Cruz skateboard, is pretty badass for a few reasons. Mills shared, "I started skating as a kid, but I had to hide it. My parents wouldn't let me and all I wanted to do was skate. I would just read skateboard and surf magazines all the time. Of course, when I was a kid I got accused of trying to be white."[12]

Mary posted the image to her blog, *The Surf and the Fury*, in 2009, and it was then discussed in an article by Chelsea Woody from the Textured Waves website, celebrating Black women who surf. Mary wasn't deterred by anyone's response to her interest in skateboarding, whether they were a friend or family member. Mary would hide skateboards in her closet and sneak out of her house to go for a session, even finding an empty pool a few miles away in West Los Angeles, which she skated until it was shut down by the owners. As an adult, Mary built herself a backyard mini-ramp and made skateboarding a bonding experience with her young son.[13]

In a conversation between *Building the Revolution* and Mary, the interviewer stated that they felt skateboarding was more inclusive and diverse than surfing and asked her opinion. Mary replied that to her, skateboarding's status as a subculture made it more accessible for her:

> [Skateboarding] has always had a largely counter-culture reality and aesthetic. It took awhile for Hollywood to notice it and Hollywood movies can never do it justice. Surfing, on the other hand, became

> a big part of the culture in the 60s with the Beach
> Blanket movies and the Beach Boys. Surf magazines
> furthered that racial narrative of surfing being a life-
> style and pastime that only white people enjoyed . . .
> Skating was harder to sell to the masses, so it remained
> underground and, in some ways, gritty.[14]

The situation with surfing, which required a beach that produced waves, expensive gear, and exposure to onlookers, was a challenge for Mary. Access to American outdoor leisure spaces for Black people has been marred by racism and violence, including segregated public pools, swimming areas that were deemed unsafe for white swimmers but were the only ones accessible to Black people, and polluted waters in Black communities.[15]

Mary had watched surfing as a kid on a TV show called *Wide World of Sports* and thought, "'I want to do that.' But there were a few things holding me back. Number one, I couldn't swim. Number two, I had straightened hair. And number three, I was a black kid. So, I was like, 'Well, I'll never do that.'"[16] But she savored the dream. At age twenty-three, Mary learned how to swim, and in her late thirties, she finally pursued surfing and excelled at it. Mary wrote that her ultimate day was surfing in the morning and skating in the afternoon without falling. And when a knee replacement meant dismantling her mini-ramp, at least she could still surf with its more forgiving terrain.[17]

Thanks to the founders of Textured Waves — Chelsea Woody, Danielle Black Lyons, and Martina Duran — a whole movement has been sparked to inspire women of color to get organized, meet up, and pursue surfing. Mary concluded her interview with Textured Waves by asserting her individuality: "What the hell! If I can't blend in, I'm going to stand way out."[18] And according to my Instagram followers, that 1984 photo of Mary skateboarding was exactly what they wanted to see and celebrate.

Stephanie Person
Pro skateboarder (1980s)

Stephanie Person is the first Black female professional skateboarder, and this title comes thanks to her own perseverance, which motivated her to spend sixteen years competing against men in Europe rather than in the United States. In 1984, when Stephanie was sixteen years old, she was living in San Jose and used to borrow a friend's chewed-up skateboard before receiving her own setup from her mom on her seventeenth birthday.[19] Stephanie was a natural talent and was soon noticed at Derby Park, a popular skateboard spot in Santa Cruz. She even appeared in the classic Bones Brigade video *Future Primitive* (1985), pulling off a boneless in front of a crowd, not unlike KZ Zapata.

In an interview conducted by Cindy Whitehead, Stephanie mentioned how she took the initiative to launch a competition at her community center when she was in high school. To gather prizes, Stephanie flipped through *TransWorld* and *Thrasher* magazines, found the phone numbers listed in their back pages, "and every company that I called donated something for the competition as prizes . . . In fact, Gullwing was my first truck sponsor because of this."[20]

From there, Stephanie began entering street contests, but with the growing popularity of vert skating, and because of her friendship with Cara-Beth Burnside, the most celebrated female vert skater, Stephanie shifted her focus away from flatland to this more extreme terrain. After she graduated from high school, "I ended up moving to Southern California and living with eight street skaters. I was skating vert at that time, but I stayed with them in that house for about six months. I was like, everyone is so sponsored, and I don't see any other girls ever except a couple, so I thought, why can't I be sponsored?"[21] Based on her early success organizing prize donations, Stephanie decided to be proactive and started making the calls to set herself up just like the guys.

I was first sponsored by Madrid back then, and a skateboard shop in San Jose was my first shop sponsor. Then Rector Pads, Speed Wheels, Venture, Billabong, and Swatch. That was very interesting because I called Swatch up and said, "you guys have a new team out, but you don't have any girls." They said they had their team, but I kept explaining that having a female team rider would bring so much more attention to their demos.[22]

Another breakthrough occurred when Stephanie was approached by the legendary slalom skater Judi Oyama at Derby Park who said, "'You should be sponsored by Santa Cruz.' I was like, 'You think?'"[23] Judi had long-standing ties to Santa Cruz and believed that Stephanie's confident style was a good match for the company. She helped make the sponsorship official.

Following in Judi's footsteps, Stephanie also advocated for other female skateboarders and published an article on the topic called "Equal Time" in the March 1989 issue of *Poweredge* magazine.

Being female is hard in its own right. But being a female who skates is down right a rarity. In the society in which we live a skateboard is seen (looked down upon) as a boys toy. So it's only obvious that being a grown female who rides a skateboard is a far cry from being normal to our society's standards. But what's even more frustrating is the fact that female skaters are not understood in the skate community. Seen but not heard is the feeling that a lot of us female skaters experience.[24]

Stephanie was revered by women skaters for her boldness — she was acknowledged in the first issue of Lauri Wong's zine *Ladies Skateworld* in April 1986 and was highlighted on the cover of Lynn

Kramer's zine *Equal Time* in April 1989. And thanks to the Women's Skateboarding Network, Stephanie became a kind of ambassador overseas, connecting isolated skaters like Nathalie Richter of Germany and Sue Hazel in England, among others, as pen pals.

And yet as a person of color, Stephanie had to face a whole other set of barriers. Yes, she was receiving recognition with ads in *Thrasher* for Thunder Trucks (February 1986), a photo by J. Grant Brittain in *TransWorld* (April 1988), another photo by George Medlock in *Thrasher* (August 1989), and a four-page interview (or should I say, feminist manifesto) in the U.K. magazine *Skateboard!* (November 1989). But behind the scenes, there were instances of racism that might make most people want to quit, and that was likely the intention.

Stephanie shared with Cindy Whitehead that while skateboarding in the South, she had members of the Ku Klux Klan show up at a skateboard ramp to intimidate her and attempt to beat her up. A famous skateboarder tried to rape her in a hotel room, a jealous teammate accused her of sleeping with her all-male team, and she had her skateboard stolen moments before a contest in Münster, Germany. "It always felt like I never had backup from a group of guys, I was always fighting my way to stay relevant and be me, and it was never easy. Everything, every single story, every single second of it was absolutely grueling and very hard."[25] To Chris Pastras, she said, "Nothing will ever be as hard as being a girl skater. Ever."[26]

Stephanie was no fool. In 1989, she recognized that for change to happen, the skateboard media and companies needed to step up: "There's a girls market out there, [the companies] are really just not willing to put their ass on the line . . . there's some kind of inspiration needed."[27] Stephanie *was* the inspiration. She forged a path for BIPOC pro skateboarders today like Samarria Brevard who was the first Black woman to be featured on cover of *Thrasher,* in January 2022; Nika Washington who followed in Stephanie's footsteps riding for Thunder Trucks; Adrianne Sloboh with her glorious interview in *Skateism* magazine from April 2023; or Beatrice Domond who is a

NYC style icon, represented by the iconic clothing brand Supreme. I would like to believe that Stephanie would also be proud of contemporary skateboarding organizations like the Brujas, froSkate, Concrete Queenz, and Bronx Girls Skate for their inclusive efforts and workshops.

Stephanie concluded her *Thrasher* interview by saying, "I did everything on my own because I wanted to and that's why skateboarding is easy to me in a life sense. You see it, you want it, you take it. I got it because I wanted it."[28]

Crystal Solomon
Professional skateboarder (2000s)

The trajectory of progress and change is never linear, and I can see this in the history of women skateboarding. There are steps forward through initiatives like the Women's Skateboarding Network and the existence of Stephanie Person in the late 1980s and early 1990s, and then steps backward when the industry reasserts itself as a boys' club through demeaning marketing tactics and limited opportunities for female skateboarders.

This rollercoaster journey means that it is important to keep honoring individuals who may not get to own the label of being "the first," recognizing that their presence was still important. For example, San Jose is not only the hometown of Stephanie Person but also Crystal Solomon, another young Black skater who had to forge her own path. It was a big deal for a female skater to be sponsored in the early 2000s, and Crystal was able to secure support from the Circle-A boardshop, Ball Hitch Ramps, and leading brands Osiris shoes and Enjoi Skateboards. She even briefly claimed professional status from Cherry Skateboards — a female-run board company founded by Emily Oliver and Shodie Lyon in 2003.

Photos of Crystal skating street by Ed Devera and Jen Valenzuela appeared in the "Skater Gurlz" section of the *Real Skate* website, and in 2006 and 2007, Crystal created her own YouTube channel called SkateboardcDOTcom. Footage of Crystal out in the streets practicing and landing technical tricks like grinds, noseslides, and flips, as well as skating switch-stance (using your less dominant foot to perform moves) demonstrated her skill. Crystal also offered tutorials for beginners, breaking down tricks into manageable components and encouraging her followers to challenge themselves by attempting tricks on different obstacles.

In her kickflip video, which included a collage of photos of Crystal as a child, including one where she is receiving a Black doll for Christmas, I noticed that the comments were turned off, and after browsing another tutorial, with the comments on, I can understand why. The comments section is like a hideous time capsule (even though online abuse is still very real) where men, some of whom are not anonymous, reveal their nauseating entitlement through derogatory remarks. There's banter questioning her gender, heckling her appearance and style, and one arsehole stated, "Ovaries should never be on a board. End of story." It was obvious the trolls never bothered to watch Crystal's video but condemned it based on their racist and sexist principles.

Thankfully, there were other comments that rose to the top along the lines of "we need more black female skaters!" "That 5-0 Back 180 was SICK," and individuals who expressed gratitude for the help Crystal was providing. My favorite comment came from a Black female follower named Efgen who exclaimed, "wow your like my idol. i have no girls that skate or even african american chicks that skate! your awesome!!!"

Crystal's profile never fully surfaced to the broader skateboarding community during her peak because she was ahead of her time. If Crystal had been skating today, her profile and videos would have gone viral, along the lines of skateboarder Briana King out of East Los Angeles whose innovative and stylish account has amassed thousands of followers.[29] Nonetheless, it's important to know that

Crystal was out there in the early 2000s, holding space and skating strong as a woman of color.

When I posted Crystal's feature on Instagram, the response was encouraging with @skatersofcolor stating, "This is mind blowing 😺 thank you for this." The best reply was from Jen Valenzuela, the Filipina skater and photographer who had documented her friend's skill. Jen wrote, "Crystal was so fun to skate and hang with! She was all about learning and mastering tech tricks . . . She also had a witty sense of humor, was a great storyteller, and had a very creative, entrepreneurial mindset."[30] Jen remembered that there was long-lost footage of Crystal on a VHS series called *Ghetto Fabulous* from 2002, which resurfaced on YouTube, and that Crystal's family had moved to Georgia and then on to Florida.[31] Hopefully, someone will find and alert Crystal to let her know that she is not forgotten.

When I searched for Georgina Matthews's video features in the university library catalog online, I could feel my irritation grow. I have a real problem with academic institutions that stonewall the public from gaining access to their archives. I can understand the exclusivity when it comes to expensive databases and wanting to lure in PhD candidates with their resources, but there should always be an equitable loophole for content that once originated in the public sphere. I'm obviously motivated and knowledgeable about these back-end systems as a librarian, and if I find this process challenging, I can't imagine how an average person could navigate these barriers.

I realized that the catalog records had fine print explaining that the *Aotearoa Skate* episodes required a special sign-in permission to receive a digital copy, so at least I knew that it was possible to receive a download. I figured I would hit up my Kiwi nephew attending a nearby university to request some kind of student access. My nephew gave it a go and forwarded me his correspondence with the university, which included a variety of policies and institutional hoops to navigate.

We were first told that we could access *some* records if I applied and paid for a membership, but the "eligibility rules and provisions" gave me the sense that my privileges were limited to visiting the campus and making photocopies of physical documents, which wasn't my request. I then messaged the librarian's helpline but immediately received a terse form letter that copyright policies prevented an exchange with an outsider and that I needed to go through "the official channels" of my library's interlibrary loan system. And finally, the Interlibrary Loan department fobbed me off saying that their service did not pertain to digitized videos in their archive.

And they thought they had gotten rid of me.

My next step was hitting up LinkedIn, finding library staff in the right departments who looked approachable, gleaning their email addresses from a staff directory, and appealing to what I assumed was a shared appreciation of access to information. I upped my game as a "fellow librarian" and milked it — how could they resist a keen Canadian wanting to celebrate one of their own?

My first connection, a digital specialist in the Research and Collections department, got me close. In her reply, she copied in some colleagues, one of whom articulated that media content was restricted to their staff and students alone — end of story. I'm going to assume that this was because institutions need to justify their high tuition rates, but no explanation was offered. The second colleague confirmed that the videos were gated, and that a library associate membership for a "legitimate research purpose" could be obtained, but application requests were decided upon by management at a six month or annual fee, and even then, usage rights weren't guaranteed.

I was feeling defeated but kept reading.

At the bottom of the email chain, there was a caveat. Turns out, one of the librarians copied in was also a skateboarder and Māori, and he felt that my project was worthwhile. This fantastic person came up with a viable solution. If I could gain permission from the original rights holders, he could provide a copy of the relevant clips. In fact, this wonderful librarian had done some digging and the production company was called XSTV Productions Limited. The only problem was the company was no longer active, according to a business directory. Almost twenty years had passed since it had produced any shows, but there was one woman's email address still listed in the directory for a Jane Allen.

Am I boring you, reader, with this backstory? I understand that institutional policy is tedious, but try to imagine how charged up I was. For a librarian, this kind of sleuthing is as close as we ever get to feeling like a superhero, poring over catalogs like a detective and scheming access to resources through any means possible. I figured that if Georgina overcame adversity and defied expectations in her day, I was going to take this as far as I could.

I thanked the librarians for their thoughtful replies and got to work. I sent out my email with nothing to lose, and Jane Allen immediately replied with full permission granted. In fact, my website was *exactly* where Jane wanted this footage to live because the "positive recognition for women skaters sits very well within the XSTV brand." Fuck yeah. I forwarded the correspondence, and it was like my skater librarian friend was just waiting for an excuse to send me the clips, because at the end of the day I had the MP4 downloads, and they were awesome.

Episode five of *Aotearoa Skate* from 2003 contained an interview with Georgina, rocking her Gallaz T-shirt, and footage that displayed her talent, kindness, and impact at only fifteen years old. Georgina gave props to all her friends, including a young girl blasting air at a local park with a cast on her arm. And she shared her vision of merging her two passions of singing and skateboarding — describing a fantasy music video scene with a skateboard ramp on a stage, her busting out moves with a headset, rocking out like Avril Lavigne. I would later learn that Georgina and her sister ended up forming a band called Daughters of Ally.

And then came the *AKA: Girl Skater* footage in episode eleven, which highlighted Georgina boardsliding handrails, clearing rooftop gaps, kickflipping sets of stairs, and grinding down obstacles, all to a Riot Grrrl soundtrack. I had previously reached out to Georgina and shared with her my website and plan to track down the two episodes featuring her, but it wasn't until she saw the footage and was tagged in a post that I heard back. Georgina was pumped, especially with all the personal messages she was receiving. She replied,

> 😲 😍 🤍 🙏 oh wow This is such an honour to be featured on this page! Thank you so much 🙏 xx I haven't seen some of this footage in years, took me back to the early days . . . 🤍 sooo cool! I am so grateful and blessed that I was able to travel around the world skating, meeting new friends that Im still in contact with and mostly been able to represent NZ. Now it's soo amazing when I go skating these days to see all the next female generation talent coming out of NZ . . . so exciting for NZ! 🤍 Skateboarding has definitely shaped the person I am today xx and I still absolutely LOVE it 🤍🙆 thank you xxx

Was the effort combatting university protocol worth it for two video clips, each approximately three and a half minutes long? Absolutely. Young skateboarders today may not realize that so much footage has been lost or buried because in pre-internet days, if something was broadcast on television, you either watched the episode or you missed it, unless someone was prepared in advance and hit record on a VCR. Thanks to my librarian friend and Jane Allen, Georgina and her family could now enjoy these videos with ease after so many years. There are other YouTube clips of Georgina available, including contest footage from the U.K. Ladies Skate Series in Manchester in 2010, but nothing quite captured her youthful enthusiasm as these clips did, being interviewed by her peers.

Back in Aotearoa, Georgina has continued to skate these past twenty years, and the skateboarding community has ramped up their efforts to honor her, describing Georgina as New Zealand's skateboarding royalty.[32] In February 2022, there was a report on the work of Surely Skate, an organization in New Zealand that provides mentorship to young female skaters.[33] Surely Skate hosted a contest at Alfred Cox Skatepark in Gisborne, and while Matthews was the oldest competitor at age thirty-four, her performance garnered serious respect. She received affirmation from random folks who remembered her skateboarding as a kid, including a parent of a young girl who had been motivated by her skill. Georgina also took home a proper check for one thousand dollars as the winner and said the reason she's still out skating "is to inspire little girls or any gender out there, up and coming, to just keep pushing."[34] Georgina understood how her presence helped make skateboarding accessible and viable for others.

If I'm going to create an archive that is rich and meaningful, I want to go the extra mile for anyone who has been historically marginalized. An academic institution throwing up barriers was an unexpected challenge, but I was grateful to discover that I was not the only rogue skater librarian in existence. There would be other instances of unexpected support, and I was encouraged by knowing that more of my peers were out there finding loopholes and opportunities to promote accessibility in their library system, not limit it.

Bonnie Blouin skating a vert ramp in the 1980s

CHAPTER SIX

WHISTLEBLOWERS
(BONNIE BLOUIN)

The skateboarding industry has gone through several cycles of boom and bust over the years. We saw a collapse in the 1960s when skateboarding, performed on sketchy homemade contraptions, was condemned as unsafe by authority figures, and then a boom in the 1970s with the evolution of quality equipment like urethane wheels and shaped boards. Companies like Hobie, Tracker, Bahne, Powerflex, Gordon & Smith, Zephyr, and Logan Earth Ski produced reputable designs, and contests became a venue to test their products. Talented skaters excelled, which resulted in sponsorships, media attention, and an explosion of for-profit skateparks. The movement started out at a grassroots level, but when it grew in popularity, it drew the attention of corporations, which led to a model of success, money-making, and opportunity.

At a superficial glance, the 1970s can look like a golden era for skateboarding, even for female skaters. It's been speculated that 25 percent of skateboarders in Southern California during this decade were women.[1] But this is California at its peak, and beyond its borders, the more common story of a singular female skater competing against the boys is what I found in newspaper clippings. It could be lonely out there. In the 1970s, even though magazines were receptive to promoting female skateboarders and companies consistently sponsored top riders on their teams, women still had their shit show of retro patriarchy to contend with. Media representation was imbalanced, contest pay was unequal, and there were rigid expectations to conform to gender roles in society at large.

Conforming to stereotypes can also be regulated by one's peers, those who would rather play by society's rules and hold on to an ounce of power than elevate their community and show support for someone trying to push the boundaries. For example, Peggy Oki would face more criticism from female skaters for her gritty surf style than any poor treatment from her male counterparts.[2] Peggy was welcomed as the only girl on the Zephyr Skate Team. The Zephyr surf and skate shop was based in Dogtown, a rundown area in Santa Monica and Venice where the team riders became commonly known as the Z-Boys of Dogtown.

In 1975, at the Del Mar Nationals, female competitors protested Oki's unconventional freestyle performance that landed her in first place. The critics wanted Peggy removed from the winner's list because her style was viewed as too aggressive and not an acceptable freestyle routine.[3] The judges disagreed, but Peggy later explained, "I faded from the scene after the first few contests. From the first, the Del Mar, I didn't like the politics."[4] Peggy decided that hanging around a contest and waiting to skate all day wasn't her idea of fun.

These early glory days faded in the late 1970s when insurance claims and waning popularity gutted the California scene, resulting in the mass demolition of skateparks, which had a ripple effect around the world. And yet this upheaval only helped better define skateboarding as a subculture. The skaters of the early 1980s continued to innovate tricks and seek out new obstacles and terrain in backyard pools, on the city streets, or with their own DIY mini-ramps. But like clockwork, when something underground is considered cool and marketable, even if it's for the second time, the boom returns. By the mid-1980s, skateboarding was lucrative again, contests were launched, new brands were established, and male pro skaters were idolized and offered publicity on MTV. A few years later, along came a recession and a shrunken economy, which rebounded into the extreme sports era of the 1990s. Up and down the popularity of skateboarding goes, which can seem unimaginable when things are going well.

There are books and websites dedicated to exploring these ebbs and flows of skateboarding history, documenting the progression of companies and products, eulogizing defunct skateparks, and rhapsodizing over the male skaters who invented certain tricks, won contests, and secured sponsors. In skateboarding magazines, it's common to find flashback articles by male historians celebrating bygone decades, highlighting who was hot and what the popular tricks were. But preserving a legacy of women skaters and providing heroes for future generations of girls to look up to was not a priority.

When an industry like skateboarding decides that young men are their target market, there's little motivation for male editors and writers to pause and remind their readership that women in the 1970s were killing it in all disciplines, including the "masculine" realm of pool-skating. Iain Borden explored how the pool became mythologized as a site of pugnacious, competitive masculinity, quoting the likes of pro skaters Tony Alva and Duane Peters who declared that to skate pool, "you had to have big balls."[5] In Alva's 1977 interview for *Skateboarder* magazine, he stated that his crew was protective of the empty pools they skated, citing an example when some random guy broke his arm during a session, called an ambulance, which tipped off the police who busted their spot.

> Now we don't allow people who can't skate to ride our spots. We keep them out for their own good... When the boys are together, you could never find a more aggressive, arrogant, rowdy, perhaps ignorant

bunch of people than me and my friends. That's just the way we are.[6]

Alva expressed appreciation for girls who skated because "they have to go out and compete against the best guys just to be able to skate. You have got to hand it to any girl who will put up with that radical sort of nature that's common to skateboarding."[7] But there was still an unspoken assumption that it was people like Alva and his friends who established the culture and its rules.

There were some extremely competent women catching air and grinding pool coping (when the metal trucks that your wheels are secured to connect with the raised lip, or coping, that surrounds a pool's perimeter). They would even sneak onto private property during a notorious California drought in the late 1970s to skate drained pools just like the guys, because the steep terrain was a proving ground regardless of gender, and it was fun.

Terry Lawrence reminisced about trespassing into empty pools and full pipes like Nukeland near a military base at San Onofre, and Pattie Hoffman said that her older brother would take her to backyard pools, which helped her progression, resulting in a sponsorship with Variflex at age twelve. Laura Thornhill remembered landing in jail for skating a pool near her home.

> It was a house that was being remodeled and the pool happened to be empty. We were ditching school for the potential day of fun and then the cops showed up. They could have taken us in for trespassing, truancy and lack of supervision, but only took us all in for lack of supervision. That was the first pool that I tiled and grinded.[8]

Cindy Whitehead also had a brush with the law during an East Coast tour organized by the World Skateboarding Association: "It was a crazy and fun time. Anything and everything could happen: getting arrested for skating empty backyard pools." They were even shot at with buckshot for trespassing and skating full-pipes in Arizona.[9]

Female skaters in the '70s were willing to break the law for a pool session, sometimes even leading the way. Canon "Bunny" Price considered herself a ringleader among a crew of boys, including her childhood boyfriend Eric Dressen, now revered as an iconic pool skater. Canon recalled organizing stealth missions to drain swimming pools at neighboring homes in nearby Palos Verdes, and when the cops caught up to her, she was brought home to face her father. She said, "My dad had to work his magic to get me off the hook,"[10] and as the more accommodating parent, he helped keep her misdemeanor a secret from her mom.

Marilyn Latta and her friend Susie Lindsay tried to drain their apartment complex pool but were caught by Marilyn's mom before a session ensued. Latta said, "The laws have to be changed . . . Right now there are too many restrictions. I don't see what's wrong with skating on public property as long as there are no people to hit."[11] Yvonne Cucci was more fortunate. When an opportunity to skate her neighbor's pool arose, "My mom wrote me a note that said we had health insurance so if I got hurt the homeowner would not be liable. I did wear complete gear and never broke anything thankfully."[12]

Further afield, Jeannie Narducci, who was inducted into the Florida Skateboard Hall of Fame in 2003, was a regular at Oaks Pool in Daytona Beach, Florida, and Sandy Chadbourn of Atlanta, Georgia, was also a dedicated backyard pool skater. In the summer 1978 issue of *Skate Rider* magazine, she was shown skating the "Mansion Pool," and in the July 1978 issue of *Skateboarder*, in an ad for her sponsor Progressive Skateboards, Sandy is seen grinding the coping of "The Blue Room" pool.

It was within a "Who's Hot!" feature for *Skateboarder* in 1977 that Brian Gillogly made a fascinating statement after observing Jana Payne skate pool, another female skater who had fond memories of trespassing. Gillogly wrote, "Jana shows a distinct preference for vertical and near-vertical skating, and particularly pool riding. If the style which she has developed there is often characterized as more masculine than feminine, perhaps it is time to reassess those terms, especially regarding a female who deals so thoroughly with radical terrain."[13] But the industry did not want to reassess these ideas, and by the 1980s there was no interest in celebrating these badass women. This disconnect from the past meant that a new generation of female skaters floundered in the dark, thinking that they were the only girls in existence. It's a scenario that has repeated itself over the decades.

Fortunately, we had Bonnie Blouin, who was a whistleblower and a truth teller. Bonnie had the guts to become *Thrasher* magazine's first female columnist in the mid-1980s, tackling issues of universal appeal to skateboarders. Her writing, full of eloquence and passion, represented female skaters who had so often been dismissed as irrelevant. When I sat down to write Bonnie's biography for the archive, I was excited because I imagined myself interviewing her and discovering shared experiences despite our difference in age, but I was in for a real shock.

As a 1990s skater, I remember when online skateboarding forums and message boards first became a popular mode of communication. I noted earlier in this book the negative response to Toy Machine's announcement of Elissa Steamer going pro, and much of that negativity lived on forums. The response was toxic bile. I pray that Elissa didn't have access to the internet in the 1990s; she was the number one target for trolls, men who were likely threatened by her talent and jealous of her sponsorship and recognition, such as her "Check Out" feature in *TransWorld* (April 1997) and interviews in *Big Brother* (August 1997) with Clyde Singleton and *Thrasher* (November 1998) with Michael Burnett (and it was thanks to Burnett that Elissa was finally honored with a cover for *Thrasher*

in March 2024). Elissa obviously received support from her close-knit crew, but the hostility online seemed unprecedented. These insecure jerks were adamant that women should remain in the kitchen or lounging in bed waiting to be of service straight out of *The Handmaid's Tale*. Skateboarding was supposed to be off limits for the "fairer sex."

Elissa was probably too busy skating to care. But I cared. I couldn't sit by and witness my heroes getting trashed, although I soon realized that it was pointless trying to debate anonymous haters. In the first issue of *Armpit* zine from 2002, I mentioned how the local guys on our skateboard forum had given me the nickname "Femi-Nazi." It's an awful term made popular by the 1990s talk show host Rush Limbaugh, but that's how they perceived me. I didn't last long in that forum because it's exhausting trying to repeatedly explain that calling female skaters *lesbians* and *whores* is tedious and unimaginative, and as an insult it's just irrational.

Luckily, I found exclusive online spaces for female skaters to banter. Denise Williams, a Canadian East Coast skater from Halifax, hosted a website and forum called Frontside Betty and edited the magazine *Push* (2002–03), which lasted for four glorious issues. Williams recognized that because we were a female subculture within a subculture, or a "scene within a scene"[14] (the title of one of her editorials), our own community regarded us as deviants, so the best thing we could do was embrace our identity and stick together. Even in these safe places there were often infiltrators trying to disrupt the community with crude, usually anonymous, comments but at least they were outnumbered, and on a forum like The Skullz (introduced in Chapter Five), it was a joy to witness feisty Australians annihilate their opponents. While I don't have nostalgic feelings for the skateboarding industry at large in the 1990s and early 2000s, I can be sentimental about those early days online which felt like a life-or-death battle to defend our right to skate and upheave a culture that was misogynist.

I was fortunate to find other young women to skate and form girl gangs with once I moved out west, but I know that many individuals depended heavily on these more inclusive forums because they were isolated in towns across North America and beyond. It's important to recognize the impact of isolation and loneliness, which is partially why I was so drawn to Bonnie Blouin's writing. Bonnie addressed these themes in her column "Skater's Edge," and I wish I had known about her when I was learning to skate in small-town Ontario. I could've used the inspiration. It turns out that Bonnie had the exact same sentiment, wishing that she had female mentors from the 1970s to give her hope and help her feel like less of an oddball in Richmond, Virginia.

When I wrote my thesis paper in 2003 and discovered Bonnie's game-changing article "Sugar and Spice . . ?" from April 1986, which was the first article of its kind in the 1980s that investigated the role that female skaters could play in the community, it was like a godsend and I quoted her thoroughly. Here was a nerdy skater just like me articulating some of my experiences. I felt aligned with Bonnie, and I often imagined meeting her.

Now that vintage *Thrasher* magazines are digitized along with select copies of zines that Bonnie contributed to like *Lapper*, *YAKK*, and *True Devotion*, I had plenty of fodder to dig into her story. Bonnie had a fantastic run in *Thrasher*, with her "Skater's Edge" column spanning from October 1987 until May 1989. While the plight of female skaters was her passion, she covered a wide range of topics each month from dealing with unstoked parents, going on road trips, dating, preventing injuries, selecting the best gear, rallying fellow skateboarders to protest injustice, handling police harassment, the works.

It all began in the mid-1980s when Bonnie sent letters alongside her zine *True Devotion* (which she originally coproduced with Gigi Gits, a punk skater also from Richmond) to *Thrasher's* zine review department. These zine connections helped Bonnie establish a rapport with the staff. Her first *Thrasher* writing credit appeared in the March 1986 issue when one of her poems was selected for the "Poetry in Motion" feature. Some of the skaters' poems were better than others, and Bonnie's was called "I See You." It describes a newbie skateboarder with their pristine board and brand-new checkered Vans shoes, too afraid to join a skate session. In rhyming verse, Bonnie encouraged the skater because even the most talented riders have had to face their fears as a beginner: "Energy is created by the power in your mind. Use that power, get that grind."[15]

I suspect Bonnie was trying to remind *Thrasher* readers to have empathy for beginners in an era that was obsessed with condemning people as "poseurs." While it's not strictly a 1980s phenomenon, the poseur label implies that a person is a pseudo-skateboarder or fraud, which is comical because everyone and everybody must start somewhere, making us all poseurs at some point. The problem is when someone is ridiculed as a poseur simply because they are a girl, as though being female automatically disqualifies someone from claiming status as a true skateboarder. The topic was on Bonnie's mind because she also had a letter printed in that same issue of *Thrasher* in support of a girl dubbed "Jane Doe" (mentioned in Chapter One) who was fed up with being mocked by the local skaters, who instead could've been offering advice to a newcomer. Bonnie totally had Jane's back and called out the guys who labeled her a poseur. She wrote, "Your attitude reflects *you* as a person. When you look at someone and make negative assumptions towards them, you're only thriving on insecurities of your own."[16]

The following month, Bonnie's first feature, a six-page article called "Sugar and Spice . . ?," was published. Her opening paragraph describes two uncomfortable experiences that made her feel out of place. At the Rock Against Reagan event, Bonnie was heckled by a guy who branded her a "betty." Being called a betty implied that you were lurking around the skate session or holding a skateboard like a fashion accessory, trying to get the attention of a guy and score a date, but not actually skating with purpose. It was a dismissive label intended to make girls, both those who skated and

GIRL GANGS, ZINES, AND POWERSLIDES

those who didn't, feel inadequate and inauthentic (the term *betty* was eventually reclaimed in the 1990s by websites like Frontside Betty, companies like OG Betty, and the 2020 HBO series *Betty* about female skaters in New York). And then at the entrance to a concert, another dude interrogated Bonnie by asking, "Hey, do you ride, or are you posin'?" even though she had arrived sweaty and filthy from a skateboard session. Bonnie was tired of these statements and said, "It's my boyfriend's board," preferring to "let the clueless remain without a clue."[17]

In the 1980s, a girl couldn't simply say she was a skateboarder; she was expected to prove it on demand by any bozo or face the consequences of being harassed. By the 1990s, the term *betty* was revamped with a more malicious edge, and one could be dismissed as a "pro ho" because it was presumed that only men were professional skaters and the girls in their vicinity were just there to seduce them. Photographer, Magdalena Wosinska remembered being called a pro ho at the skatepark in the early 1990s. "And I was like, 'what's that?' I didn't know what that was. I was twelve. I didn't even know what sex was."[18] To add insult to injury, if you were able to competently perform the classic kickflip, the accomplishment would be mocked as a "chickflip." Even pro skateboarder Elissa Steamer reported having her kickflip dismissed as a chickflip by someone revered in the industry, implying that she lacked a certain style that only men possessed.[19] Good lord, help us.

At the time of "Sugar and Spice . . ?" Bonnie had only skated with three girls: Gigi Gits, Deirdre "Dee Dee" Devine, and Trish Wright. Bonnie was always searching and hoping to find other girls because when you're without any peers,

> you don't have any way to "measure" your ability or progression. You always know when you are progressing or jelling, but you wonder, "Gee, can I really do that?" If there were other girls around who you could see shredding, you'd have no doubts, 'cause they paved

the way . . . I know there are girls out there who ride and take it seriously. I wonder all the time what they are like, how they are progressing and if they have the same thought that I do as a girl in a guy's game . . . I saw [Stephanie Person] doing a boneless in the new Powell video and I was like, "Hey, wow, that's a girl, rewind it." No one else even noticed.[20]

Bonnie then speculates why many girls are reluctant to skate and determines that society is fixated on this idea of women being cute and sexy, and that aggression in sport is "unfeminine." She even notes that some guys are threatened by her presence as if she is part of a ploy to undermine their manliness, especially if she learns a trick before they do. Bonnie expresses her frustration because she was not skating to impress anyone, and she wasn't interested in being told that she was pretty good "for a girl."[21] Bonnie just wanted to ride, but she was also weary of being alone.

It was destiny for Bonnie to write "Sugar and Spice . . ?" because it opened a whole new range of possibilities. The article was enhanced with photos that *Thrasher* had sourced of West Coast female skaters, including April Hoffman, Babs Fahrney, Michelle Sanderson, Stephanie Person, and KZ Zapata, whom Bonnie had never heard of. Bonnie and the women of the 1980s were pre-internet and had to resort to being pen pals and distributing zines as means of communication with friends; long-distance phone calls were a real expense. Because Zapata was also a zine writer, the two skaters recognized their shared values and began corresponding.

Two years later, in her follow-up article on the topic of female skateboarders for her "Skater's Edge" column, Bonnie was pleased to report that her "Sugar and Spice . . ?" article had resulted in a positive response, and that her network had grown thanks to the development of the Women's Skateboarding Club. Bonnie even took a trip out west to meet and skate with KZ Zapata and Amy Paul, and she was overjoyed with the experience of ripping around town with a gang of female friends. Bonnie loved being part of a collective, "blowing people away with your mere existence. Most of all, you have someone to share your hopes, your fears and your dreams with, and that, in itself, is an indescribable priviledge [sic]."[22] Bonnie also experienced the "if she can do it, I can"[23] way of thinking while skating with her new friends, which helped her improve, like she had always hoped to experience.

But then the article took a dive. Bonnie revealed to her *Thrasher* readers what it was like returning home after her time out west. As I read through her thoughts on isolation, the lack of opportunities, the lack of desire to compete and prove herself against the guys, I could feel the ache of her loneliness.

> I no longer wonder why more girls don't skate. Unless a girl has the total strength and desire within herself to ride and to keep riding, there is truly nothing to keep her motivated. In fact, society and a lot of guy skaters prevent girls from skating.
>
> Laura Thornhill, Vicki Vickers and Patti[e] Hoffman are three women whose faces are deeply embedded in my mind. Yes, they were true pioneers, an inspiration to us by way of example, but they are not involved now. They cannot flow advice to girls who may need it . . . Skateboarding has evolved for males into what it is today because kids have been able to learn from their role models.[24]

There was a hint of bitterness toward female skaters of the 1970s, whom Bonnie seems to have felt abandoned by. I can understand her disappointment, but Bonnie didn't have the resources to explore why these women might have disappeared, or even if they were still skateboarding. For example, Laura Thornhill, who was the world freestyle and slalom champion in the mid-1970s and the first competitive female skater with a signature skateboard model for Logan Earth Ski, experienced a jarring injury, but this wasn't the end of her connection to and love of skateboarding. And Pattie Hoffman, who dominated the pro contests in bowl skating, had only taken a pause. She had been discouraged by the prize discrepancies between the guys and girls, one thousand dollars to her one hundred. And when her sponsor Variflex shot down her hope of a signature board in the early 1980s, saying that a girl's board wouldn't sell, Pattie needed to disconnect.[25] Pattie would eventually reappear, skating in the 1992 video *SK8HERS*. But how was Bonnie to know all this?

It was in her powerful critique about the state of contests in California — where Bonnie had discovered a concentration of female skaters — that she shined as a whistleblower: "I am totally blown away that there are no women's divisions at contests. Contest organizers argue that there aren't enough girls entering to warrant a women's division. It takes a lot of guts to stand out there and face 50 burly dudes who'd just as soon run over you as take their turn."[26] Bonnie tried to impress upon her readers how it might feel to be 115 pounds and get bulldozed by a half-crazed, six-foot monster at 185 pounds. Bonnie said no thanks, she was perfectly capable of injuring herself.

> Many girls will not enter contests for this reason. It is very intimidating. Males seem to think it is "their problem" and something "they" will have to overcome if "they" want to ride, but the point is, it shouldn't be that way. If a women's division was created and publicized in time the blank pages would fill in quite rapidly . . . We need only the chance to excel at our own pace, to progress in our own league and to be recognized for our achievements as females on our own terms.[27]

Bonnie felt that instead of seeing women's participation as an enhancement to skateboarding, the contest organizers considered this lack of opportunity the girls' problem. Female skateboarders just had to suck it up and overcome their fears, but Bonnie wasn't buying it. A women's division needed to be established as an opportunity for inclusion to help skateboarding evolve.

Bonnie's writing resonated with many young women, some of whom voiced their support in the Mail Drop section of *Thrasher* throughout the years she was a columnist. For example, a skater named Kim M. wrote,

> I want to thank Bonnie Blouin for writing an article about girl skaters. She's right. It is hard for girls to get out there and shred without getting criticized by some stuck-up skater. Let me tell you skater dudes something I know for a fact: some guys don't want us around, but tuff. We are here to stay and we're going to be out there shredding too.[28]

Bonnie's efforts gave women permission to talk about their experiences. She provided a glimpse of what was happening in the underground network of women skateboarders and rallied for change. And by being vulnerable in such a public platform as *Thrasher*, Bonnie helped her female readers feel less alone.

WOMEN'S LIB

Cindy Berryman
Journalist (1970s)

Cindy Berryman began reporting on the skateboarding scene in the 1970s when Warren Bolster, a photographer and editor of *Skateboarder* magazine, invited her to contribute. Cindy was pursuing law school at the time but took time off to develop her writing.

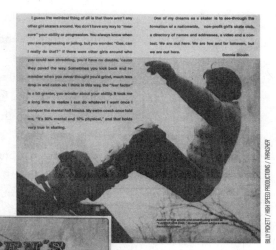

Thrasher columnist Bonnie Blouin is photographed by Billy Pickett for her article "Sugar and Spice..?" April 1986

Vicki Vickers is featured in the "Special Women's Section" of the June 1978 issue of the *National Skateboard Review*, by Glenn Miyoda

In the book *Urethane Revolution*, author John O'Malley joked that Bolster intentionally derailed Cindy's career path because "in 1976, finding a skateboarder to put together one thousand words on deadline was a very tall order, so Warren was happy to grow the talent that he needed where he could."[29]

While Cindy dabbled in skateboarding and was part of the crew at Black Hill at La Costa, a mecca for skateboarders and product innovators in the mid-1970s, it was her kid sister, Ellen Berryman, who competed as a professional alongside all the rising stars of the era. Cindy was Ellen's greatest supporter and had been her primary caregiver. Their father was paralyzed from the waist down, often struggling to support the family while he was in hospital for long periods, and their mother lived with schizophrenia.[30]

Cindy decided to write a key article called "Let's Hear it for the Ladies" in the August 1976 edition of *Skateboarder* to draw attention to the growing talent of female riders, their concerns, and accomplishments.[31] The introduction states, "Just setting pen to paper to write an article on the skate ladies is an admission that there is something different about the women."[32] Berryman discusses the debate around gender roles in skateboarding, noting that while women were typically revered for their grace, balance, and freestyle rhythm, aggression is often necessary when skating banks and bowls, and it shouldn't be pigeonholed as a masculine behavior. Berryman also expresses concern about how some women appeared to accentuate their femininity when not competing to overcompensate for being active in a male-dominated activity.

The article is accompanied by photos of skaters like Kim Cespedes cruising the bowl at Carlsbad, high jump and freestyle ace Desiree Von Essen, Francine Hill and Dodie Hackemack ripping around the deep ends of some gnarly pools, Robin Logan and Laura Thornhill claiming space at their local park, and even a six-year-old girl named Jennifer Dimon flying off a small launch ramp.

Even with all this progress, Cindy felt that contest standards for female skateboarders took them back to the Stone Age. Cindy echoed Von Essen who described how organizers would either schedule their events at the end of the day, "or they schedule us for free-style while the men do slalom, so we're never noticed."[33] A similar scenario would repeat itself for women well into the 2000s. And then there was the Belmont Park Freestyle Contest in San Diego where all the girls and women, regardless of age or experience, were lumped together. The women's winner won a trip to San Diego, where the contest was held, even though they were promised San Francisco, and the men's winner won a trip for two to Hawaii.

After competitive skater Robin Alaway earned 775 dollars less than her male counterpart at a contest, she said, "Maybe the day will arrive when all we skate ladies will see the light and organize ourselves to form a stronger union. But remember, there is strength in numbers, so come on, ladies, and get involved."[34] Berryman concluded that the power behind the skateboard industry was primarily male but insisted that there was still a place for women: "They're a significant factor in skateboarding, and their accomplishments are not to be overlooked."[35]

Cindy's sister, Ellen, would win the first Free Former World Freestyle Championships in 1976, among many contests, perform in front of a crowd of 70,000 Jethro Tull fans at the L.A. Coliseum,[36] and be inducted into the Skateboarding Hall of Fame in 2016. And while Ellen is the more recognizable name, Cindy still holds a place of honor, at least to me, as a whistleblower. Cindy would go on to write a column for the *Wild World of Skateboarding* magazine called "Footnotes" and contribute to several surfing publications, including one from Australia, providing reports on the scene in Southern California and Hawaii.

Leslie Jo Ritzma
"World's Fastest Female Skateboarder" (1977)

Leslie Jo Ritzma from Redondo Beach started skateboarding in 1964 in second grade by nailing her roller skate wheels onto a two-by-four.[37] She ended up breaking her arm thanks to that DIY setup, but the injury didn't deter her nor did being told that skateboarding was "too dangerous" for a child. In 1977, at age twenty, Leslie Jo decided that she wanted to enter the notorious Signal Hill

Speed Run race that boasted a 30-degree incline, even though she was told, again, that it was "too dangerous" for a woman.

A *Los Angeles Times* historical piece about the Signal Hill contest quotes Leslie Jo:

> "I asked if there were women in the race, and I was told they weren't allowed to enter. I thought that was stupid." . . . After appealing, she was allowed to compete, but she'd never done any downhill skateboarding. She had enough time to practice before the event, with generous helpings of road rash. She did well in the race and her 51 mph put her in the Guinness Book as the world's fastest female skateboarder.[38]

The article makes it sound like Leslie Jo was a novice, but she was sponsored by 41st Ave Skateboards and Tunnel Wheels and a competent skater.

Leslie Jo didn't take the comment lightly that women were forbidden from competing. In an interview with Tunnel Skateboards, she shared, "It was the '70s and women's rights were going on, so I contacted the Women's Equal Action League in Washington, D.C., and *CBS Sports Spectacular* who filmed at Signal Hill. They put pressure on the organizers to allow women."[39]

Leslie Jo was successful in her bid and found herself at the start line but admitted that she was nervous about plunging down this epic hill on a skateboard that was more like a luge or skeleton sled in front of thousands of bloodthirsty spectators. "I was laying down, face forward, on my stomach. We made some metal pieces shaped in an 'L', and we bolted pieces of tire onto those, so when I pushed my feet down, it slowed me down. Very primitive brakes."[40] Leslie Jo made it down the hill intact and in good time. She tied for sixth place overall and could officially call herself the fastest female skateboarder in the world for her death-defying achievement.

Leslie Jo was acknowledged in the June 1977 issue of the *National Skateboard Review* with a letter explaining that while her Guinness record was a result of being the one and only female racing, she ended up beating more than half the men competing. It was then stated that Leslie Jo's skateboarding fiancé was so nervous about being overtaken, that she was pressured not to take a second run just in case she beat his time.[41] The situation spoke volumes about the kind of era the 1970s was with its momentous strides toward equitable treatment contrasted with ingrained beliefs about women's place in society. I was relieved to find out that Leslie Jo eventually remarried and took up motorcycle riding, pursuing her love of speed and adrenaline.[42]

Vicki Vickers
Pro skateboarder (1970s)

While attending the national surfing championships in Port Isabel, Texas, fourteen-year-old Vicki Vickers overheard Dogtown Z-Boy skater Nathan Pratt declare that "girls can't skate." In her "Who's Hot!" profile in the December 1978 issue of *Skateboarder*, then eighteen-year-old Vicki told Jim Goodrich that she took Pratt's statement seriously and immediately started skateboarding.[43] Vicki would be a vocal advocate for equal pay and support for women skateboarders throughout her career.

Originally from Pensacola, Florida, Vicki moved to Texas and eventually to Los Angeles to seek her skateboarding fortune. Vicki began competing in freestyle but preferred riding reservoirs because it was the most fun, which led her into the terrain of pools and bowl riding.[44] With her move out west, Vicki found sponsorship with Pepsi, Hobie, Sims, and Kryptonics. Pepsi even took her on tour to Mexico, where she was photographed doing a powerslide on a plexiglass ramp for the first issue of Mexico's first skateboard magazine, *Roller*. Vicki also made a great discovery in

GIRL GANGS, ZINES, AND POWERSLIDES

Mexico, finding a local ripper named Stephanie. I would later determine that this was Stephanie Fernández on team SERISA — she became Mexico's first national female champion. This mention of Stephanie was another eureka moment that helped me build a global perspective of women's skateboard history, thanks to Vicki.

Vicki was always looking for opportunities to acknowledge her fellow female skaters, like Jana Payne, Lori Rarey, and Ellen Oneal. She celebrated these three women as early influences in her "Who's Hot!" feature. The article was full of praise for Vicki, concluding, "Her determination and skill is certainly equal to that of her male counterparts in the sport; and I think most would have to agree that, though she may be quite a lady, she is definitely more than a pretty face."[45] The "pretty face" comment was then duplicated as a photo caption for added emphasis.

A year later, in a six-page interview for *Skateboarder*, Vicki posed for a glamour shot, which grabbed the readers' attention, and then used the opportunity to share her frustrations. There were times when she showed up at a demonstration and everyone assumed that she was there to perform a flatland freestyle routine rather than barge into the pool with skill and determination. Her biggest beef was regarding contests where the girls' events were left to the end of the day and only run "if we have time," or when the women were expected to show up at the skatepark at seven in the morning for practice and compete without any spectators.[46]

> And the money isn't the same. I'll be damned if we're not out there breakin' our necks just like the guys . . . We're catchin' air, we're coming out of the pool and we're comin' on strong, but we're gonna fade out . . . if that's what the media coverage wants . . . I mean, I'm pissed! Why can't I say that — it's my interview! I want to tell the whole world that we're being screwed over . . . I don't care if there's no money, there's always coverage, there's always the media!

> How many issues has it been since you've seen a
> girl's face? About five.[47]

Women were pushing the limits, but as Vicki predicted, it was as if the media wanted their presence to fade because that's exactly what happened the following decade.

Again, Vicki acknowledged her fellow competitors in her interview, all of whom were skating strongly in pools and bowl: Terry Lawrence, Lori Rarey, Brenda Devine, Leilani Kiyabu, Kim Cespedes, and Vicki's protégé, Canon "Bunny" Price. She felt that the one person in the industry who was elevating women in skateboarding at the time was (surprise) another woman, Denise Barter, the team manager of Sims Skateboards. "She always keeps up the girls' morale because the girls get so depressed so often because we are taken advantage of."[48]

Vicki had an interesting set of opinions, and she wasn't shy about expressing them in her interview. She was often sarcastic, even pretending that basket-weaving and ant farming were her hobbies, so it's sometimes hard to know when Vicki was messing with her interviewer. One minute Vicki declared that she would become the "Billie Jean King of skateboarding," and the next she would be advising girls to clean up their acts by dieting and appearing feminine. She demanded that "girls have got to be respected," but then cracked a joke about being willing to skate in a string bikini for attention, even after having stated that it was upsetting hearing people assess female skaters' appearances by commenting on "whose shorts are tighter."

From a staunch feminist perspective, Vicki's observations may seem problematic, but I found her fascinating as someone who was transparent and honest. I recognize that she was navigating her role as a talented skateboarder and someone who was accountable to her female friends, all the while operating in a male-dominated culture. As a vivacious blonde, she did have the privilege of being viewed as conventionally attractive, but she still sought out opportunities to leverage her voice for women skateboarders. Vicki was also human. She worried about how people would perceive her ideas, wondering out loud, What if "everything I say is wrong?"[49] And everyone can relate to that feeling.

Vicki concluded her interview by making a jab at *Skateboarder* magazine, telling Goodrich that it was about time he interviewed another girl. She also hoped that her interview and kickass photos, looking like a pissed-off Farrah Fawcett on wheels, would raise awareness that women could succeed as skaters. In 2017, Vicki was celebrated by her peers and inducted into the Skateboarding Hall of Fame.

I think it's fair to say that we all contain contradictions and hidden struggles. When I had first read Bonnie Blouin's writing, I decided that here was a person who possessed deep confidence and self-awareness, a true leader, unfazed by snide comments, willing to defend her peers and promote skateboarding unabashedly. This judgment may be true, but I will never fully know Bonnie's perspective or the internal battles she faced.

I assumed that getting in touch with Bonnie would be easy. With my connection to her old pen pal KZ Zapata, I felt certain that when I found Bonnie's social media profile, she would graciously accept an interview. I began imagining what I would ask her: What gave her the idea to start her first zine? Did people treat her differently once she became a columnist for *Thrasher*? What was she most proud of? But when I started my search and stumbled upon an article called "Bonnie Blouin: A Trailblazing Skater and Writer,"[50] it took me a moment to realize that it was a memorial. And I'm going to pause here to say, just as I wrote in her online bio, that the next few paragraphs are sad and may be triggering.

At age thirty-two, Bonnie took her own life. Her memorial states, "For *Thrasher* readers of the late '80s, especially girls and women, her voice and even her very existence was world-expanding, enriching and inspirational. Lest we forget, Bonnie Blouin."[51] I can't even type this paragraph without weeping, and I never even met her. It hit me that, the summer I started to skate, Bonnie was nearing the end, and I've wondered what would have changed if I had heard about her and written to her at that time. This kind of magical thinking can seem stupid, but it's also an expression of grief and heartbreak.

It wasn't the first time I had discovered that a skateboarding legend had passed away, but those women, while still being a great loss, had died surrounded by loved ones as they combatted an illness like cancer. I didn't know the details of what had happened to Bonnie, except that she chose suicide, which meant something was wrong. I felt like I had lost a sister and then remembered again that I had never met her and never would. It would take me weeks to write Bonnie's feature for the archive, and this chapter has been a stumbling block for me all over again.

I wasn't sure how to traverse the sensitive topic of suicide on a website that I had imagined would be purely celebratory. All I could do was try to remind the reader that "life is good, and skateboarding is freedom, and to anyone reading this last paragraph, who has any doubt please remember you are unique to this world, and you are loved. Reach out to a friend or a professional if things are feeling dark, and find the light to sustain you, and that flicker of hope that things will change for the better." [52]

It's hard to discuss suicide, so I'm grateful that bold steps are being made among skateboarders to address this topic, such as pro skater John Rattray's initiative Why So Sad? and the Ben Raemers Foundation. Rattray's campaign began in 2017 after he lost his sister Katrina to suicide and was dealing with his own depression. The Why So Sad? storytelling platform invites conversation and aims to help skaters feel less isolated. The Ben Raemers Foundation, in honor of its namesake, a professional skater from the U.K., was established after Ben took his life during a time when he was perceived to be at the top of his career. The foundation offers suicide prevention training and focuses on ending the stigma around mental health challenges through promotions online and by encouraging people to develop positive coping strategies and the confidence to reach out when they are struggling. These efforts remind us that suicide is a preventable cause of death and that there are support networks available.

The skateboarding industry often projects a lifestyle of extremes, such as partying and drinking and stupid pranks on par with a *Jackass* production. While there's an element of fun involved, there comes a point when it's worth questioning if this lifestyle is masking something problematic. It requires courage for someone to take a time-out, be vulnerable, and acknowledge that there can be heavy repercussions to this behavior when there are no checks in place. Skateboarding is not a self-help model that can fix a person's problems, but it is a great outlet and can provide community. And the best kind of community is made up of individuals willing to step up and have hard conversations, knowing that it's for their friend's well-being.

It was evident that Bonnie was a deep thinker, perhaps a sensitive soul, and part of what bothers me, what I'm hesitant to talk about, is that I wonder if I have more than just a passion for writing and skateboarding in common with her. I don't have any record of what Bonnie's life was like at age thirty-two, so I won't compare our situations. When I was thirty-two, I was in a dark place. I entertained the idea of finding a final escape to end destructive behaviors that I was ashamed of but couldn't control. I was tired of feeling trapped in negative thinking, my brain like a broken record rehashing instances of rejection and humiliation over and over. Fortunately, I was directed toward EMDR therapy and group counseling by a mentor who supported me in making some drastic changes.

Bonnie embraced her role as mentor and happily shared words of wisdom with others, reminding *Thrasher* readers to have a positive mindset. In her column, she wrote,

> Sometimes the mind must be trained and even forced
> to think positively. This is also put into action by the

soul. The mind can be trained through the repetition of positive encounters (making a new trick) that counterbalance the negative ones (slamming). The already dedicated and stoked soul assists the mind in reaching a high level of self confidence, which leads to positiveness in day to day skating and in life, for that matter.[53]

Bonnie's thoughts are not diminished because of how she passed; they just land differently imagining her writing these sentiments with conviction but struggling to adhere to them.

I am always updating the archive with newly acquired content such as photos and video, but I am especially diligent when it comes to Bonnie. The most cherished items in my collection are her two handwritten letters to *Thrasher*, responding to Jane Doe's letter, and when she submitted issues four and five of her *True Devotion* zine. Her immaculate, childlike penmanship in all-caps and friendly expressions like "Hey-O" with the occasional underline for emphasis feel so alive. I am eternally grateful for this gift of letters that was offered to me.

Bonnie's love of skateboarding shines through her words. She wanted equitable treatment of female skaters and skaters in general, and she despised stereotypes that portrayed us as delinquents, causing parents to be irrational and city officials to establish vindictive rules. All this motivated her to write, and I respect that. I just wish that she was here right now, witnessing the incredible opportunities available to girls and women in skateboarding today. She could never have dreamed of the efforts being made to improve inclusivity. It is indeed a good time to be a skateboarder, and Bonnie helped make this change possible.

I'll repeat my sentiments from my original post here for good measure. Rest in peace, Bonnie, you beautiful, radiant skateboarder! WE SEE YOU and we won't forget you.

Lynn Kramer lambasts the UCSD mini's lip.

UCSD RAMP

For an article in the August 1989 issue of *Thrasher*, Lynn Kramer grinds the coping of the UCSD mini-ramp

CHAPTER SEVEN

BETTER TOGETHER
(LYNN KRAMER)

A critical step in any skateboarders' progression is the drop-in. This is when you position the tail of the skateboard on the coping of a mini-ramp or quarter-pipe, which resembles the raised lip of a pool perimeter, and then fearlessly shift your body weight forward, pushing down on the front of your board to ride the ramp's transition without bailing. To convince yourself to take the plunge, it helps if you have someone demonstrate the motion and a group of supporters to cheer you on. In skateboarding, we call this a hype team, and it refers to the bystanders waiting in anticipation for their friend to successfully complete a trick before going ape shit in response.

While it's awe-inspiring to witness flawless contest runs by the leading pros, there are times I would rather watch a video of the first time a beginner drops in or lands a kickflip. There's a buildup of tension with every failed attempt, and I become invested in their progress. And when the moment arrives and the trick is accomplished, the expression on the skater's face goes from stunned to ecstatic when they realize their battle is over. It's a combination of pure relief and exhilaration, enhanced by an explosive reaction from friends or family who encouraged them through the ordeal. Skateboards are winged into the air, and there are group hugs like after a game-winning goal at the Women's World Cup.

A celebration with your hype team is one of the best things about being a skateboarder. And these roles often reverse. It's expected that you would reciprocate and bring the same energy and enthusiasm to a session for your fellow skater. A hype team is critical when a barrier seems insurmountable, whether it is a physical, mental, or even a societal barrier. The crew might heckle you in fun and place a few bets, but they are consistently telling you to keep going and try again. When an injury busts up the session, they reassure you that you'll be back and next time you will *nail that trick.*

Learning to skate transition such as a mini-ramp, let alone a vert ramp, is a privilege for many skateboarders because it requires access and opportunity. Ramps are not cheap to build; they require space (usually covered to protect them from the elements) and accommodating neighbors because of the noise. Lynn Kramer had the opportunity to skate a mini-ramp while studying engineering at the University of California, San Diego (UCSD) in the mid-1980s, and she discovered her first skateboarding friends in the process of building one.

Lynn is best known as the seventeen-time world slalom champion (as of 2023), dodging cones downhill with strength, speed, and precision and representing Sk8Kings as their first female rider to have a signature slalom board. This history of Lynn as a mini-ramp skater may be surprising, because slalom-racing is a very different discipline that tends to be a solo affair, even though there's a supportive community of slalom skaters. A mini-ramp session is more of a communal experience since it is a shared obstacle with skaters waiting their turns to perform a line and cheering for each other, if it's an inclusive group. I think it makes sense that Lynn's origin story revolves around a mini-ramp because it aligns with her character and how she encourages others to be their best. I can just imagine her at those sessions in university, hyping up her friends and setting the standard of camaraderie and respect.

I am terrible at skating mini-ramps. I blame this one skatepark in Ontario from the 1990s, which was a ramshackle collection of rotting wood obstacles in a tennis court covered in rusty sheet metal, thanks to melting snow that accumulated over winter. Even with its limited scope, I was grateful to go there because it was the only skatepark around. My mom would graciously loan me her car to drive the forty-minute commute. I didn't mind the drive because I would crank up Pennywise and the Beastie Boys to get psyched and was usually transporting some buddies from my high school.

While I was able to learn how to drop in on a small quarter-pipe relatively unharmed, the mini-ramp was a death trap. If you fell, the sheet metal would either burn you in the heat of summer or cut you because the layers had begun to curl and the screws holding each sheet in place were stripped and constantly popping out. The mini-ramp would've made a fine mafia boss. As a beginner, I preferred practicing tricks on flat banks and curbs after being winded and sliced on the mini-ramp.

My avoidance of the mini-ramp meant that when I got older, I often felt intimidated at group skate sessions. The only times I made progress on a ramp was when I was surrounded by trusted friends. In 2002, I wrote in my journal that a group of girls and I had rented access to a small four-foot bowl inside a skateboard shop called Underworld in Montréal. I remarked that my friend Julie Lévesque was a "ripper" and seeing her skate got me pumped: "It was cool because I started to get angry with myself for not doing rock to fakies and forced myself to do them! This one trick has prevented me from skating the mini-ramp and now I can't wait to learn more!"

Our crew of skaters had a range of abilities, but the mutual effort to learn meant that any attempt to try something new was appreciated with raucous yelling and tail-tapping — hitting wood boards against metal coping — as a form of applause. Being part of a group of like-minded friends can make you feel indestructible and help squash negative thinking that may be blocking your progress. As Bonnie Blouin explained, when you witness a friend land a trick, you know that it's attainable and will want to do the same. And this hopeful attitude extends to other projects like building a skatepark, demanding inclusive skateboarding contests, and beyond.

When I first began this project, I recognized Lynn Kramer's name as the editor of the *Equal Time* zine (originally called *Girls Who Grind*), the official publication of the Women's Skateboarding Network (WSN) from 1988 to 1992. According to Patty Segovia in her book *Skater Girl*, WSN's motto was "no nuts, just guts" and boasted 250 members with representation from around the world.[1] When I read this in 2007, I was fascinated. In my mind, *Equal Time* seemed like some mythical legend and finding copies would be on par with the discovery of the *Epic of Gilgamesh*. Meanwhile, in 2022, all it took was a quick message to Lynn via Instagram for an interview to unfold, and PDF scans of the zine were floated to my inbox like magic and revealed a gold mine of history.

Lynn was a dedicated athlete as a kid, taking up football, tennis, BMX riding, and Little League baseball, even asserting her right to play softball in junior high against the boys and encouraging her female friends to join in.[2] Lynn had dabbled with skateboarding at age seven, but her parents were wary after she chipped her tooth while knee-boarding on a friend's board. Eventually, she received a proper setup at age twelve, but it wasn't until after high school that her interest in skateboarding flourished.[3]

> When I got to UCSD, the first thing I saw were skateboards. Skateboards everywhere. It was 1985, and skateboarding was at a high. My apartment was on a major walkway, and I would sit outside waiting for

people on skateboards to go by, so I could hijack their boards. I met some skaters and borrowed a board for a couple weeks, until they told me it was time to get my own.

My sister Bobbie (RIP) took me to a skate shop in Pacific Beach, and we put together a Powell Peralta Skull and Sword with Tracker Trucks and Bones III wheels, complete with rails, a tail skid, copers, a lapper, and a nose guard. That was it. I skated every day for the next three years.[4]

But she did more than just skate. Lynn joined the UCSD Ready to Shred skate club and helped organize the first-ever campus skatepark, learning to build a mini-ramp before learning to skate it. Lynn wrote about the experience, the highs and lows of dealing with an institution's red tape, for *Thrasher* in August 1989, which included a photo of Lynn grinding the coping.[5]

Lynn insisted that she was "not very good at skateboarding" because it took her six months to learn how to ollie and two years to learn how to pump the transition in the mini-ramp, "but I had the heart, and good bones."[6] The UCSD community was supportive and nonjudgmental, and thanks to the mini-ramp, Lynn made friends with skateboarder Lisa Forman. In the early 1980s, Lisa had represented SkaterCross skatepark and competed against Cara-Beth Burnside as a youth in the Association of Skatepark Owners contest series before they scratched the girls' divisions. Lynn shared that Lisa "ripped on vert, with inverts and laybacks. She traveled with us for Women's Skateboard Network stories and was often featured in *Equal Time*."[7]

Around 1988, Lynn was encouraged to take the reins and reinvigorate the Women's Skateboarding Club, which Lora Lyons and Lauri Kuulei Wong had initiated two years prior, rebranding it as the Women's Skateboarding Network. The best way to garner interest was obviously through a zine. In December 1988, the *Girls*

Who Grind zine was launched, and it contained letters from skaters from Arkansas to West Germany, coverage of the Street Life contest, a story about a road trip to Northern California, and a list of World Skateboarding Association contests that promised to include separate women's divisions.

Girls Who Grind looks like a scrappy, slapdash publication with grainy photos and simple line drawings, but from a historian's perspective, this zine is a diamond in the rough, providing some of the only published photos of core female street skaters of the late 1980s. First off, the story about the Street Life contest epitomized the vibe of what it was like for a young woman to boldly exit the safety of a community scene, like UCSD, and enter the snake pit.

> On November 19, 1988, Street Life held an amateur streetstyle contest in San Diego, CA. Included in the contest was a women's division. Five women showed up to skate that day, and skate they did . . .
>
> One thing can be complained about. The timing of the women's division. The women competed at the end of the day, right between the sponsored ams' preliminary and final heats. The [amateur men] were less than gentlemen when the girls went out to practice, refusing to get off the course. About ten or fifteen of them even had the balls, or lack of, to skate DURING the girls runs.[8]

I bristled with irritation when I read about this entitled behavior.

Lynn printed a photo of Christy Jordahl, a sponsored rider for Santa Monica Airlines, boardsliding down a sketchy wooden obstacle during her contest run, which made me feel better.[9] The thought of Christy also landing kickflips and tailslides, which were impressive for 1988, and keeping those little shitheads in line gave me great satisfaction. I had heard of Christy's existence because she was acknowledged two decades later in a *Check It Out* interview with Saecha Clarke, who credited Christy with arranging her sponsorship with World Industries. But this was the first photo of Christy I'd found and it proved that she wasn't a mythical unicorn. I was ecstatic.[10] Christy would later confirm in an interview how important that friendship with Saecha was, whom she verified as being the first female skater to boardslide handrails — a huge milestone for women.

While the title *Girls Who Grind* was catchy, a name change was in order after Lynn had a breakthrough that would upgrade the sketchy Xeroxed zine to a large newsprint format. This improvement was thanks to Henry Hester and Steve Cathey at the Gordon & Smith (G&S) skateboard office, who provided access to their printing press. The new publication was made on a Commodore computer, retitled *Equal Time*, and had a circulation of one thousand copies. *Equal Time* kicked off in April 1989 with Stephanie Person gracing the cover skating a vert ramp. The new name was in reference to Stephanie's article "Equal Time" from the previous month in *Poweredge* magazine, a popular publication in the late 1980s that was considered an alternative to *TransWorld* and *Thrasher*. *Poweredge* even printed a letter by Lynn to generate interest in *Equal Time*:

> I'm putting together a zine called Women's Skateboarding Clubzine. Only girls can be in it, but it's for everyone to read. If you're a girl who skates, you can be in this zine. Just send me stories, photos, and art. If you don't have anything to put in it, but want to join the club, that's okay too. It's a chance to meet other girls who skate, and promote women in skating.[11]

Jennifer Sells, contributing writer for *Equal Time*, shared some reflection on Stephanie's article, and the zine's name change in

GIRL GANGS, ZINES, AND POWERSLIDES

an insightful piece called "We Are Progressing Aren't We?"[12] Sells asked why women and girls, with all the right motivation and desire, still weren't hitting ten-foot-high airs and boardsliding eight-foot-long handrails. She wrote, "I think it has to do partially with the fact that we aren't sessioning every day with a posse of girls. We are so few and spread out that it's hard to keep motivated."[13] Jennifer's concluding statements made me smile because she speculated that if there were the same number of girls skating as men, "it would take away some of the fun of searching for each other and it wouldn't be as stokin' as it is now when girls session together . . . We are progressing, so smile, complement yourself on how far you have come and always look to the future! We are getting there! Rage like there's no tomorrow and demand your equal time!"[14] And then the letters from female skaters started pouring in. Lynn said,

> Some of the first letters I got were from Joyce Wheldrake who owned Hogtown [skate shop] in Toronto, JoAnn Gillespie (Rawkmom), and Patty Segovia, who went on to run the All Girl Skate Jam. From the letters, George [Medlock] and I would plan road trips. We visited Seattle, Phoenix, Santa Barbara, and Santa Cruz. I even visited Stacey (Stace the Ace) and Jax Roper in New Zealand. It was all word of mouth. Someone would see our zine in a shop and tell the one girl in town who skated.[15]

Those singular skater girls in towns around the world began to add up, and I'm glad that Lynn mentioned Stacey "Stace the Ace" Roper — who became Georgina Matthews's mentor in Aotearoa. When I posted Lynn's feature on Instagram, Stacey immediately commented:

> Oh man, my *Equal Time* mags are some of my most prized possessions! I think I found out about the

176

world women's skateboarding network from an interview on Sue Hazel. There must have been an address. I'd been skating for so long and the only girl skaters I'd see were my sisters. When they quit I roamed New Zealand for 8 years before I saw another skateboarder that was a girl!

Those mags and the mailing list (I still have) were the only things that reminded me I wasn't alone in the world . . . cause I was so isolated and imagine how excited I was when Lynn came to visit! I'm so glad we've stayed in touch for over 35 years and I've enjoyed watching Lynn absolutely still kill it on a skateboard! Congrats Lynn and thank you so much for writing me back when you did![16]

The WSN even initiated what Lynn believes to be the first all-female contest in September 1989, advertised in *Equal Time* and organized by and for women skaters exclusively. There would be no early morning start, no waiting around for the guys, and no being cut off by jerks on wheels. The contest was called the Labor Day Skate Jam,[17] and Lynn recalled seven skaters entering, including a German skater named Chris Reis who was then featured in the zine.

The *Equal Time* masthead of contributing photographers, writers, and artists kept growing, as well as the gratitude from female skaters. They were finally seeing women in competitions and hearing from their heroes like Anita Tessensohn of Powell Peralta fame, who was on the cover of volume one, issue three showcasing her street-skating prowess. In 2023, this evidence from *Equal Time* helped solidify her status as a legend, and it was fitting that Anita, along with fellow street skater Saecha Clarke and Lynn Kramer, who included interviews and photos of both women in her zine, were all reunited at the 2024 Hall of Fame ceremony as inductees. I was honored to provide commentary for these three skaters in their celebration videos, summarizing their accomplishments.

Subscribers to *Equal Time* knew that there's just something special about skating with *your* people. As Jennifer Sells put it, "We can relate to other girl skaters so much easier."[18] You have an unspoken bond, a trusted hype team, and you can be yourself without that pressure to justify your presence. And in the 1980s, *Equal Time* was there to remind isolated skaters that they were part of an important movement and helped fill a void perpetuated by mainstream skateboarding publications.

GIRL GANGS

La Femme
First girl gang (formed in 1963)

Hands down, the coolest thing that happened in the 1960s was the organic coming-together of the first girl's skateboard gang called La Femme Skateboard Team, based out of the Pacific Palisades, California. A girl gang is a special thing because it means solidarity, friendship, courage, and progression, and this dynamic was appreciated all the way back in 1963. The local skateboard teams, the Palisades and Hobie, initially only recruited boys, so Colleen Boyd and her friends from school, Donna Cash and Suzie Rowland, rallied together as La Femme, naming themselves after a local women's clothing shop. The shop provided the girls with matching plaid windbreaker jackets, adorned with custom-made, ten-inch back patches designed by Suzie's mom.[19] The jackets were worn with pride while the girls skated around town.

Colleen shared with the *Encinitas Advocate* that she was five years old when she first set foot on a skateboard. It was 1956, and her big brother Greg hammered Mickey Mouse roller skate wheels

Stephanie Person representing Santa Cruz on the cover of *Equal Time* zine in 1989

to a two-by-four: "[Greg] plopped me down on my butt on the board at the top of the driveway and gave me a push."[20] Colleen's parents were supportive of her athletic pursuits, including surfing and volleyball, and by junior high she decided to focus on skateboarding along with her friends, a story she included in her 2021 Skateboarding Hall of Fame inductee video.[21]

The girls had a great time inventing new skateboarding tricks, like carrying each other on their shoulders and balancing on top of a trash can on top of a skateboard while moving.[22] Any innovation was fair game in the 1960s. When the first International Skateboard Championships was hosted at La Palma Stadium in Anaheim in May 1965, Colleen, Donna, and Suzie all entered, with Colleen taking second place overall behind Laurie Turner. Suzie was a solid fourth place overall, and Donna had her best result in the tricks contest, placing seventh. Photographs of the girls competing were printed in the August 1965 issue of *Skateboarder* magazine.

The contest propelled skateboarding into the consciousness of the American public thanks to the thorough coverage of the event by ABC's *Wide World of Sports*, which offered equal airtime of the male and female competitors. When the footage became public domain and shared on YouTube, Colleen was delighted to finally see herself skating barefoot in front of the crowd fifty years after the fact. In her *Encinitas Advocate* interview, Colleen said, "I hope I can be an inspiration to young women athletes . . . When boys didn't take us in, we started our own group. We skated no matter what and we didn't let any obstacles get in our way."[23]

The Hags
Girl gang (1983–84)

The Hags were an all-female punk skate crew formed in 1983 in west Los Angeles, and their name evokes rebellion and anarchy, which was exactly their intention. The girl gang was the creation of Sevie Bates and her friends Gardia Fox, "Little Kim," Amanda Brix Toland, Elizabeth Devries, Michel Miller, Keren Sacks, Mimi Claire, Sara Johnson, and Nancy Sefton.[24] Many of the Hags were part of the local skate scene at Venice Beach before joining forces, but they recognized that forming a girl gang could have impact.

Sevie received her first skateboard in the early 1970s at age nine — a wooden board with clay wheels branded "The Black Knight."[25] In *Bust* magazine, Emily Savage wrote,

> By her late teens, Bates was an aggressive and talented street skater who frequently got into scuffles in then-crime-ridden Venice Beach, and says she was always pushing back against what was expected of her as a girl. She had a motorcycle, a skateboard, and short hair . . .

She was often looked at curiously because of the large, light-red birthmark that sits on one side of her face. As a reaction to all this and more, she gathered up a crew of women she'd become friendly with and started the Hags. "I had a lot of rage and a lot of aggression, so I didn't take shit from anyone. That's what led me to the Hags," says Bates.[26]

Sevie had originally requested membership in the Jaks, the dominant punk skater gang in Los Angeles. She was a better skater than most of the guys, but her bid was denied because the Jaks considered themselves a "dude thing." Sevie briefly considered calling her group "The Jills" to compliment the Jaks, as their female equivalent, but the girls decided that they were better off distinguishing themselves with their own unique identity.

The Hags were photographed with the Jaks in 1984 for a *Los Angeles Times* article called "Head over Heels in Love with Skateboarding" by Ann Japenga. In the article, it was shared that to be a Hags member and worthy of wearing a custom-made patch on your denim vest, the rules were quite simple. "'You don't have to be a really good skater,' said Fox, 'but you do have to skate. A lot of girls want to be Hags, but they don't want to skate.'"[27] Nicknames and DIY back patches were core elements of the Hags' identity, and the imagery came from the band Iron Maiden's Eddie the Head mascot. Gardia Fox was especially pleased when her patch was christened with blood after she bailed on her skateboard.

The Hags had tons of fun ripping around parking garages at night and hanging out at their clubhouse — a rental property owned by Nancy Sefton's dad, which became a safe house for their friends. Bates explained "we were like a gang — and we'd skate around Hollywood Boulevard. Mostly, it was about going to clubs, partying, and drinking . . . Everything is more fun in groups, and it was good to have the girl power thing."[28]

The women looked out for each other. Keren Sacks, who was dubbed "Rag Girl" by her neighbor Tony Alva for tying pieces of fabric into her dreadlocked mohawk, broke her leg skateboarding and was set up with a mattress on the floor of Sefton's house to avoid having to climb into her loft bed.[29] An all-ages benefit concert for her surgery was then organized at the Cathay de Grande club in Hollywood featuring Tony's band, the Skoundrelz, plus the Screamin' Sirens and the Lethal Arms. A poster was designed for the event that read "Poor Raggie ate shit on her board . . . time to rock out and help her out now!" The poster, along with a variety of other memorabilia, was shared on a Facebook page for the members to keep in touch and reminisce about this critical time in their lives, decades later.

The mainstream media's fascination with the Hags even paved the way for a popular film about skateboarding. Film writer Alan Sacks admitted that he never would've written about skateboarding if a profile about him hadn't been published opposite to an article featuring the Hags in the *LA Weekly*.[30] Sacks was referring to his script called *Skate or Die*, which became the cult classic movie *Thrashin'* (1986) — a kind of *West Side Story* meets skateboarding romance. Even though the Hags were his inspiration, the film doesn't mention any all-girl skater gang. Instead, only the men skate in a gang. The Hags were invited to be extras as punk girls hanging around the guys, to create a sense of authenticity, but they were not offered active roles, let alone dialogue in the film.

A review of the movie on YouTube channel Bread and Cinemas called out the inequity: "Their visibility can be counted in fractions of seconds."[31] The only other reference to the crew was some graffiti on a wall which said "Flow or Go Home," which was the Hags' motto, as displayed above the door of their headquarters. The movie failed to represent the ethos of these badass skaters, and the existence of female skateboarders was minimized. Plus, Mimi's board was stolen during the chaos of filming a scene, which added insult to injury.

The story of the Hags is slowly coming to light, with rumor of a possible documentary. They were an official girl gang for just a year, but in such a brief time they had enormous impact. Feminist scholar Lauraine Leblanc once wrote, "This resistance against gender roles must be considered when we examine girls' deviance. While it may be true that males use subcultures to explore masculinity, it is also the case that some females use subcultures to repudiate or reconstruct femininity."[32] The Hags epitomized deviance, but in a joyous way that was centered on cultivating a unique community with skateboarding at its heart.

Rookie
Skateboard company owned and operated by women (1996)

Back in the 1990s, an innovative company called Rookie based out of New York City created its brand by sponsoring a mixed gender team, and the concept was revolutionary for that decade. Rookie-sponsored skater Jessie Van Roechoudt said it best: "Today people say Rookie Skateboards was ahead of its time — though it's more appropriate to say that Rookie's inclusive team roster, brand identity, and art direction were on point, and the rest of the skate industry just took 25 years to catch up."[33]

In 1996, Catharine Lyons and Elska Sandor, with early contributions by Jung Kwan, founded Rookie out of Kwan's Chinatown loft on Canal Street in Manhattan. Originally, Catharine considered herself a "pure betty," driving her boyfriend to the skate ramp, watching him skate from the sidelines, and bringing him home: "Finally, after yet another breakup with the same skater boyfriend, Catharine got out the skateboard he'd given her for Christmas. 'I just decided: I'm gonna get on this board and ride to work and back . . . And then it bit me. Nothing had made me feel that good.'"[34]

Catharine had never met another female skater until she bumped into Elska at the launch of a vert ramp and art installation inside the

Brooklyn Bridge Anchorage.[35] The coming together of these two isolated women at this venue felt profound. Catharine said,

> The plywood ramp was overflowing with exuberant young men shuffling to claim and hold an inch at the coping and get a chance to drop in, slapping their boards in solidarity after someone landed a good trick. Only the most assertive could get a turn to skate, and not one female skater was on that ramp.[36]

Catharine even talked to the installation artist, Maura Sheehan, to see if there "was some secret time that girls could come in and have access because it was so ridiculous! New York didn't have any other skateparks, so it was just packed with these guys that had been skating since they were 10 and here I was at 22 being like, 'Can I get on?'"[37] In a zine called *Mimi's Revenge*, Sheehan was interviewed and reported that a girls' night was organized on Thursdays from 9 p.m. to 1 a.m., thanks to Catharine's request during that lone summer the ramp was available.[38]

After the ramp event, Catharine and Elska kept conversing and learned that they were both working at skateboard shops. They instantly connected, especially around how the skateboarding industry ignored the existence of female skaters. In 2000, Catharine said, "Our idea was just that there might be this huge market of women that either want to skateboard, or don't know they want to skateboard because they haven't even considered it."[39] Twenty years later, Catharine explained that "the most tangible female presence in the skateboarding industry was overtly sexualized: non-skating images found in graphics and advertising. We saw a glaring absence of female riders in any skate media, very little support for female skaters, and a conspicuous lack of product with female skaters in mind."[40]

In an interview for *Punk Planet*, which documented the "growing girls' revolution in skateboarding" in the 1990s, Elska said,

By 1995, we really wanted to start a company. We'd started doing things like silkscreening our own T-shirts and that sort of thing. By about 1996, we had gotten sick of just talking about it. We pooled together absolutely a minimum amount of funds and opened a bank account, registered ourselves and just kind of went for it . . . We struggled a little bit but we were lucky because in the first year, people caught on to it.[41]

After launching Rookie, Catharine and Elska headed west to the Action Sports Retailer trade expo in San Diego and claimed a booth. According to Catharine, "All the bigger companies were just looking at us like, 'What is this? What are you trying to do?'"[42] regarding them as a threat to the establishment. But Rookie was a resounding success. In a *New York Times* article from 1997, it was reported that they sold close to 100,000 dollars' worth of gear at that trade show.[43] Catharine said, "We wanted to create a diverse and inclusive skate company. Creating a way for women to be represented and included in the industry was a part of that. Rookie didn't see themselves as a 'girl's company,' even though that was kind of how it got interpreted by the majority of the skate industry in California."[44]

With their success came concerns that major companies would co-opt the idea of catering to girls and shut Rookie out of business. There were bigger brands testing out the waters of this female market, but female skateboarders were devoted to Rookie. Rookie wasn't trying to impose a vision of what a male executive thought a girl skater should look like; instead they intentionally produced gear in smaller sizes without gimmick or frill. They catered to us because they *were* us. Away from the skatepark, skateboarders tend to notice visual cues that someone skates, for example, scuffed-up shoes that prove the wear and tear of ollying and flicking your board against the sandpaper surface of griptape. If you were a female skateboarder in the mid-1990s and you saw someone wearing a

Rookie T-shirt or hoodie or someone riding their branded skateboard, that was a surefire sign that the person was "in the know" and someone to befriend.

Rookie sponsored a strong representation of women including Jaime Reyes, Lauren Mollica, Kyla Duffy, Lisa Whitaker, Jessie Van Roechoudt, Stefanie Thomas, Amy Caron, and Monica Shaw. They weren't just a team; they were like a family, and that message was expressed in many of their promotions. Rookie's advertisements in *Slap* magazine were painstakingly cut out and taped to our walls, and female skaters collected their stickers, determining their placement on our skateboards with great consideration.

And yet witnessing the progress of Rookie was threatening to some. A letter to *Thrasher* in August 1999 stated,

> What I want to know is, why do girls skate? They might do a flip trick or a shove-it here and there, but guess what? I got some news for you: they still suck. The Rookie team? Who the hell are those people? Girls should stick to painting their faces and looking good for us men. Leave skateboarding for the men. It's our sport and it always will be. Brindle Pit. San Francisco, CA.[45]

How wrong was Brindle Pit. Even though there was no editorial response to the letter, a thoughtful reply from a woman named Ally in Anchorage, Alaska, was printed reminding "Brindle Pit" that "skating's not about how good you are, it's about how much fun you have doing it."[46]

There had been earlier short-lived commercial efforts to cater to women within the skateboarding scene like Poot!, which was a clothing brand trademarked in 1993 by Keva Marie Dine and Tod Swank of Foundation Skateboards, but Rookie was still an anomaly as a female-owned board company. Thanks to Elska and Catharine's initiative, more woman-owned board companies emerged like Cherry Skateboards, founded by Emily Oliver and Shodie Lyon in 2003; Hoopla Skateboards in 2008 owned by Cara-Beth Burnside and Mimi Knoop; and Meow Skateboards, which was established by Rookie-sponsored skater Lisa Whitaker in 2012 and is still thriving today. There's been comparable companies overseas like Rogue Skateboards, launched in 2005 by Jenna Selby in the U.K., and Sunny Skateboard, the first brand to be created by Japanese women skaters Chihiro Ueno and Miho Miyamoto in 2012 (who is now Japan's national coach). All these companies helped fill a void by supporting the leading female skateboarders who didn't have board sponsors and weren't being marketed or celebrated. They also set an example for what women business owners can accomplish today, like Cat Tamez in Austin, Texas, who started the first female-owned wheel company in 2022 called Cherries Wheels.

When you have an opportunity to skate with a legend, you do not pass it by. On my first trip to San Diego, for a surfing and skateboarding history conference in April 2023, I skated with Lynn Kramer. I had never skated with a woman older than my forty-five years. I chose to ignore a minor concern that my travel insurance may not cover a skateboarding injury in the United States and let Lynn show me a day in the life of a world champion. Tacos were a must, plus an hour of fine-tuning her slalom board setup, and then it was game time.

At a local skatepark, Lynn was killing it and had her lines dialed. And I surprised myself. When Lynn dropped into a pool, I did too. The last time I had access to a skateable pool was twenty years prior, but here was my chance. When Lynn took me to a slalom training session with members of La Costa Racing Team, I thought, *Hell yes!* I geared up, tried out Lynn's custom board, and weaved my way through the slalom cones. And I had no idea what a rush it was to don a pair of slide gloves (which have a hard hockey-puck-like

GIRL GANGS, ZINES, AND POWERSLIDES

block embedded on the palms) to screech out a pushup slide or powerslide: hands on concrete, board swiveling like a pendulum.

Learning how to properly perform a powerslide triggered a special flashback. The first time I stepped on a skateboard, around age ten or eleven in the late 1980s, I was in front of my childhood home on our dead-end street. Every day after school, the neighborhood kids would gather on this short stretch of pavement to ride bicycles, play a round of street hockey, or organize a game of capture the flag because our street backed onto a forested extension of the Niagara Escarpment. One day, my older brothers introduced a skateboard, best described as a yellow banana board, to the mix of options.

Our outdoor activity was rarely supervised by adults. When I took my turn on the skateboard, there came the inevitable moment when I wobbled and bailed, not knowing a proper foot stance or how to roll with stability. To protect my face, I broke my fall with my hands, which became a fulcrum while my feet stayed planted on the board, pushing it against the concrete in the wrong direction. The hideous sound of skateboard wheels scraping against the pavement accompanied my fall and let everyone know what had happened.

My brain had to immediately choose whether I would start crying or steel myself and hide my shame. I was embarrassed because sharp grit was embedded in the palms of my hands and would soon start bleeding. But my one brother shouted out, "Sick powerslide!" in response to my awkward performance. It caused me to pause. When I realized that I was not being made fun of, the pain instantly evaporated. I had cluelessly executed a powerslide, and my brother approved. Everything was right in the world.

I wouldn't actively pursue skateboarding until my teen years, being preoccupied with competitive long-distance running, but this introduction was important. It's also an excuse for me to write that there have been and currently are boys and men — brothers, friends, and dads — who have chosen to be allies of female and non-traditional skateboarders. Their role is important, and I applaud them, especially when men use their own platform to demand accountability from their male peers relating to violence against girls and women and not excuse someone's hurtful behavior because of their ability to throw down epic video parts. This collective effort helps to validate the victim and encourages others to step forward, and this is a new development in skateboarding because typically it has been the women banding together, like the Women's Skateboarding Network, to move things forward and create change.

Back in San Diego, the slalom team welcomed my presence and efforts to learn, and why wouldn't they? Lynn had set a model for how people were to be treated — with acceptance and encouragement. I didn't expect her to attend my conference presentation, but she came out and offered support of my project. I felt humbled having her there in the audience.

There's an article from the *Everything Skateboarding* blog regarding Lynn's success as a slalom racer, and I had to laugh reading it because it felt as if the author, Ron Barbagallo, was speaking directly to me.

> When future generations of skate historians finally get their act together, and write the complete and comprehensive history of skateboarding . . . I think they'll end up agreeing with me on this one. No woman, anywhere, has dominated any field of skateboarding, more than Lynn Kramer has dominated the world of slalom.[47]

Barbagallo bemoaned how historians spotlighted Laura Thornhill for representing the 1970s, Cara-Beth Burnside for being the leader in vert from the 1980s and onward, and Elissa Steamer as the 1990s hero of street-skating, and have called this scant representation "a history." Barbagallo wanted to demonstrate that there were women like Lynn Kramer who evoked "The Fear of God" in her competitors regardless of gender.[48] While I agree that Lynn's story needs to be elevated, all these women are amazing and deserving of respect, and they have all shattered their respective glass ceilings. But I understand his point and am fully on board to create a more fulsome picture of women's skateboarding history. I'm less interested in debating which female skaters can destroy their male peers and grind them to a pulp, but it did bring a smile to my face imagining Lynn on course.

Lynn has dominated slalom, but for me her legacy goes much deeper. When I returned home from San Diego, I kept thinking about why I admired Lynn so much because it wasn't just her competitive accomplishments. And then I stumbled upon a letter she wrote to *TransWorld* printed back in October 1989. It was in response to some parents who were giving their kid a hard time, suggesting that skateboarding was a delinquent activity and would harm their son's grades. Lynn calmly explained that the opposite was true, and when she was injured and couldn't skate, her grades at UCSD fell, in contrast to when she had a positive outlet like skateboarding.

It occurred to me that when I was around Lynn, I didn't need to justify myself and I didn't feel the urge to grill her about her chosen path because we were aligned. Lynn was a skater nerd at university, she wrote letters to magazines, and she supported her friends by establishing the Women's Skateboarding Network and by honoring their experiences in the *Equal Time* zine, which I consider to be an essential primary document. I also liked Lynn's consistent style over the years — cropped hair, athletic gear, no-nonsense, and not a hint of being anything but herself.

Even after dedicating this chapter to Lynn, her contributions to skateboarding feel immeasurable and a thousand trophies and a closet full of shoeboxes crammed with medals could not encompass how grateful I am for her. She's the kind of person you want at every skate session — offering guidance, but not in a condescending way, and there to celebrate you when the magic happens and progress is made. Her legacy is a masterclass in how to build skateboarding community.

Sue Hazel (forty) was photographed by Wig Worland skating vert for a feature in the U.K. magazine *Sidewalk* (July 2001)

CHAPTER EIGHT

INFILTRATORS
(SUE HAZEL)

In recent years, a genre of historical books and films that shine a light on unsung women of the past has seen a rise in popularity. For example, *Code Girls* (2017) by Liza Mundy explores the history of approximately eleven thousand American women codebreakers in World War II who helped decipher Nazi military codes, followed by a flurry of comparable titles like *Code Name: Lise, D-Day Girls*, and *The Woman All Spies Fear*. Many of these women endured contempt and hostility, even segregation, as described in the book and film *Hidden Figures* (2016) by Margot Lee Shetterly, which celebrates Black women mathematicians at NASA. It's fascinating to learn about the critical roles women played, infiltrating male-dominated professions alongside major triumphs in science and espionage.

I have no idea what the process is to access a World War II archive and sort through the stealth missions of a spy, but I wonder how many researchers passed over these women until the right person came along and appreciated their value. And from there, it still takes a multitude of dedicated champions including archivists, academics, journalists, and editors for these stories to be acknowledged, let alone featured, in a podcast, added to Wikipedia, and represented in a book or film. These people are my kindred spirits.

While the intensity of life as a female codebreaker in wartime and as a contemporary skateboarder is vastly different, I still think comparisons can be made because we've all seen progress gained and lost over the years. Women during World War II experienced a flush of opportunity by entering the workforce in positions previously reserved for men to maintain production, but when the men returned from war, they demanded their jobs back and many women were expected to reembrace domesticity without complaint. In skateboarding, we've had an industry decide that girls can't skate and aren't worth promoting and a society that tells us to grow up and become a "real" adult by going to college, getting a proper job, and fulfilling our child-rearing duties. But when we've had a taste of the freedom and fun that comes with skateboarding, we're not going to abandon ship so easily.

One person who was unimpressed by such traditional notions is the now legendary British skater Sue Hazel, who took up skateboarding in 1977. Sue's path to nonconformity wasn't a Johnny Rotten punk-inspired frenzy, but a more discreet *screw you* to the masses. Sue is a renaissance woman who enjoys rock-climbing, snowboarding, kite-surfing, running, yoga, and cycling, and she would probably make an incredible spy. She has such a gracious, unassuming manner that you would never know how talented and gritty she was as a competitive skateboarder. Her personal mantra? "Do what you believe in. Life's not what society wants you to conform to. Enjoy your life, as long as you don't harm yourself and others. Do everything you can to the highest level and don't be put off by what others think of it."[1]

I woke up this morning at 5:30 a.m. with a distinct memory of the moment I realized that skateboarding had existed in the 1970s and that women had been a part of it. It was 1998, after I had moved out west for university. My gang of skateboarding friends were younger, still in high school or about to graduate, and I sometimes found myself hanging out at their parents' homes. One evening, a group of us girls were in New Westminster in the basement of a parent's heritage home, perhaps relaxing after skating the new (now defunct) local skatepark. I'm sure we were bantering about guys and the next party that two of the girls loved to arrange at my derelict, cockroach-riddled house that I shared with other university students, when one of the girls produced some vintage *Skateboarder* magazines from the 1970s that her dad had unearthed from his collection.

The conversation faded as I started flipping pages, mesmerized by what was unfolding before me. I'm confident that one of the issues had a photo of Laura Thornhill, the competitive freestyle skateboarder often documented by the late Warren Bolster, because my friend Laura Piasta, who was the most talented in our crew, looked uncannily like her with long blond hair. I also got a kick out of stumbling upon Cara-Beth Burnside's name listed in a bowl riding contest in the thirteen and under category. But Cara-Beth was the only name I recognized among the twenty-five odd female skaters listed in contest results and handful of photos, including one of Vicki Vickers slashing the pool coping at Marina del Rey like a boss. My interest in skateboarding history was ignited that day.

A few years later, I would write a chapter in my thesis about women in skateboarding history to provide context for the progression that occurred in the late 1990s and early 2000s. During my studies, I had mail-ordered a CD-ROM from Russ Howell (a professional freestyle skateboarder from the 1970s) because he had scanned old issues of *Skateboarder* magazine, which published a regular "Who's Hot!" feature of up-and-coming skateboarders, including the occasional woman. Thanks to these magazine scans, Iain Borden's book *Skateboarding, Space and the City: Architecture and the Body* (2001), and *The Concrete Wave* (1999) and *Skate Legends* (2002), both by Michael Brooke, I was able to piece together some semblance of a 1970s backstory but had no obvious route to contact the women I was learning about. There was, of course, no social media back in 2002 to help make those connections.

My memory of pawing through those vintage *Skateboarder* magazines was a good reminder that in order to do this work, as diligent as I am in my research, I am still dependent on others. And if these journalists, editors, photographers, collectors, academics, and random Instagram followers are "my people," I need to express gratitude. Without their efforts to take photos, conduct interviews, add a hashtag, and even include the contest results from a women's event in their publication, I would be hard-pressed to develop a bio for a skater. Every breadcrumb of information helps.

I think of Kim Cespedes, a skateboarder who was in her prime during the 1970s; she received reasonable coverage but isn't a big name today outside knowledgeable skateboarding circles. Kim had the best style for the era with laidback grinds and powerslides in rugged, derelict settings, and her progress skating pools and bowls showed what determined women could achieve. I wrote a massive website post about Kim, and if it hadn't been for Dr. Neftalie Williams and his PhD thesis, "Colour in the Lines: The Racial Politics and Possibilities of US Skateboarding Culture,"[2] I would never have known about Kim's heritage.

Kim's family was from Guam, an island in Micronesia that offered residents American citizenship because of military reclamation. In conversation with Neftalie, Cespedes spoke candidly about her experience as a skateboarder watching blue-eyed and blonde-haired Californian girls receive significant sponsorships even though they were sometimes less skilled: "My dad always said I could do anything I wanted, no matter the color of my skin, and no matter who thought otherwise. If your dream is in your heart, you go out and get it."[3] And that's exactly what Kim did by winning contests despite odd comments in her "Who's Hot!" feature about her dark complexion, with a suggestion that her aggressive style was a "classic Polynesian" trait.[4] Williams's thesis offers a more nuanced understanding of Kim's story as a person of color skating in a scene dominated by whiteness, which I'm grateful for.

In many of my posts, I can point to someone I've tagged, or someone who preferred anonymity, who helped make the discovery happen. For example, much of the content about international skaters has been thanks to Instagram followers, because how else would I know about Aina Maria Oliver in Mallorca, Spain, in the 1970s; freestyle champion Elisabeth "Eli" Meyers of Belgium; MaryAnne Uyemura on Team Pepsi in the Philippines in 1978; slalom skater Antonella Ferrero in Italy in the 1980s; and Zhenya Arguelles in Russia from 1990. There's even a comparable initiative to @womxnsk8history in Brazil called @skatemaniabrasil presenting local heroes like Gini Gonçalves, Monica Polistchuk, and Renata Paschini, who all deserve respect.

There have been many times when I've reached out to Kevin Marks, founder of the Look Back Library in Encinitas, requesting his help to confirm the existence of a particular article or to source a better scan of a magazine image. The Look Back Library is a nonprofit initiative created in 2015 and is the largest collection of skateboarding-related print material. Kevin sources and shares magazines by traveling across America in his van to create micro-libraries at skate shops, and he maintains a core library at home. It is a heroic effort, and I'm fortunate to consider Kevin an ally for my own cause.

Researching and writing history is always going to be a collaborative effort, especially for someone like me who is geographically isolated in the Pacific Northwest. As one person with limited access and opportunity outside my regular work, I need all the help I can get. Interviewing is the ideal method for gleaning the facts, but it's not always viable. I also experience anxiety reaching out to skateboarders that I revere; even if they're not a household name, they have significance to me. Sometimes I just need an introduction or a push.

Sue Hazel was someone that I could never imagine just casually reaching out to — in my mind, she's practically British royalty. Fortunately, Lynn Kramer had no qualms about emailing Sue and forwarding her my contact information. Sue was a friend from Lynn's *Equal Time* zine-writing days, and both women still skate and keep in touch. Unexpectedly, in the fall of 2022, an email arrived in my inbox from the one and only.

GIRL GANGS, ZINES, AND POWERSLIDES

Hi Natalie,

Lynn Kramer pointed me your way.

What an excellent idea in creating your library of women skaters.

I see some of my old contacts in there, plus a whole lot of others spring to mind from my time in the sport who I can't find anything about online.

I didn't know Bonnie Blouin was no longer with us, shame to read that.

I still skate a bit (just turned 60) but was most active between 1977 & early 00's.

Best Regards,
Sue

I had known about Sue ever since my thesis-writing days, but without access to vintage British skateboard magazines, I had yet to deliver a full-fledged biography. And now I had my chance. Fueled by adrenaline, trepidation, and excitement, I immediately responded to Sue at approximately 6 a.m. I should have been starting my morning routine to ensure that I would be caffeinated and on time for my early shift at the library, but I figured that a response to Sue was priority.

I was ecstatic to be in Sue's orbit. She promptly replied and forwarded old articles, interviews, and core memories. Throughout the week, Sue and I collaboratively wrote her feature for the website, and this was the first time someone had been so thoroughly engaged with their bio, offering suggestions and edits. Within a few weeks, I had one beast of a post celebrating Sue and, thanks to her sister, Nicky, a great selection of retro photos and home videos.

You might be wondering what the big deal is. A nice British lady emailed me and reminisced about the past, but that's the thing with Sue: it's not just the past because she never stopped. Sue never caved to an idea that skateboarding was inappropriate for a girl, let alone a "woman her age." I regard Sue as the British equivalent to Cara-Beth Burnside as they both persevered in skateboarding for over four decades.

My bio for Sue expanded after an older skater named Joachim "YoYo" Schulz began supporting my efforts via Instagram. He relayed a fantastic article called "80's Research Lab: Sue Hazel" from *Sidewalk* magazine in July 2001. The interviewer described Sue as "a little thing, and appears to be built of string, whipcord, and muscle with an inquisitive face, and a pair of Vans that look like they've been partially eaten by a pack of starving belt-sanders."[5] The description of Sue's mangled shoes tells the reader *heads up this woman is still killing it on a skateboard*, but her age was never explicitly stated. And despite the article's title, the three prominent photos of Sue that accompany her article, taken by Wig Worland, are not from her 1980s glory days — they were current, taken in 2001. The photos show Sue destroying a vert ramp with hand-plants, backside grabs, and big air with a small selection of thumbnail photos from previous years. When I clued in that Sue was forty years old at that time, I was blown away.

Over the decades, Sue not only retained her skateboarding skills, but she continued to improve with practically zero affirmation from her local community and with minimal instruction let alone financial support. It's fantastic that we're seeing more women over forty being celebrated on social media for starting to skateboard or returning to skateboarding after a prolonged absence (featured in Chapter Ten), but there's only a handful of women from the 1970s who never altered their course and steadily progressed, and Sue is one of them.

Sue was born in New Forest, Hampshire, and even though finances were tight, her parents encouraged athleticism. When the skateboarding craze hit the U.K. in the late 1970s, Sue "saved up and got my first board and was the immensely proud owner of a 'Surf Flyer.' This board would be seen as the pits now, but to me at the time; it was the first magical step into something which would change my world and shape my life for years to come."[6] Sue was quickly consumed with skateboarding and would diligently practice. She even made her own skateboard decks with her dad using a concave board press based on a how-to article from a magazine.[7] Sue found inspiration in magazines, and it's possible she was aware of Sheenagh Burdell of Southport, who was skating pools with authority and appeared in the U.K. magazine *Skateboard!* in December 1978 and the "Kate the Skate" articles from *Skateboard Scene* magazine, a one-of-a-kind column just for girls.

DOCUMENTED

Kate the Skate
Skateboard column written by Kate Mahony (January–August 1978)

A regular female-focused column in a skateboarding magazine was a unique concept back in 1978, but Kate Mahony decided to propose such an idea to a British publication called *Skateboard Scene*. In her first article from January 1978, "Kate the Skate" explained how it had been a battle for the column to see the light of day, but she convinced the editors that the effort was worth it. Kate wrote, "There's a dreadful rumor going around that girls just aren't bothered about skateboarding, and that they're just not a force to be reckoned with. Rubbish! I say that the girls can prove to be just as good as the guys any day, and this page in *Skateboard Scene* is all set to prove it each month."[8] Kate observed that women had excelled in skiing, surfing, tennis, and ice-skating, so why not skateboarding?

The rumor Kate was referring to came from a dismissive article in the *Skateboard Special*, a review printed in September 1977, which covered Britain's first national championships at Crystal Palace in London. The organizers had chosen not to include a category for girls, which Kate described as "depressing," although several women didn't get the memo or perhaps chose to ignore the male monopoly and showed up ready to skate. The contest reporter stated,

> Among those who turned up then were four dishy ladies from the Emotion Bristol Skateboarding Centre store. The girls who all live in Bristol were former Bunny girl Lynne Shillingford, Janie Wilmot, Lizzie Melling, and Helen Thomas. "People seem to think girls aren't interested in skateboarding — but they're completely wrong," said 21-year-old Helen, who lives in Victoria Square, Bristol . . . Well, we'd be interested to hear whether that's the case. All we can say is that we didn't see a great many girls around at Crystal Palace.[9]

And yet the U.K. was chock-full of female skaters emulating the scene in California, and Kate Mahony tracked many of them down, including those "dishy ladies" of the Bristol team. Kate's column also documented the Skate City Girls from London; Thea Cutts, who was possibly the first U.K. girl to stomp a kickflip; the STP Toomer Zoomer team, which sponsored Sue Slade and Janet Adams; and best friends Michelle Lee and Debra Brown who had been tearing up their local half-pipe in Kettering.

In her February 1978 editorial, Kate reminded readers, "This is the page that challenges you girls to make your mark in the most exciting, fastest-growing sport the world has ever seen! If you have the misfortune to be bugged by one kid brother laughing hysterically at the sight of you wobbling against your mate's shoulder as you attempt to push off to greatness, ignore him."[10] Kate proved her point by interviewing successful American female skaters and writing a feature on Liz Karlsen who was a skateboarding reporter on a London-based television show. She also acknowledged two British girls who were looking for pen pals to set up an all-female skate club.

I was especially grateful to see Kate's feature on Londoner Minh Duc Tran — the first Vietnamese skater I had come across and the only British female skater of color I had found in 1970s photos who still skates today. I had stumbled upon a tiny article about Minh in the August 1977 issue of U.K.'s first skateboarding magazine, *Skateboard!*, in which she is described as "the hottest female on wheels."[11] Minh had been keenly anticipating competing in the nationals at Crystal Palace and must have been disappointed that she had been excluded. At least Minh met the American legend Ellen Berryman on tour and was even more motivated to skate, launching herself off ramps, catching air and grabs, and dreaming of sponsorship.

Skateboard Scene magazine folded by the end of the year, but based on the enthusiastic letters Mahony published, her efforts to be inclusive made an impression. Thanks to social media, I was able to track down Kate and express gratitude for her early work as a young journalist and skateboard enthusiast. Kate is still a writer and now lives in New Zealand, known for her short stories and historical fiction called *Secrets of the Land* (2023).

National Skateboard Review
Skateboard journal edited by Di Dootson Rose (1976–79)

In 1975, Di Dootson Rose moved into a house in Cardiff-by-the Sea, California, with her brother Craig and their childhood friend Dave Dominy, who all had a passion for surfing and skateboarding. They were fortunate in that "La Costa's Black Hill was close by with empty and spectacular brand new streets all over a hill — a perfect spot for downhill."[12] The trio would go skate there after work along with many other talented skaters and entrepreneurs to share their knowledge and enjoy the freshly paved concrete.

The scene at La Costa began to get competitive as word got out about this skateboarding oasis, and because Di was an organizer, she soon established a weekly contest series. Di monitored the race results and started to post them as a single-sheet newsletter in 1976. Di then expanded the endeavor into the *National Skateboard Review* (*NSR*), which she called "my monthly grass roots newspaper that published contest results, photos, interviews, cartoons, and letters from all over the country."[13]

The *NSR* was consistently balanced in its celebration of male and female skateboarders, but Di went above and beyond to celebrate her friends in the June 1978 issue, which featured Judith Cohen on the cover at the Carlsbad skatepark. Di created a "Special Women's Section," highlighting legends like Deanna Calkins, Ellen Oneal, Gale Webb, Judi Oyama, Kathy Bomeisler, Kim Cespedes, Laura Thornhill, Robin Logan, Terry Brown, and Vicki Vickers, as well as many lesser known skaters. For this issue, Di encouraged companies to cater their ads to female readers by celebrating the women on their teams, which was a savvy approach. Companies like Hobie, Santa Cruz, G&S, Tracker Trucks, and Logan Earth Ski stepped up to the challenge.

Thanks to digitization, all the *National Skateboard Review* issues are available online, as well as physically preserved by the Smithsonian Museum. By painstakingly going through each issue, I was able to create a directory of every instance a female skater's name appeared, whether in contest results, advertisements, letters, or photos. Along with the digitized issues of *Skateboarder* and *Thrasher*, these sources became the foundation of my archive and continue to be a springboard for research. For example, the name "Laura Engel — Heemsteede, Holland" was listed as a member of the International Skateboard Association in the back pages of a 1978 *NSR* issue. Her location prompted my curiosity and an internet deep dive, which led to a family connection via LinkedIn and then an interview with Laura, who turned out to be the first female Dutch skateboard champion in 1978 and 1979.

It's remarkable how far one can go these days toward uncovering a legacy with just a name and a connection to skateboarding, but someone had to make that initial effort decades prior to drop those clues. I'm eternally grateful to Di for her motivation and drive to document a unique time and place in skateboarding history with integrity, while organizing contests simultaneously. Her lifetime achievement award as a skateboarding icon, presented at the 2024 Skateboarding Hall of Fame celebrations, was long overdue.

"Girls Who Skate"
Article in *Thrasher* (February 1995)

On a rare occasion in the 1990s, an editor at *Thrasher* threw his arms up in defeat and allowed a feature about female skateboarders to be printed, perhaps thinking that the token gesture would be good enough to hold us off for another five years and quench the flow of angry letters.

The six-page-long "Girls Who Skate" article from the February 1995 issue is an onslaught and should be read while listening to a Riot Grrrl playlist. It was a freakish collage of photos and letters crammed together to appease the women. And while it's wonderful that the article happened, a steady supply of coverage would have been preferable with clearly tagged names and photographers, but still, it was a start.[14] The feature included primarily unknown and isolated skaters, but I can now spot some recognizable pros like Jen O'Brien and Jaime Reyes. And more recently, I've identified other influential skaters like Sally Affleck from Australia and Rhonda Doyle from Colorado, best known for her snowboarding skills.

The *Thrasher* issue began with a letter by someone who called herself "Poison Ivy of Pussyville, CT" in the Mail Drop section, which set the tone for the "Girls Who Skate" article:

Chauvinist pigs, you called? Yes, I am a girl skater. If you don't like it, tough shit! Go and skate somewhere else. I like smashing stereotypes and male egos . . . To all the guys — sure I'll skate with you, but "Ladies first!" There really are a lot of girl skaters out there, in the shadows of the guys, practicing and waiting to come out . . . If you don't like to watch me skate, close your eyes and leave . . .[15]

And then we get to the goods. So many raging letters with a few sentimental feelings about skateboarding, some anonymous, some not. Shamsia Razaq of San Jose had a rant about a bunch of dickheads who were hassling her with their questions: "as soon as I answered all their f*ckface questions and they see me make a totally down kickflip, they decided to cut on me! What asses!" Airra Dalmacio of Hercules, California, also had a few choice words to share:

I just want to say a few things to the a$$holes out there who think girls can't skate . . . They should just shut the f*ck up and get a life. The stereotype that skateboarding is only for guys is bullshit. Girl skaters deserve the same rights as guy skaters, like getting sponsored. All the skate companies should sponsor girl skaters. Thrasher Mag should encourage girl skaters, not as sex objects or toys, but as skillful and able-bodied skaters. Thanks for hearing me out.

More letters kept coming. Allison O'Brien of Yonkers, New York, challenged "all you boy skaters out there whose egos won't fit through the door" to come to her town and prove themselves. Sasha Liege of Westminster, California, expressed some major fury, at herself for having low self-esteem and at other women, but concluded, "Chicks aren't always posers [sic]." This fear of being labeled a poseur came up frequently in the letters, and the pressure to prove themselves as being worthy to occupy space was a real battle.

Athena Pascal of Vancouver was introduced to skateboarding by her brother, pro skater Rick Howard. She observed that "there aren't a lot of younger girl skaters like twelve or thirteen, and I think more younger and older girls should get into it. What I really want to say is wake up, guys, it's the nineties — girls do skate." Sofia Lauren Moberly of Tulsa, Oklahoma, highlighted a hero of hers, skater Lori Rigsbee from the early 1990s, and wrote, "I wonder what [Lori] is doing now. Does she still skate? Where did she go? Will I ever get to meet her or even skate with her?" Sofia's questions were left unanswered, but she had an interesting vision of the future and a warning for male skaters. "Before long, female skaters will have their own teams, magazines, parks, videos, and clothes, and you will be left out. Right now we're just using you and your products. Yep, we've got it all planned out, and in the end we will have absolute gynarchy. Call me 'betty' now, but soon it will be 'Queen Betty.'"

The women writing in to *Thrasher* were committed to skateboarding but frustrated with the industry and how they were being unfairly treated. The letter that impacted me most was by Patricia Wodecki of Lithonia, Georgia, who wrote,

> I basically do my own thing. I don't copy anyone. My life is going just fine right now, but I wish that the "guy" skaters would talk to me and invite me to go places with them. I love skating, and no matter what anybody says, I'm not quitting. I just want everyone to respect me for what I like to do, skate.

What a simple request, to be respected. It would soon dawn on these skaters that because the male majority were unwilling to be respectful, they would have to ignore them and do things themselves in line with the Riot Grrrl movement. At least this article demonstrated that they weren't alone.

As a new skateboarder, Sue Hazel's first challenge was keeping the peace with her refined neighbors who disapproved of the noise she made practicing in her laneway. Sue's parents also became concerned with respectability and whether skateboarding was a "worthy activity to pursue, in spite of the great effort it took to master it."[16] But Sue was undeterred, and "every fortnight, I'd put my pocket money towards a bus ride to Southsea Skatepark, to meet other local skaters and learn to ride bowls . . . Seeing any other female skaters was always an inspiration, there weren't too many."[17]

When the skateboarding frenzy of the 1970s started to wane, Sue was unfazed because even if the industry was struggling, it didn't mean that individual skaters had to give up. Thanks to the English Skateboard Association (ESA), which forged on, hosting fun contests for the devoted few, Sue began to compete in 1983 in both freestyle and vert ramp. In 1984, Sue took first place for freestyle in the "B Group" at the Farnborough contest. The event was covered by *Thrasher* in a two-page report called "England Skates" in the October 1984 issue but fails to mention Sue's performance, besides the results' listings. Instead, the author Billy Runaway was more intent on describing the underage girls who were lurking around the ramp in a creepy, clichéd fashion.

Sue was oblivious to the fact that her name had been listed in *Thrasher*. Instead, she was systematically learning new tricks by breaking them down, analyzing the elements, starting low on a ramp, then trying a trick higher or faster and visualizing success. She said,

> I remember the first time I really committed to coming in backwards out of a rock fakie on the Farnborough vert ramp — I slammed so hard on my back! After a while sitting out recovering, I got on the board again to get it wired, just made darn sure in future attempts I didn't let my wheels hang up on the coping.[18]

Sue learned from her mistakes and opted to wear safety gear, even if it outed her for being uncool by the fashion-sensitive crowd of skateboarders in the 1980s.

Sue's practice paid off and the timing was perfect because Vancouver's Expo 86 included the Transworld Skateboarding competition, and there would be a team representing England that Sue was destined for.

> The theme of [Expo 86] was transport of all things, and they used skateboarding as a showcase for it. The parade at the start was good. Olympic style, with all these skaters representing their respective countries, flags and team colours, and of course, being skaters everyone mixed themselves up because they were friends with each other. It was a howl![19]

It was good to hear Sue's perspective because my only point of reference for the event was the 1986 Transworld video called *Radical Moves* (dir. Larry Dean), which covered the entire contest via the mind-numbing dialogue of Kim Blackett — a young male skater seeking fame and sponsorship. The film was laced with degrading banter directed at the female participants, and it's sadly a reflection of the times that persisted into the 1990s.

For some reason, the women were only offered a flatland freestyle competition at Expo, even though they were perfectly capable of skating the vert ramp. The female competitor who won was Corina "GoGo" Spreiter of Switzerland. Kim Blackett states, "In warm-ups, GoGo was wearing her old skate shirts that she cut up. They barely covered the essentials. She said she didn't do it to be sexy, it was hot in her country, and it was the only way she could get a tan like that. They were pretty interesting — it made it even more fun to watch."[20] Blackett's comments suggested that female skaters were just a sideshow to amuse Transworld's prime audience — prepubescent, heterosexual boys. Meanwhile, the outfits of the male competitors, which included crotch-clutching short-shorts, went unacknowledged.

Partway through *Radical Moves*, the location shifted to Seylynn skatepark in North Vancouver for a bowl contest. Blackett introduces Michelle Sanderson's brother, Gary, who placed third in the amateur bowl: "Gary Sanderson was an all-round nice guy and had a lot of friends and took his skating seriously. His sister Michelle competed in the women's freestyle. I think she got first place — for best legs." Evidently, the brother took skateboarding seriously, while the sister was a punchline for a joke. At least I spotted Stephanie Person in the distant background, tearing up the skatepark and claiming her rightful space.

Sue's freestyle performance managed to avoid toxic scrutiny in the film, and she placed second behind Spreiter, and ahead of April Hoffman, Sophie Bourgeois, Michelle Sanderson, and Stephanie Person. A photo of Sue is in the December 1986 issue of *Thrasher* in the coverage of the event by John Lucero. In small print, Lucero wrote that the contest organizers decided not to count the women's contest results as part of the overall team points for each country like you would at the Olympic Games because they were a "separate event."[21] This decision to withdraw the women's points toward a team prize implied that their efforts were of no value and inconsequential to the whole global vision of the Expo. What a burn. The only observation that Kim Blackett nailed in his commentary of Expo 86 was the fact that the women "stuck together." Of course they did. They had to.

Meanwhile, the guys in Britain were fully aware of Sue's skill — that she was holding her own and representing her country with exceptional talent. In addition to Canada, Sue was competing at events all over the world including in France, Germany, Sweden, and the U.S., in particular New York, North Carolina, Texas, and California. Back home in England, in 1988 at the Southsea Skate Contest, Sue placed fifth as the lone female competing in freestyle on a cold winter's day, illuminated by floodlights. The contest was covered in an article called "Double Your Money" in *R.A.D.*

magazine's January 1989 issue, but again there was no celebration of Sue's presence. You would think that there might be curiosity about Sue, whose name kept infiltrating the guys' contest results.

It was later speculated in *Sidewalk* magazine that British magazine editors like Tim Leighton-Boyce of *R.A.D.* were fearful that by giving Sue special coverage, or even a photo, it would imply bias.

> Boyce stuck with boys and played safe . . . [he] stayed away despite her prowess at vert and freestyle, and the woman consistently rated highly in the ESA's amateur freestyle contests and apart from her name in the results gained not one ounce of credit for it.
>
> The well meaning reissued (but ultimately doomed) *Skateboard Mag* finally gave her some time in the latter part of the eighties as did the likes of vert masters like Lance Mountain and Neil Blender. They were struck dumb by her ability . . . Where have you been hiding this woman? A similar reaction was from Santa Cruz's Stephanie Person: Sponsor her![22]

Read that again. Lance Mountain and Neil Blender, who were revered professional American vert skaters, were "struck dumb" when they saw Sue skate. It makes me want to scream.

Stephanie's sponsors stepped up to help Sue, and besides the Southsea Skateshop, she rode for Brand X, Santa Cruz Speed Wheels, and Vans shoes when she competed in the U.S. for an extended period.[23] During one of her trips to the U.S. to visit Stephanie, Sue remembered skating JoAnn Gillespie's backyard mini-ramp and meeting Lynn Kramer and Cara-Beth Burnside, who would acknowledge the British skater in her October 1991 *Thrasher* interview. Sue said that the trip "was a great opportunity to actually find other women that skated."[24] Lynn also gave Sue some limelight with a photo in *Equal Time* zine to compensate for the minimal coverage back in the U.K.

Sue reciprocated Lynn's generosity in an interview for *Skateboard!* magazine in November 1989, which was a brave attempt by a U.K. editor to produce a "girls' issue." The issue included interviews with Sue, Stephanie Person, and Glasgow's vert skater Michelle Ticktin. The interviews were enlightening and the cover was pink, but the magazine still gave a dude the cover shot. Sue used the opportunity to explain how essential Kramer's zine, *Equal Time*, was for putting women in touch "with other girls for travelling around and somewhere to stay . . . Not many people realise there are hundreds of girls worldwide."[25]

In *Skateboard!*, Sue was asked about how the industry might go about changing attitudes toward girl skaters. Sue suggested the obvious:

> Perhaps more coverage in magazines. When a girl opens a mag she just sees all these guys and it gives skating a real macho image. You don't have to be all macho and aggressive to skate so I think there is a place for girl skaters . . . It would be nice to compete against more girls. The first time was in '86 in Vancouver. It was really enjoyable, a good atmosphere of real camaraderie.[26]

Regrettably, even with its flaws, the Expo 86 contest would not be replicated for years, and an event like Slam City Jam, established in 1994, did not include a girls' division from the beginning, as discussed in Chapter Three.

Along came the 1990s, and in spite of film productions like *SK8HERS* in 1992, female skateboarders were again ignored, and the industry struggled from the fallout of another recession. But women like Sue kept calm and carried on. Perhaps we didn't all keep calm.

Female skateboarders were desperate to be validated rather than denigrated as poseurs or token novelties (hence all the vehement letters in *Thrasher's* "Girls Who Skate" article). The idea to create exclusive, safe spaces for women in subcultures, whether it was punk concerts or skate contests, began to take hold.

Patty Segovia had experienced the impact of the Women's Skateboard Network in the late 1980s and kept the momentum going by launching the All Girl Skate Jam (AGSJ) in Chula Vista, California, at the Graffix warehouse on September 7, 1997, with divisions for street and vert that drew twenty-five competitors. She said, "I had to create a revolution . . . Guys were like, 'What do you think you're doing? You can't do this. There are not even enough girl skaters to do an all-girl event.'"[27] How wrong they were — the series would go on tour to cities around the world from 1997 to 2012.

Cara-Beth Burnside competed at the inaugural AGSJ and said, "It was awesome, like, I had such a good time . . . Everyone there was there to see *you*. They weren't there because they came to see the guys, 'cause there were no guys skating."[28] This was Patty's vision: to draw attention away from the men and offer opportunity for the women to shine. She said,

> Our motto is all ages, all girls, all abilities, where you don't have to have a sponsor. You can come and sign up the same day, show up and skate. It's real important to try and help these girls because you don't want them to give up. So many times Cara-Beth wanted to give up. She was frustrated but she stuck to it and that's the difference, and Cara-Beth was a major reason why I started the All Girl Skate Jam . . . That was the start of a revolution.[29]

That 1997 AGSJ contest was even featured in issue six of the Beastie Boys' magazine *Grand Royal*, with portraits of all the participants taken by skateboarder Charmaine Hunter of Vancouver as a historical record of this momentous event.

Vert skater Holly Lyons remembered her first AGSJ with enthusiasm:

> [Cara-Beth Burnside] told me of an all girl's skateboard contest in San Diego. I had to go! As far as I knew at the time, there were about five girls I knew that skated. I went to the event and was blown away. There were so many girls. I told myself I wanted to start going to every girls skate contest, so I could meet more girls like myself.[30]

Another participant named Kyla Duffy, who was sponsored by Rookie, said the experience was amazing. "Everybody was so happy, and everybody felt the same way: 'This is great, we're doin' it for the girls.'"[31]

Tony Hawk was interviewed at the 2000 AGSJ in San Diego after the contest had proven that it wasn't a flash in the pan but was becoming stronger with more sponsorships and increasing cash prizes. Tony said, "[The women are] sort of pushed aside and not really taken seriously, and something like this, it shows that there is support for it and I think that this type of event will grow and eventually, probably it'll make it into the X Games."[32] The AGSJ continued to evolve and merged with the Vans Warped Tour as a sponsor and venue, and the results were always shared by Lisa Whitaker on the Girls Skate Network website.

The concept of celebrating female skaters in a welcoming yet competitive environment was then replicated with a pool and bowl series called Wicked Wahine (2004–09) by organizers Tammy "Bam Bam" Williams and Liz Brandenburg. Outside the U.S., similar events followed like the Gallaz Skate Jam in Australia and the Ride Like a Girl series in Canada, which I attended with the Skirtboarders in 2003, embarking on a road trip from Quebec to Ontario to compete.

I had always been gutted that I missed out on the first All Girl Skate Jam back in 1997. My friends were able to travel south, but since it was in September, my university classes and expenses prevented me from attending. So, when the Ride Like a Girl contest was announced, I was not going to be denied. Being part of an exclusively female group of competitors felt defiant as we took over the entire Iceland skatepark in Mississauga, inappropriately named after the nearby ice rink. We skated in the sweltering heat next to the roaring Highway 403, breathing in the fumes, but we were still enthusiastic. The contest was such a different vibe than being a weird spectacle at Slam City Jam on a Sunday morning in 1998 for hungover spectators.

Britain followed suit with the Girls Skate Out (GSO) contest series, and I was delighted to read that in 2003, a surprise guest made an appearance. Jenna Selby, who would go on to direct the first European all-female skateboarding documentary, *As If, And What?* (2009) followed by *Days Like These* (2015), had initiated the GSO jam at the Epic skatepark in Birmingham. Jenna was reporting on round two for *Check It Out* magazine and noticed that after the beginners had wrapped up their session, a familiar yet mysterious woman asked to register for the contest.

> There was a sudden realization that it was Sue Hazel . . . It turned out that she drove to Birmingham the night before and spent the night in her car just to participate in the 2nd Annual "Girls Skate Out." After getting padded up, Sue headed straight for the vert ramp. Despite the fact she hadn't skated in six months, it was really impressive to watch her drop-in straight into a frontside air then eggplant. This is a skater who still uses rails on her board to slide![33]

Sue would win the GSO mini-ramp and vert contests two years in a row and would remain a supportive presence for British skaters. She is an example to all that a woman can embrace skateboarding throughout her adult life, especially if she's rocking safety gear, and of how important it is to have these senior mentors representing the past and the future.

Recently, there have been some incredible opportunities for female and non-binary skateboarders to gather, compete, and celebrate. The two largest annual events are the Wheels of Fortune contest in Seattle by the nonprofit group Skate Like a Girl, which is always a highly anticipated festival of fun and debauchery, and the Exposure contest initiated by Olympian Amelia Brodka and cofounded with Lesli Cohen. Exposure is hosted every November to help fundraise for survivors of gender-based violence while drawing attention to up-and-coming skateboarders from around the world. There are many community-based offerings as well, including the Stop, Drop, and Roll event in Vancouver organized by Indigenous pro skater and advocate Rose Archie from Tsq'escen' (Canim Lake) of the Secwépemc Nation.

It's also exciting to see that there's a whole new arena of possibility for individuals who never quite fit the mold of being a contest skater. Thanks to improved video production and social media, a skateboarder can reject the rigors of the contest circuit and instead create innovative video parts for their sponsor, going on tour with their team, offering demos, and cultivating a following of devoted fans. I'm thinking about Nora Vasconcellos, Maité Steenhoudt (aka Club Maiteee), Vitória Mendonça, Leo Baker, Beatrice Domond, Briana King, and many others who are revered for their unique style and character but are not necessarily vying for Olympic glory.

Sue Hazel shared that she was impressed by the standard of skating today, but said, "Skaters growing up these days have a very different introduction to the sport. There was such public hostility to us. It seems a bit ridiculous now to look back at the massive shift in public opinion."[34] I fullheartedly agree with Sue. In 1995, while I was practicing alone in a church parking lot, I was jolted by the sound of a revving engine and squealing tires moments before an old man tried to run me down in his crappy brown sedan. I dodged his attempt at manslaughter behind a church pillar but then had to listen to his tirade about me trespassing on holy ground. If I had been a kid with a hockey stick and puck, would the old man have behaved the same way? Probably not. There was just something about skateboarding that triggered Grandpa's rage. The man's behavior was surreal and extreme but not unexpected in an era when skaters were labeled as delinquents, intent on destroying public property.

The overall level of public hostility toward skateboarders has softened today, and the learning environment has improved, and a big part of this is because parents of young girls are seeing opportunities for their daughters rather than viewing skateboarding as a dead end or an embarrassment, which was the case in the 1980s and '90s, and totally valid. What rational parent would want their daughter participating in a crude, male-dominated subculture that came across like *Lord of the Flies*?

Sue was drawn to skateboarding because of her drive to carve out her own path, rather than succumb to societal expectations or her parents' concerns over her neighbor's opinions. She said,

> It's nice to be into something a bit different. Making your individuality and getting on with it. Not feeling like you have to be a sheep . . . It wasn't a conscious thought in my mind that I was being different. Sometimes you got vibed by people for doing something they perceived as immature, but the overriding passion, belief and excitement in doing something so unique carried me through all that. It wasn't something that I ever thought about giving up.[35]

Sue liked that skateboarding wasn't easy, and she even joked that skateboarding was a "hopelessly addictive affliction . . . I may have missed out on the run of the mill things, like nightclubbing and going down the pub,"[36] but there were no regrets. Sue concluded her interview for *Sidewalk* magazine by stating, "I hope the girls reading this take note and start enjoying skating for what it is. Ignore what people perceive women should be doing with their lives and go for it!"[37]

And Sue has been true to her words. Sue skated throughout her fifties, and these days, in her sixties, even though she is battling breast cancer and undergoing chemotherapy, she sneaks out for a skate session, ripping around the concrete waves of a pump-track, or a climbing day when she's able and the weather aligns. Sue explained that the chemo and its side effects like nausea, migraine, and extreme fatigue are brutal, but she is getting through it.[38] Again, Sue steps up to model and mentor us through life's challenges with courage, and I'm so pleased that interest in her story has emerged. She is now being referred to as "the First Lady of U.K. Skateboarding" online, which seems like a fitting title after an era of indifference.

Just like the female mathematicians, code breakers, and spies of the past, Sue infiltrated skateboarding on her own terms. The best part is that Sue has never expected anything in return from the skateboarding industry; meeting new people, traveling, and having novel experiences were enough for her. You won't find Sue on social media trying to elevate her personal platform as a legend, and while there are individuals rallying for her to be recognized, perhaps even with a Skateboarding Hall of Fame induction, that's not her motivation. There was a time when a company proposed designing a freestyle board for Sue as a signature product, but it never panned out. "I didn't really mind . . . It would have been nice but skating isn't about sponsorship is it? Get on and enjoy it and ignore the paraphernalia that goes with it."[39] Amen.

JoAnn Gillespie skating her mini-ramp in 1991, documented by the late Scott Starr (RIP)

CHAPTER NINE

REBELS
(JOANN GILLESPIE)

For a youth subculture to thrive and be appealing, there needs to be an element of fun, a sense of identity, and some tension with mainstream society. There's a reciprocal relationship between authority figures, like teachers, parents, police officers, and city policy makers, and teenagers. Authority figures exert power by imposing rules and regulations, and teenagers need an outlet to assert their independence and question the values being imposed upon them. A classic example of this dynamic is the punk movement.

Lauraine Leblanc in *Pretty in Punk: Girls' Gender Resistance in a Boys' Subculture* looked at both the British and American interpretations of punk to understand why young women were drawn to the scene. She was curious because, as one of her interviewees explained, "a lot of people associate [punk] with a certain aggressiveness with the music and with the scene . . . and that's been associated with male behavior and maleness."[1] And because punk was constructed as masculine, the male punks would typically establish the "rules of engagement" within the subculture. These rules were focused on authenticity, "who is a real punk and who is a poseur . . . with reference to who most closely approximates the masculinity of the ideal punk."[2] Sound familiar?

There are many parallels between punk and skateboarding including this association with masculine identity and aggression as a necessary trait. This pigeonholing is problematic for several reasons. Sue Hazel certainly didn't think that aggressive behavior was required to be successful. To her, it was more about analysis, trial, and error, with a bit of stubborn determination thrown in to perfect a move. But what about the women who are naturally aggressive and use this aspect of their personality to thrive and progress in skateboarding? It seems absurd to suggest that one gender encapsulates this characteristic, while implying that it's inappropriate for another.

No matter your gender expression, sometimes you want a fierce, rebellious friend at a skateboard session to back you up and get you stoked. For example, in 1978, competitive skateboarder Robin Logan shared her inspirations with journalist Kate Mahony for a "Kate the Skate" article. Robin said, "Kim Cespedes who is a great buddy of mine and lives on my street — she's what I call a really aggressive skateboarder . . . she puts the guys to shame, they'll get out of the pool to let her ride."[3] Robin was thrilled to have a friend stepping up at the skatepark and holding her own. There was no suggestion that Robin felt inferior, or wished she was more like Kim, it was, *This is who we are, and we both skateboard, and if the guys can't handle it, they can get out of the way.*

I was reminded of JoAnn Gillespie, otherwise known as Rawkmom, who skated in the late 1980s and early 1990s; she exuded passion, courage, and kindness as a skateboarder, musician, and mom. JoAnn became interested in skateboarding because of the way it provided an adrenaline rush, combined with its association with punk music and youthful rebellion. JoAnn also took on the role of mama bear and channeled her punk defiance to support and protect her friends. I write "mama bear" because her Instagram profile picture literally features the Mama Bear logo, used by proud mothers of transgender children. JoAnn is a rebel, and a mom, with a cause.

Skateboarding has an interesting history of being labeled as a rebellious pursuit, sometimes by authority figures, sometimes by the skateboarding industry as a marketing ploy, and other times enhanced and sensationalized by news outlets focusing on a few seedy characters in the scene prone to drug dealing and murder.[4] The attitude toward skateboarding by newspaper editors, journalists, and city officials as early as the 1950s and '60s fluctuated seemingly daily from celebration to condemnation, all depending on who was doing the talking and what their motivation was.

In the May 14, 1965, issue of *Life* magazine, Bill Eppridge's photos capturing the joyful energy of skateboarding around New York City's Central Park in the 1960s were printed. The photos featured kids, and some adults, of diverse economic backgrounds, genders, and ethnicities, all united in their pursuit of chaos and fun as skateboarders. But the photos were juxtaposed with an article by Ben Cosgrove called "Skateboard Mania — and Menace: A Teeter-Totter on Wheels Is the Risky New Fad." The title alone proves that skepticism and disapproval were the reigning attitudes toward skateboarding by newsmakers, even with Patti McGee's iconic handstand on the cover and her advocacy for safety while on tour across America.

The early DIY skateboards were precarious with little turning flexibility, but the kids were having a blast. Yes, they were scraping skin and breaking bones, but their enthusiasm was irrepressible. In news stories, doctors were consulted, issuing expert words of advice, and yet there was something else, something sinister that adults couldn't quite pinpoint besides the obvious fact that injuries were a regular occurrence. Then came *The Devil's Toy*, a short film by Claude Jutra subtitled in English in 1969; it explored a growing stigma around skateboarding. An original abstract from the National Film Board of Canada explained that the documentary was "filmed in 1966 on Montréal streets before the elongated roller skate was banned, this film captures the exuberance of boys and girls having the time of their lives in free-wheeling downhill locomotion."[5]

The skaters in the film bombed down Mont Royal hill as a high-spirited mob, seemingly without a care in the world, but they were also dealing with negative repercussions from disapproving adults. Skateboarding, to them, was disorganized, not regimented by rules or confined to a field or ice rink, but out in the streets, in cul-de-sacs or local schoolyards, where adults couldn't monitor or dictate the kids' behavior.

In an article published on April 9, 1965, called "Salina 'Surfers' Soar and Suffer," I had a laugh-out-loud moment when Mr. Ray Miller had the nerve to point out an interesting fact: "Surprisingly, it is adults who are suffering the more serious hurts. The injuries are sustained while attempting to 'demonstrate' the use of the skateboard to children . . . The new sport, which could surpass the hula hoop craze in its scope of interest, has caused concern among doctors and parents."[6] This was the first time I had considered the possibility that injured adults were the liability swaying the statistics.

Sadly, the fate of five-year-old skater Clarissa Carter ended up being a lead story to help solidify the decline of skateboarding in the 1960s. Carter was killed on April 30, 1965, by a speeding police car near Central Park in New York City while skateboarding. There were over one hundred newspapers that carried the story, and most of the headlines pinned the cause of Clarissa's death on her skateboard: "Skateboard Causes Little Girl's Death," "Child, 5, Victim of Skateboard," and "Little Girl on Skateboard Killed." There were two publications that added a hint of neutrality, stating that "Car Kills Girl on Skateboard" and "Girl, 5 Killed by Car in Skateboard Accident." Only three newspapers chose headings that acknowledged the police's responsibility: "Girl 5, on Skateboard Killed by Police Car," "N.Y. Police Car Kills Girl, 5, On Skateboard," and finally, "Fake Bomb Report Fatal to Child, 5, Hit by Police Car."

The articles are repetitive and conclude with an ominous quote from the Greater New York Safety Council, which demanded that "parents control their youngsters in riding skateboards." The situation was obviously heartbreaking but fixing the blame entirely on skateboards and parents seems unfair. It's also worth noting that in a Cleveland newspaper, Clarissa's story was followed by an article about a boy named James Demko who was also hit by a car with the heading "Cyclist, 12, Killed" that same night. Sounds like speeding cars were the true devil's toy.

Regardless, skateboarding was officially condemned in the mid- to late 1960s by city officials, and the practice was banned on streets, sidewalks, parks, and even one's own driveway by cities and municipalities across North America. These bylaws certainly weren't as bad as the situation in Norway, where the import, sale, purchase, and use of skateboards was illegal for over a decade,[7] but the police, as seen in *The Devil's Toy*, were endowed with new rights to enforce traffic laws against skateboarders, distribute tickets, and confiscate skateboards at whim.

While it can be fun to play the rebel with a gang of friends, the luster wears off when your skateboard gets seized, and that's followed by a lecture from your parents. It's no wonder skateboarding took a dive in popularity with these kinds of restrictions in the 1960s. And yet skateboarding persisted, and a boom-and-bust pattern would unfold over the decades, dependent on a variety of factors: the financial health of the skateboarding industry, the preference for different styles of skating (for example, street-skating is often more popular than vert because of its accessibility), affiliations with other subcultures like punk and hip-hop, and mainstream validation, such as its recent inclusion as an Olympic sport. These elements might result in rejection or acceptance by popular culture, and depending on the individual, that general opinion might be a repellant or a draw.

GIRL GANGS, ZINES, AND POWERSLIDES

Like any segment of society, there are people in skateboarding with criminal intent that you genuinely do not want to mess with, but for the most part skateboarders are focused on having benign fun with their friends. JoAnn Gillespie personified this spirit, and again thanks to Lynn Kramer with her Women's Skateboard Network connections, I was pointed in JoAnn's direction and encouraged to seek her out.

In 1990, when Lynn was the editor of *Equal Time* zine, she published a letter from JoAnn, which illustrated a brutal skateboarding accident in graphic detail. JoAnn had ollied over a railroad tie but instead of landing on a horizontal board and riding away, it flipped vertically between her legs, and JoAnn had to get "12 stitches *you know where*." The zine was the perfect venue for the letter, as I'm sure other female skaters could relate to or at least empathize with the injury. JoAnn also didn't filter the fact that her incident happened at the Powell Peralta company picnic, "so it was really embarrassing and very bloody. I can't skate for awhile but I plan to skate. I miss my skate even though it hurt me."[8] JoAnn's letter was a perfect example of how straight-up she is, and I got to experience this dynamic firsthand via Zoom.

I always have nervous energy before interviewing someone, and I wondered what someone nicknamed Rawkmom would think of a nerdy librarian like me. I also have a limited knowledge of punk music, although I'll never forget the first time I heard the Clash as a preteen. In the room next to mine, my brother blasted "Should I Stay or Should I Go" and I immediately barged through his door wanting to know what I was hearing and why I felt instantly possessed to thrash about like a puppy with a new toy. Joe Strummer's voice was tormented, upbeat, hypnotic, and cool, and I wanted to hear more. But the closest I came to embracing a punk style was threatening to shave my head like Sinéad O'Connor in a tense moment with my mom, who said "Go for it," which meant that I never followed through.

I virtually entered JoAnn's living room, a glorious white loft space with skylights, and discovered a woman about ten years my senior with flowing blond hair, glasses, and a variety of intricate tattoos covering her shoulders. She was sipping tea from a massive mug featuring Milo, the cartoon mascot from the punk band the Descendents. Seeing Milo, the patron saint of nerdy punks, reminded me of being introduced to the band by a roommate in my first year of university. I immediately felt at ease.

JoAnn launched into a bubbly introduction — she was so pumped for us to meet. She said, "I can't believe you're doing this. I'm like, 'Oh my God, what a unicorn!' You're gonna archive all this?"[9] Her warmth was infectious. Did she intuitively know that I was part of an all-girl motorcycle club called the Majestic Unicorns? JoAnn loved unicorns, and so we hit it off like fireworks. She recounted how as a kid with boundless energy, growing up in the East Bay area, her young parents tried to find outlets that would sustain her need for action, and horse-jumping was initially it. JoAnn said it was no surprise that she sought out daring sports because her dad was a race car driver, and her uncle was a flat-track Harley-Davidson biker. In fact, Frank and Doug Gillespie appear in the classic documentary *On Any Sunday* (1971), featuring the "King of Cool" Steve McQueen, racing their motorcycles.

In high school, JoAnn cultivated a taste for punk music and skate punk boyfriends. She remembered sitting on a vert ramp in Orinda in 1984, rocking a mohawk, smoking clove cigarettes, and watching the guys. She described having a great time at the ramp, talking shit all day, but her preference was still horse-jumping rather than skateboarding. When JoAnn went off to college in Santa Barbara, she no longer had access to horses. JoAnn had chosen Santa Barbara because the town had a great punk rock scene including the hardcore band RKL, "Rich Kids on LSD." JoAnn said the lead singer "was an amazing skateboarder, had a vert ramp in his parents' backyard in Montecito . . . and that band really spoke to me as a kid. To this day, it's one of my favorite bands."

That first fall day at college, JoAnn pulled into her apartment parking space in her beat-up Volkswagen Golf, packed to the brim and plastered in band stickers. When she turned off the motor, JoAnn was confused because she could still hear punk music blaring, but it wasn't coming from her stereo. The source was a car parked next to hers where a kid sat rocking a full set of braces and listening to the same radio channel. JoAnn introduced herself. The young punk was her new neighbor, living in a skaters' house across the street. The residents would go on to become members of Lagwagon — a popular skate punk band from Goleta, in a similar vein to Green Day, the Offspring, and Rancid.

The Isla Vista neighborhood was so contained that it made more sense for JoAnn to rip around on a skateboard than to drive. She picked one up from a friend and immediately embraced it. Word soon got around that this rad skater chick owned a car and had an appreciation for punk music. Preteen skaters like Kit Erickson and Frankie Hill would be waiting for her every day. "They're literally thirteen-year-old groms sitting on my couch every time I got home from class. I'm like, 'How are you guys still here?' And they're like, 'We're waiting for you, we need to go skating.'"[10] Without a driver's license, Kit and Frankie insisted that JoAnn take them skateboarding to their favorite spots, which meant that she was initiated into the scene by going to some gnarly locations. They were the perfect definition of groms, which is a term surfers and skaters use for precocious kids always lurking at skate spots, often more talented than their senior mentors.

JoAnn fell in love with skateboarding by skating dirt ditches, empty pools, and rugged reservoirs like the Tea Gardens, while dodging rent-a-cops or bribing them with a joint to turn a blind eye as the skaters trespassed. She soon connected with one of her early skateboarding idols, Krishna Swenson, who was fortunate to have a mini-ramp at her parent's house in downtown Santa Barbara. Their friendship was inevitable because Krishna also loved horses, creating an instant bond. JoAnn became aware of a whole network of backyard mini-ramps where parties and skate sessions happened, even crossing paths with KZ Zapata, being a fellow skater and drummer in the punk band PMS, also attending university. With all these fun distractions, college became quite the ordeal for JoAnn, especially once she got her own ramp.

While there was a wealth of backyard mini-ramps in the area, it made sense to JoAnn to have a ramp of one's own, to paraphrase Virginia Woolf. Skateboard sessions with a mob of dudes were more like snake sessions, where you had to aggressively assert your skateboard in the lineup and charge forward if you wanted to get your turn. JoAnn was perfectly capable of participating in these sessions, especially with her experience galloping around on a thousand-pound beast with a bunch of horse-jumping kids, prepping for a show. But if she had her own ramp, she could mess around for hours, doing whatever she wanted and provide her friends with a welcoming space to learn.

JoAnn's first ramp was made of inferior materials and the calculations were off, which triggered complaints, but the next attempt "was just butter!" and she gave Lagwagon drummer Derrick Plourde credit for his ramp-building skills. JoAnn still enjoyed skating curbs in the streets and launching herself off sets of stairs, but the fluid nature of skating ramp was more her style. JoAnn liked grinding coping, dropping in on over-vert walls, and clearing the spine of a ramp, which is when two ramps are connected to create a peaked obstacle in the middle.

The four-foot-high ramp that JoAnn owned was heavily filmed by Ethan Fox for *SK8HERS* (1992) and eventually became known as the "Equal Time" ramp. JoAnn was always inviting her friends to join in on a session, and she even modified the ramp by screwing in wood blocks at a lower level for beginners to learn to drop in more comfortably. JoAnn also loved hosting friends from afar, inviting travelers to crash on her couch and skate to their heart's content, including Sue Hazel, all the way from England, who experienced skating with a women's collective for the first time.

In our interview, JoAnn vaguely remembered stumbling upon an early issue of *Equal Time* with Lynn Kramer as editor, possibly at a local skate shop. Not long after, Lynn took a road trip to Santa Barbara and enjoyed JoAnn's ramp, writing an article about the experience in the December 1989 issue. While skating the Tea Gardens, Lynn noticed that "JoAnn had the place wired. She could carve up the steep face to the catwalk, and she knew all the speed lines through the holes made by dynamite (the city's contribution)."[11] Apparently, "the city of Santa Barbara planted TNT throughout various sections of the bowls and blew large sections out. They also dumped a bunch of soil in the bowls to further deter skaters. Yet this did not stop people from skating it."[12]

JoAnn was grateful for her friendship with Lynn and said, "I brag about [Lynn] all the time because she is my hero . . . Academically, she's a badass — super smart and administratively quick as a whip . . . She was and still is completely obsessed [with skateboarding]. She's the fastest woman in the world!" When Lynn was ready to hand over the Women's Skateboard Network and *Equal Time* zine in 1992, she chose JoAnn to be the new editor.[13] In JoAnn's video part for *SK8HERS*, Cara-Beth Burnside used the opportunity to promote the initiative. Cara-Beth said, "This is JoAnn Gillespie, she's from Santa Barbara, California. Here she is riding her backyard ramp and the Powell Skate Zone. JoAnn also has her own zine that's called *Equal Time*. It features many girls as well as guys, so if you're interested, write to her, and send some photos."[14]

JoAnn released only one issue of *Equal Time*, which was also the fourth and final issue, and because they were all about equal opportunity, Frankie Hill was the cover-boy. The zine was substantial and the effort to create, copy, and distribute the DIY publication couldn't be sustained. It was noted decades later in the book *Skater Girl* (2006) that the economic recession in the early 1990s made the zine difficult to produce on a shoestring budget, but progress was still made, and many of the women kept in touch, some to this very day.[15]

Unfortunately, the equal opportunity attitude wasn't always shared. When JoAnn and her friends ventured over to the Powell

Skate Zone, away from the communal spirit of her backyard mini-ramp, they experienced negative vibes from male skaters, who were often outsiders to the local scene. It's possible that these guys had never skated with women, but that was no excuse for thoughtless behavior. For example, one of JoAnn's friends who was "tough as nails and blind in one eye" kept getting run off the ramp by a legendary pro skater visiting town. JoAnn said that she threw a fit and demanded an apology. Someone's status as an original Z-boy from Dogtown was meaningless to JoAnn if they weren't being respectful.

A comparable incident happened at a contest in Reno, Nevada, in 1990, which was held at the Nevada State Fair and arranged by the National Skateboard Association. Patty Segovia had successfully proposed a small competition to the organizer, Frank Hawk, as a kind of "All Girl Skate Jam," to showcase female talent. JoAnn traveled to the event with Patty, Cara-Beth Burnside, and Rhonda Doyle, who all appeared in the *SK8HERS* film. Before their contest run, while they were trying to warm up on the ramp, the women kept getting rudely heckled by several male professional skaters. One of these pros was a youth from Canada, a prodigy on the vert ramp, whom I'll refrain from naming because of his ongoing affiliation with skateboarding and coaching today. JoAnn was so enraged by the vitriol this kid was spewing that she came close to punching him out; she hurled a skateboard at him instead.

The Reno contest was reviewed in the December 1990 issue of *Thrasher*, and in the six pages there was no mention of the women, but the top ten men in the streetstyle, freestyle, mini-ramp, and vert contests were all listed. On the All Girl Skate Jam Facebook page, Segovia posted that Cara-Beth received a child's pink scooter for winning the event. A scooter for a badass female vert skater!

JoAnn's response to the Reno contest experience? "I just stopped talking to dudes. I was like, 'I'm just done.' There wasn't any love for us, believe me." Twenty years later, one of the rude perpetrators, who had been "judging" the contest, approached JoAnn and apologized to her. He recognized, now that he had matured and was a parent, that his behavior and that of his friends was pathetic. JoAnn accepted the apology but felt that this kind of self-reflection and accountability was a rarity. She may have stopped talking to the dudes, but it didn't prevent her from venting through letters. "I got pissed off in the '90s with *Thrasher* and *Big Brother*. I wrote so many letters!" JoAnn could see a direct correlation between the arrogant behavior of young male skaters in the 1990s and the way that skateboard magazines and companies privileged teen boys, rebranding mainstream misogyny as a form of rebelliousness.

An outsider looking in at the American skateboard community was Michelle Ticktin, a Scottish vert skater who traveled from Glasgow to California with a female friend to soak up the scene in the early 1990s. Michelle was fascinated that the industry was run by twenty-year-old men and said that rumors about Mark "Gator" Rogowski's violence had been "flying around for ages but nothing had been done. Most of the men had warped ways of thinking and there was so much casual violence around."[16] Michelle didn't expand on examples of this casual violence in that interview, but wrote to me, "A year later Gator confessed to brutally killing a young woman . . . So, the story a young female skater had told me was tragically proved to be grounded in reality."[17] Michelle's trip to SoCal left her feeling disillusioned and disturbed, and after her trip, she quit skateboarding for a year before her friends coaxed her into returning. In an interview from 1994, Michelle said, "the reason there is such a warped mentality [in skateboarding] is that there are so few females involved to even it out," and her solution was to pursue journalism with the understanding that control over the media and its portrayal of skaters would be a way to "counteract the gender imbalances in the culture."[18]

Meanwhile, JoAnn and her friends opted to take a temporary time-out from trying to effect change from inside the dominant skateboarding scene, where toxic attitudes were given free reign. Even in a cursory review of interviews and reports in skateboarding magazines and videos during the 1990s, there are constant references to and celebrations of violence like attacking security guards, predatory sexual encounters at skateboarding contests and parties, and blatant sexism and homophobia.

What's depressing is that a similar scenario to Rogowski's crime repeated itself. Professional vert skater Ben Pappas from Melbourne, Australia, moved to the U.S. in the 1990s, along with his brother Tas Pappas. The brothers had a tumultuous upbringing but found refuge in skateboarding and were dominating contests by 1996, giving Tony Hawk a run for his money.[19] Their descent from rockstar status into drug addiction and cocaine smuggling was explored in the 2014 documentary *All This Mayhem* (dir. Eddie Martin). After murdering his girlfriend, Lynette Phillips, Ben died by suicide in 2007.

A report from *The Guardian* suggested Ben's motivation for murdering Lynette was that he had "found out she was a prostitute," which is the only detail about her life included in the article.[20] Through a brief online search, I discovered that while she had her struggles, Lynette had been studying to become a drug and alcohol counselor. She had taken out two intervention orders against Pappas to protect herself from unwanted behaviors, evidence that he had displayed a history of physical violence and controlling behavior, which one doctor failed to act upon because he had been in awe of the former professional skater, despite the fact that Ben had become psychotic and depressed.[21]

All This Mayhem reveals how ugly things had become in skateboarding — again. It's this repetitive story of a talented yet messed-up young man being delivered fame, money, drugs, free time, and zero accountability, while being surrounded by people who idolize his destructive behavior and hang off his every word, words that are so often expressing sentiments like, "Girls shouldn't skate, they just hurt themselves too much. They should just watch."[22] Skateboarding loves a rebel, and there's no expectation for a pro skater to become an upright citizen after achieving success, but even so, it's in all our best interests to not turn a blind eye when someone is negatively impacting others and going down a path that typically leads to discontentment, isolation, and far worse.

Needless to say, female skateboarders had their work cut out for them to interrupt this dysfunctional scene and dismissive attitude toward women, which was, of course, a reflection of society at large. After the success of the Women's Skateboarding Network and the launch of the celebratory *SK8HERS* video, the continuation of skateboarding as a frat club must have been disheartening. But there was hope, and the Riot Grrrls had a part to play in this slow and unsteady transformation.

TRAIL BLAZING

Terry Lawrence
Pro skateboarder and renowned trans skater (1970s)

The legacy of pro skater Terry Lawrence and his skateboarding journey is game-changing. In 2020, he said, "I'm 57 years-old, my pronouns are he/him/his and I'm transgender. I was a professional skater in the '70s and early part of the '80s, when I was skating, I was skating as a female."[23] Before I even had a chance to reach out, Terry graciously wrote to me via the @womxnsk8history account, thanking me for creating a respectful virtual space. He offered me permission to celebrate his story with the understanding that I would use his name and pronouns and still acknowledge his time and influence as a female competitor. I was happy to oblige.

Acknowledging Terry's presence in skateboarding is vital because it speaks to a realization that queer skaters have always

REBELS (JOANN GILLESPIE)

Cyndy Pendergast skating The Turf in 1983

BELOW: Kim Adrian catching some proper air back in 1979 at Skatopia

BELOW: Terry Lawrence competing at Lakewood skatepark in 1979, by James Cassimus

participated, whether society or the skateboard industry supported their choices or were aware of their existence. After receiving a skateboard for Christmas at age eight, Terry quickly progressed and became sponsored in 1976 by Pepsi and skateboarding companies Vans, Independent, and Powerflex, who released Terry's signature board.[24] Cara-Beth Burnside remembered seeing Terry and the Powerflex team at the Big O Skatepark, which inspired her to ditch the roller skates and start skateboarding.[25]

In the late 1970s, Terry consistently won pool and bowl contests like the ISA Northern California Pro championship at Winchester skatepark, the Lakewood World Pro Halfpipe contest, and the Hester Pro Bowl series. *Skateboarder* magazine gave Terry a "Who's Hot!" interview in the June 1979 issue as someone to pay attention to. Terry, sixteen, shared,

> I started at the Concrete Wave about a year ago when I first saw Jana Payne. I just wanted to do what she was doing so I started riding there every day . . . Finally, I started riding pools and vertical. Then I heard about the Hester [Pro Bowl contest] at Newark and that Leilani [Kiyabu] won and what she was doing; so I thought I would give the next contest a try. That was the Hester/Big 'O' and I ended up with first place.[26]

The caption under Terry's photo appropriately read that he was "closing the gap between male and female potential in the realm of vertical skating."[27]

Terry was a rebel during his youth, but it wouldn't be until much later that Terry would gain an awareness of what trans identities were and challenge the status quo. For *Skateism* magazine, Terry explained that "I didn't know any trans skater, or even gay skaters that were out," [28] but he fell in love with skateboarding because it gave him a sense of freedom and a means to express himself as a competitive, aggressive youth.

Terry also appreciated the skateboard scene in the '70s because "so much was new and exciting. In a lot of ways, it was developing its own culture, its own voice. It was the sense you could be and do whatever you wanted, it had that rebellious aspect."[29] In contrast, Terry felt that the 1980s was "male-dominated and heteronormative. It was a lot of 'this is gay, you're a fag, you're a dyke.' When you grow up in that kind of environment, there is a lot of fear, kids shut down, they don't feel safe to be who they are."[30] For Terry, rebellion was the ability to embrace any identity your heart desires.

Skateboarding still empowered Terry, and he transitioned five years prior to being featured on Jeff Grosso's "Loveletter to LGBTQ+," the most courageous episode of the televised series *Loveletters to Skateboarding*. To Grosso, Terry said, "Queer skating is awesome, I really like to see the diversity that's happening. I hope that the environment continues to be safer, and safer for folks that are not only like me, but the whole spectrum of the community and for everyone because to me, skating has given me a great life and a great perspective on everything I've done."[31]

Kim Adrian
Skateboarder (1970s)

Kim Adrian is a "skater's skater" — someone who skates for the love of it, committed to the actual doing of skateboarding, which I respect. When Kim sent me unpublished photos from 1978 and 1979 of her blasting out of pools and bowls with serious amplitude, I was blown away, delighted, and angry all at once. This woman should have been on the cover of skateboard magazines, and I was pissed that she wasn't known as a legend. The photos revealed that Kim had so much airtime she could perform a variety of grabs, holding her board in different positions, oblivious to gravity and the hard concrete below. The photos made me think that she was one of the most underrated female skaters of the 1970s.

In 1976, Kim began skateboarding in Lakewood, California, after noticing some boys practicing freestyle moves in her neighborhood. Kim said,

> They were just doing nose wheelies, jumps, handstands. So, I just go, "Hey, I wanna skate with you guys!" So, I got a skateboard and just started learning the basics . . . and then somehow, I got a ramp, a little ramp in the front yard. It was just like a piece of wood. So that means in '76 I was already learning transitions that first year.[32]

Kim then discovered the Concrete Wave skatepark in Anaheim and was sponsored by C&D Skateshop under the guidance of Chuck Dunn. Chuck was designing skateboarding products, which meant that Kim got to test new wheels and share her input. Chuck respected her perspective, and Kim is still in touch with him as a result.

Kim's most influential mentor was Erich "Shreddi" Repas. In 1977, Kim was skating with Shreddi at Brookhurst Park, which had unusual features like concrete flowerpot obstacles: "He does a frontside air off the little two-foot curved blocks around one of the trees. I go, 'Oh my god, that's so cool. I gotta learn how to do a frontside air,' and that's what inspired me to do it . . . Shreddi helped me a lot because he was very advanced compared to me and he just pushed me, and I just went for it." Kim became consumed with catching air and sought out steeper terrain.

Kim was then offered a sponsorship by Sims Skateboards, although she wasn't impressed by their pitch. One of the team's requirements was a signed declaration to abstain from marijuana, which Kim thought was absurd. "Of course, we all smoked pot back then — we all did! Everybody smoked pot. That's what you did back in the '70s." Kim went along with it, but Sims was not a good match. On the Sims team, Kim racked up a mass of first place finishes making her the 1979 overall point winner for the USASA

Big Five Series for women aged sixteen to nineteen, but she had little interest in dwelling on these accomplishments. "I didn't think I'd ever compete or be on a team; I just wanted to skate. I didn't care about being popular."

Instead, Kim was obsessed with skating vert, especially Lakewood Park, and taking her skills to a new level. She asked me,

> Have you talked to anyone that has ridden that half-pipe? Did they tell you how big it is? The half-pipe was very shallow in the beginning, and progressively got deeper, was slightly downhill, and then at the end of it, the bowl was like twenty, thirty feet deep. So, if you needed to step up your game, that's where you're gonna be able to do it. You could get so much speed if you had the right equipment, and you could really get that amplitude — catapult yourself into the stratosphere. And that keyhole! There was a north keyhole and a south keyhole. The one you see me doing the air in and the carve grind is the north one.

Even today, Kim wakes from skateboarding dreams remembering that feeling of weightlessness from launching herself out of a pool, and the last tricks that she was learning — a frontside invert and alley-oop. Sadly, Kim hyperextended her knee in 1979 trying to avoid a bail, which meant a six-month recovery from her injury. "I really needed more like two to three years off. After six months or so, I came back, and I just had to be careful it didn't pop out . . . I had entered the pro circuit, but I was still recovering from the knee injury at that time."

The skateboarding industry in the '70s wasn't established to support injured riders. Of her sponsor, Kim said, "They just gave me equipment. I had a sense that they didn't care that much." Once her injury healed and the Skate City Whittier Park opened, Kim focused solely on her progression, taking advantage of the full pipe and pools. Kim stopped skating in 1980, partially to pursue her education but also because of an attitude "that once you were over eighteen you were too old to skate! I'm serious, people thought you can't skate after eighteen or nineteen because you're too old. I don't know — that's young now to skate . . . I almost wish I could have been born forty years later and get more into it 'cause the girls are just killing it today."

While it's always discouraging to think, *If only things had been different*, Kim still appreciated her formative years as a skater. It was a privilege to speak with her and become more aware of the progress made by women at that time, especially to be gifted photographic proof from the past. Kim also explained that her black-and-white photos from Lakewood were taken by an unknown female photographer, another mystery person perhaps harboring a cardboard box of evidence in an attic that could help fill a void. The prospect keeps me motivated.

Cyndy Pendergast
Skateboarder (1970s–80s)

In skateboarding history, there's a tendency to not only focus on influential male skateboarders but those who resided in California, often regarded as the birthplace of skateboarding. In the 1970s, there was a plethora of talented female skaters in California, as well as across the United States with a concentration in Florida (Crystal Loges, Jeannie Narducci, Kelly Marsh, Lisa Muir, Lulu Hart, Peggy Turner) and Hawaii (Michelle Kenney, Sharon Powell, Wendy Bedell), a whole fleet of slalom racers in Colorado, and a smattering of individuals in other states like Beth Fishman (New Jersey), Kim Kinsley (New Mexico), and Sandy Chadbourn (Georgia). And then there was Cyndy Pendergast, skating hard in the Midwest.

Thanks to the *Ragged Edge* zine collection online, I found two blurry photos of Cyndy in a zine called *EDO* out of Springfield,

Virginia, from 1986, getting inverted and catching air at a contest. The photographer was Marla Rainey of Clarendon Hills, Illinois, who stated, "There are five female skaters in the area: Cyndy Pendergast came in seventh place Division A at M.A.R.S. (Midwest Amateur Ramp Series)."[33] The results showed that Cyndy went up against pro skaters John Lucero and Neil Blender, who are both Skateboarding Hall of Fame inductees. I was hooked. I had to find this woman.

When I'm having little luck sourcing information about a person, I'll explore other avenues because it's possible that instead of skateboarding, it's surfing or snowboarding where they received the most affirmation. In Cyndy's case, it was motorcycles. The lone image of Cyndy on Facebook was a photo of her forging a river on her KLR650 motorbike with a woman-owned motorcycle tour group. Cyndy wasn't on social media, but the owner of ADV Woman was a friend of hers and quickly got us connected for an interview.

Cyndy recalled barely surviving her childhood because of her tendency to bomb down hills with fearless abandon on a blue plastic skateboard with clay wheels, purchased by her mom. Her life expectancy improved when urethane wheels hit the market in the 1970s before she reached high school. "I fell in love with skateboarding, even more so when I learned vert skating a couple years later."[34] Cyndy moved away from street-skating, frequenting the Rainbow Skatepark, best known as the "Rainbo Rink," in Chicago and the Turf Skatepark in Greenfield, Wisconsin, which had concrete pools. Cyndy even sent me a whole stash of kickass photos of her skating the pools and bowls at the Turf, taken by Marla Rainey.

When asked if the other skateboarders were supportive of her efforts as a female skater, Cyndy felt that in the 1970s the kids didn't care about gender, but the "occasional kid would look at me in wonder since I look very genderqueer and was usually seen to be male to the point people would argue with me that I must be a boy."[35] This debate would happen all through Cyndy's life, which she explained could be both difficult and humorous as a lesbian, but at the Turf she was accepted. "I was a good skater, and I would get guys coming up to me to ask what I was riding, they wanted to know what board I was on. When I competed against guys — since I was usually the only girl there — I would place [top three] pretty consistently in bowl contests."

Cyndy felt that it was in these competitive environments that her abilities progressed. "I don't think anybody cared who won the contests or where you placed; the contests just motivated us all to jam as hard as we could and to use the energy to air higher. We just enjoyed the energy and ripped around the pools." Cyndy remembered having the privilege of meeting pro skater Pattie Hoffman on tour from California, and she knew some other girls who skated, but they tended to prefer the street scene, finding secret banks to skate. While the Chicago girls weren't an official crew, Cyndy wanted them to be celebrated and sent photos that Marla had taken to *Thrasher* of their skateboarding missions to Rockfords' Reservoir and Evanston Banks. *Thrasher* chose one photo for the October 1982 issue including an explanation that Cyndy was tired of only seeing male skaters represented.

And then things got weird. In the 1980s, a male pro from a California-based company asked Cyndy to join the team after witnessing her skate. She was told that she was now sponsored, given stickers, and promised a skateboard, but the moment she needed a replacement board, the managers became rude over the phone and promptly dropped her. Cyndy then wrote another company, sending them photos of her catching air in the deep keyhole pool, along with her contest placings. In their reply, the company reps "were extremely sexist in their turn down of me . . . commenting on my body in the photos rather than my skating ability," and they told her to grow out her short hair to look more feminine.

Cyndy had had enough with industry bullshit. "I'm beating guys in pool contests and they are worried about my hair length? Yeah . . . 'Sponsors' really suck and can kiss my ass is pretty much how I feel . . . This is where the sexism showed up. And the rejections were very nasty." As a result, Cyndy refused to support certain brands, and after she purchased a board, she would promptly spray-paint over the company logo and board graphics as an act of rebellion. She referred to Californian industry dudes in the '80s as "total asshats." When it came to magazines, Cyndy preferred underground zines like *The Monthly Shredder*, which printed a whole page of photos featuring Cyndy in October 1982. Cyndy said that zines "were way cooler than the mainstream so that's where other female skaters and I would learn of each other and sometimes write each other." Cyndy had skateboarding pen pals as far away as Florida and Scotland, who would swap Polaroids and letters to motivate each other to keep skating.

My interview and correspondence with Cyndy were refreshing and another great example of someone pushing gender boundaries and refusing to conform or be swayed by the industry mainstream, which means, in my eyes, she's pure punk. Cyndy wanted her story known: "I keep hearing from young skaters how women's skating is just picking up now and I am like, naw, we were there back in the '70s, '80s, we've always been there skating . . . this is not new for women. I tell them what is new is that you are now hearing more about women skaters." [36] Cyndy is closing in on sixty, has a high-pressure job in IT, but still loves an adrenaline rush, getting out snowboarding in the winter and riding her dual sport motorcycle in the summer. And when I told Cyndy that her former stomping grounds, the Turf Skatepark, was being restored by a group of dedicated skateboarders, she was delighted by the prospect of recreating some of her old photos. My list of senior women heroes steadily grows.

JoAnn Gillespie and her friends must have been dismayed by the persistent sexist behavior from their so-called community. In the

1990s, some female skaters, for their own safety and sanity, pursued snowboarding instead, which was gradually becoming more receptive to sponsoring women. For example, Cara-Beth Burnside took a detour into snowboarding and found herself representing the U.S. at the Nagano 1998 Olympic Games, placing fourth in half-pipe. And others, like JoAnn, forged on in the music scene.

At the Vans Warped Tour — a festival initiated in 1995 that merged skateboarding demonstrations with punk bands like NOFX, Suicidal Tendencies, and Pennywise — JoAnn had the responsibility of overseeing "The Ladies' Lounge," which was described in 1998 by MTV as an area featuring "booths, displays, speakers, and riders in an attempt to spotlight females in action sports. Professional vert skater Jen O'Brien and pro snowboarder Morgan Lafonte will be among the athletes featured in the Lounge."[37] JoAnn performed in her own bands, skateboarded in the demos, and breastfed her new baby throughout the tour like the badass she is. By pushing the boundaries of two male-dominated subcultures at once, JoAnn was unique as a female skater punk, but she was not alone.

In *Pretty in Punk*, feminist writer Lauraine Leblanc critiqued the double standards facing female punks in the 1990s; rebellion was supposed to be the ethos, unless it encroached on a male punk's vision of masculinity. Leblanc explained, "In theory, [male] punks oppose the norms and values of mainstream culture. In practice, punks adopt many of the gender codes and conventions of mainstream adolescent culture."[38] Leblanc's observations are also reflected in skateboarding because in theory, it is a counterculture that challenges the norms and values of authority figures, but in practice, the industry has reproduced and even exaggerated attitudes like sexism, homophobia, and racism. Skateboarding might claim to embrace misfits, but often only those who fit its brand and target audience.

In Leblanc's interviews for her book, a young woman named Lola said, "We have to fight ten times harder in a [mosh] pit, just because you're a female . . . I seen L7 at the Pantheon a year ago, and they had to stop the show and [Suzi Gardner] started cussing out the guys . . . because there was a couple of girls there and the guys were literally forefront and beating the shit out of them."[39] The band L7 formed when musicians Suzi Gardner and Donita Sparks met in Los Angeles in 1985. While they preceded the Riot Grrrls movement, they were embraced as punk feminists for being outspoken against the violence directed toward women in the scene. They even graced the stage of the Vans Warped Tour in 1995.

The response by Gardner at the Pantheon reminded me of when the Hags in Los Angeles made their first appearance as a girl gang in 1983. They decided to skate together as a crew to a Grandmaster Flash show and lined up in the front row, holding their boards in the air like an extended fist. Gardia Fox said she knew that "it was a feminist statement. We wanted to encourage girls to skate, and show we weren't just girlfriends of skaters."[40] Girls to the front, indeed.

The Hags were the quintessential skater punk girl gang, but there were others who shared their vision. In the 1980s, there was a group of six skaters called the SkateBettys in Anchorage, Alaska, who were interviewed in the July 1984 issue of the punk zine *Warning*. The SkateBettys had their own logo — a modification of the *Thrasher* pentagram with the pagan "skate goat" symbol, but with fallopian tubes, breasts, and skateboards instead, "the only things that matter,"[41] according to Shel, then aged sixteen. Their motto was "Skate Muff or Go Home," and when dudes heckled them on the streets, Laura, aged sixteen, dismissed the response, joking about how it must upset men to see them tearing around on a skateboard, a "definite phallic symbol."[42]

In New York City, Thalia Zelnik became an unintentional punk mascot for Placebo Records and the band JFA (Jodie Foster's Army) by starring in several of their ads, including one that landed in the February 1987 issue of *Thrasher*. Thalia remembered that when the manager of JFA took her photo, holding a skateboard wearing her knee pads, cut-off vest, and studded bracelets, "I didn't realize that it was going to be in *Thrasher* — I think one of my friends pointed it out to me. I had no idea what kind of impact this was going to have, right? And I started being recognized . . . it was just a surprise thing and apparently it withstood the test of time."[43] Thalia's iconic photo was featured in a JFA music video, a music catalog, and the book *Full Bleed: New York City Skateboard Photography* (2010), which commemorated thirty years of skateboarding in the city's streets.

Tobi Vail, the drummer of Riot Grrrl bands Bikini Kill and the Frumpies, reached out to me via Instagram to share that she had been in an all-girl skater gang named the Skate Bunneys in the early '80s and that they were mentioned in the Beastie Boys' magazine, *Grand Royal*.[44] Later, the Frumpies, which included Vail, Kathi Wilcox, Billy Karren, Molly Neuman, and Michelle Mae, had close ties to skateboarding and were interviewed for the July 1994 issue of *Thrasher*: "The Frumpies live in a city where they have to deconstruct the law to skate. There is a No Skateboarding ordinance in the soggy city of Olympia, Washington's state capitol, but The Frumpies skated to the interview any way."[45] In classic Riot Grrrl form, members of the Frumpies produced a manifesto called "Nu Skate Movement," because they were tired of the gender barriers that existed in skating and punk. Tobi wrote, "We are sick of being insulted by the usual boy criticisms/suspicions/disses" and encouraged everyone to "skate creatively, skate to entertain, skate to challenge accepted skating norms."[46]

In the 1990s, just as women in punk music cultivated the Riot Grrrl ethos out of frustration with the sexism in their environment, women like Patty Segovia chose to persevere with a vision of safe and inclusive opportunities in skateboarding. Despite the negative experience of the Reno contest in 1990, which frustrated the female skaters who competed, Patty organized the All Girl Skate Jam in 1997 so that girls and women could learn how to skate and compete against each other without harassment. Patty even reached out to JoAnn for assistance, and she became the music director for the event, which was another means to enhance this celebration of rebellious women, with DJs and bands to get the skaters psyched.

Skateboarding took its toll on JoAnn physically, but she used the opportunities that came with it and combined with her passion for music to keep building community. JoAnn established Rawkmom Productions, organizing shows like Rawkmom's Gutterball Bash, and created a fun crew called the East Bay Punk Rock Riders, punk enthusiasts who really love riding horses. JoAnn has sung vocals and played drums in the bands Womentors, Hurting Crew, Dynamite 8, Lazerwolf, and the Angry Amputees, who were included on the Tony Hawk's *Underground* video game soundtrack. All of this while raising a child and becoming the proud owner of Rawking Horse Ranch.

I had been delighted when JoAnn described standing up to a disrespectful Dogtown Z-Boy legend and her performance at the Reno demo, when she winged her skateboard at one of the hecklers, but I was even more appreciative of how she stayed true to herself over the years and to her keen sense of justice and equity. Throughout our interview, JoAnn was constantly encouraging me to take note of skaters' names, like the various women who skated her Equal Time half-pipe, to ensure that her friends would also have their contributions documented in the skate history archive. JoAnn truly encompassed the equal opportunity mentality demonstrated in her zine.

More recently, JoAnn loved witnessing skateboarding in the Olympics — she found the standard of tricks to be mind-blowing and had no patience for anyone shitting on the event. "So, everyone was like, 'Pooh-pooh the Olympics.' Oh well, pooh-pooh you! I don't care. It's a different thing, it's a different sport, it will be different. There'll be all these different forms of skateboarding, but this is amazing. It's all valid — it's elevating the cause." *What cause?* you might ask. Working toward a global awareness of skateboarding and increased opportunities for everyone to participate, whether it results in them becoming a champion skater or not.

JoAnn also appreciated the changing attitudes in the skateboarding community toward gender non-conforming skaters, partly because her daughter is trans. "Skateboarding is definitely going through a renaissance," she said, especially compared to the past when, as Terry Lawrence articulated, derogatory language was used to condemn, isolate, and shame queer people. And these changes are thanks to a growing movement of skaters recognizing their own privilege, demanding accountability in all arenas of life while carving out opportunities for their friends. For example, There Skateboards is a contemporary brand created by an inclusive queer collective called Unity initiated by Jeffrey Cheung and his partner, celebrating and sponsoring diverse LGBTQ2S+ skaters. Jeffrey explained,

> I started Unity Skateboarding as a DIY and a personal way of supporting myself and my queer friends because I loved skating but always felt like I had to hide being queer ... When queer, trans, and people of color simply exist visibly, are active in their communities, and take up public space, they can change the narrative both in and outside of skateboarding.[47]

In the same way that Lauraine Leblanc saw value in punk for girls on the margins to bond together, enabling them to become a "revolutionary force,"[48] skateboarders are also recognizing their power as collectives to enact change. Instead of being a youth subculture pitted against parents or security guards, skateboarders are looking outward, using their voices and their networks to call out hypocrisy on a broader scale. For example, Isa Ostos and Romina Palmero, who oversee the grassroots organization Tutifruti, offer workshops that emphasize gender diversity, sexual education, and inclusion, in conjunction with skateboarding lessons in Florida — the epicenter of queer book banning.[49] Even a skateboard shop like Antisocial in Vancouver has been a site for social justice for over twenty years, fundraising and protesting issues like the lack of access to clean water for Indigenous communities, racist violence perpetuated by police, colonial theft of land, and the genocide in Palestine.

When we unite and support each other, change might come slowly and even backpedal at times, but the overall effect is irreversible. In today's world, it seems like selfless actions, empathy, and resistance to misinformation are the true indicators of countercultural activity, and by embracing this path, skateboarders are extending their rebellious reputation in an honorable fashion.

Beth Fishman with her grandma Rose (eighty-five) after winning the Eastern Skateboard Association Championships in 1977

CHAPTER TEN

MATRIARCHS
(BETH FISHMAN)

Lately, when senior women appear in pop culture and mainstream media as revered matriarchs, from cover models, athletes, musicians, politicians, to activists, there's a buzz of approval. One of my favorite moments was when the 106-year-old Indigenous tattoo artist Apo Whang-Od appeared on the cover of *Vogue Philippines*. Apo wore a black singlet that revealed her traditional Batok tattoos on her chest, arms, and hand. She radiated beauty and dignity while holding a reflective pose, with her hand resting against her chin, gazing intently at the photographer. Her portrait suggested a lifetime of accumulated wisdom.

In skateboarding, there's been a series of matriarchs in the traditional sense who are recognized in the community and even inducted into the Skateboarding Hall of Fame. Barbara Logan, the single mother to Robin Logan and her brothers Brian, Bruce, and Brad, supported her children's introduction to skateboarding in the 1960s and 1970s. Barbara was the foundation of the family business, the Logan Earth Ski skateboard company, which started in 1974 and continues to be maintained by Robin, sponsoring young riders.[1] And then there's Gale Webb. She was dubbed "Mrs. Skateboard," "The Skateboarding Mom," and "America's Sports Mom" in magazines like *Wild World of Skateboarding* and *The National Skateboard Review* as early as 1977 and throughout the 1980s, titles which she embraced.

Gale took up skateboarding along with her son in 1976 because she was a natural athlete, competing at a pro level in motocross, softball, and BMX riding. Not long afterward, she was sponsored by Powerflex skateboards and Vans, competed briefly in pool and bowl, and became a team manager.[2] Gale had survived a near-death parachute jump gone wrong as a youth and gained a reputation as an advocate for skateboarding safety. Gale had her "skateboarding family" performing demonstrations at schools, fairs, and malls thanks to a portable half-pipe.[3] She operated these demos for decades, traveling across America with young athletes, showcasing a variety of extreme sports, and now there's a Gale Webb Action Sports Park in Menifee, California, to honor her.

While Gale was considered a novelty as a parent pursuing dangerous activities alongside her child, there's momentum gathering today among skateboarders who still rip it up as adults, many of whom are moms, and some are well into their senior years. Groups like Late Bloomers Skate Club, The Real Hot Skate Moms, Brooklyn Skate Moms, and Later Skaters Gang are organizing meetups, retreats, and contests, amassing followers and bucking the trend that skateboarding is exclusive to young people. Returning to skateboarding after a long hiatus or taking it up for the first time in your twenties, thirties, forties, and beyond is becoming less unusual and even encouraged.

This resurgence is mostly due to individuals asking themselves, *Why do I have to abandon something I love because someone thinks it's inappropriate for an adult? Why should I be excluded from having fun?* And when they see other older adults documenting and celebrating their progress with friends and making news headlines, skateboarding becomes very appealing.[4] I can't picture skateboarding being on par with pickleball as a popular pursuit for seniors, as it can be quite punishing to the body. But I'm glad that more older skaters are finding community and making connections, even if the spring in our legs has diminished and we need to consume multiple aspirins after every session.

I'm mindful that I cannot assume that skateboarding is no longer a significant part of my interviewees' lives. In most cases, the person is shocked and delighted that I've stumbled upon vintage photos from their heyday, and our conversation is an opportunity to reflect on the past, but others still feel intimately bound to skateboarding. They still dream about it, notice unique locations in their town for a skate session, and even film themselves on board for social media. I learned early on not to jump to conclusions thanks to my connection with Beth Fishman, as well as to always expect the unexpected.

While preparing for Beth's interview, I thought I could predict the trajectory and content of our discussion before I had even met her. I had the audacity to think that there were no more surprises in wait for me. I had found Beth's name in the December 1977 issue of the *National Skateboard Review* in an article covering the three-day Eastern Skateboard Association championships in Asbury Park, New Jersey. The article portrayed a classic situation of lone girl beats boys and gains her fifteen minutes of fame, but there was so much more to unpack.

In 2024, I received an enthusiastic message via the contact form of my Womxn Skate History website from a woman who had seen an article about my project in our community magazine. She wanted to see if I was interested in going skateboarding. The woman was two years older than me at age forty-eight, and after a twenty-year break, she was returning to skateboarding and looking for motivation. I immediately wrote her back, we exchanged phone numbers, and then an opportunity arrived to meet. The November rains had stopped momentarily, and the skatepark would likely be dry. I'm not sure why I felt nervous, I had nothing to lose, but as I texted this woman, I secretly hoped that she would be the friend I needed.

I'm happily married and eternally grateful for this late-in-life relationship because it was my husband who bought me Mariah

Duran's pro board by Meow Skateboards with a pizza-eating cartoon cat graphic and who encouraged me to skate as an adult, but it's not a passion we share. This is not a criticism — I find it healthy having our own unique interests — yet I had always experienced skateboarding with a community, and it's been strange relearning my old tricks mostly alone. Without any judgment, while my friends pursued motherhood over the years, I've found that I am often outside a circle of knowledge and conversation. Was it selfish to hope that this new skateboarding friend would be child-free? Probably. Plus, there were some women in my town with kids who were occasionally able to reserve time for a skate session. I just wanted one friend my age who "got me."

When I first arrived in Powell River and was meeting new people, I had the strangest experience. I had gone for coffee with a woman who shared a mutual acquaintance and then bumped into her at a music festival on the beach not long after. She turned to a lady standing beside her and said, "This is Natalie — she doesn't have children." I was speechless. The tone of her voice had a hint of scorn, and it didn't spark any further conversation. I interpreted the comment as implying that these women, as members of some elite birthing cult, were above me and I felt stupid standing there. I had never been introduced in this manner. What if I was unable to have children and had been trying in vain for years, or what if my child had died? This statement could have been extremely hurtful, but all it did was make me irritated. I could have been presented as "the librarian" or "new to town," but being called out as a childless woman felt tactless.

At least the local skateboarders were friendly. There has been the odd interaction that left me cold, like last summer when some dude showed up at the skatepark with porn images pasted to the bottom of his skateboard, giving me flashbacks to 1999. Apparently, there were not enough sexy board graphics to purchase so he had to customize his own. But overall, it's a great mix of skaters — there are older guys who sometimes perform new tricks for me to attempt, and I've loved witnessing the progress of young skaters as they gain confidence in their skills. I just hadn't met a fellow middle-aged skater woman who was as consumed with skateboarding as I was. But I always had hope, and thanks to social media and my cumulative interviews for the archive, I knew I wasn't alone.

What caught my attention in the coverage of the 1977 Eastern Skateboard Association championship was a photo and a feel-good story about an eighty-five-year-old grandmother named Rose Fishman. The senior citizen

> was so thrilled by her ten-year-old granddaughter's win in the amateur freestyle competition for 9-to-11-year-olds that she is ready to compete next year. 'I have to learn how to skate first,' said Mrs. Fishman after congratulating her granddaughter, Beth Fishman, of Bradley Beach, New Jersey, for her win against an all-male field of competition.[5]

In the photo, not only was Rose holding her granddaughter's skateboard, but she was wearing a hockey helmet, all geared up and ready to go.

The quaint story was confirmed when I found Beth's Facebook account; she had posted the charming black-and-white photo of herself next to her grandmother at the contest. Beth wrote,

> Going through [a] box and found this gem. Me and my grandma Rose. I had just come in first place in a skateboard contest. Some photographer took one of my helmets and put it on her head for the shot. Priceless. Oh and I'm in wearing a puka bead necklace. Late '70s. I want to add that my grandma started

her life in a small village in Russia, fled to this country, learned some English and lived her life in a seaside town in New Jersey. You never know the arc of your life and I think its so cool she ended up at a skateboard contest in this photo with her grand daughter.[6]

This tidbit about Beth's grandma's journey and heritage intrigued me, and the photo truly was "priceless," as Beth described.

I tracked down an additional four-page article about Beth from the April 1978 issue of *Wild World of Skateboarding*. The writer discussed Beth's pretty appearance in a cringeworthy fashion, but still included a wide range of skateboarding photos from powerslides to kickflips and captured her freestyle prowess.[7] The article summarized how Beth had borrowed her older brother's skateboard, decided that it was fun, learned the basics, and then insisted her parents take her to a skatepark before taking out all the boys in her age group at the contest. With all this content, it seemed like the bio would write itself, but I decided to contact Beth, who immediately agreed to an interview. I'm glad I did because I could never have imagined Beth's story beyond her contest win, which ended up being a librarian's dream.

QUEEN BEES

Judi Oyama
Skateboarder (1970s–present)

Judi Oyama is living life to the max. At age sixty-three, she qualified for the 2024 USA Slalom Skateboarding team, and not just in a "masters" division. In the *Santa Cruz Sentinel*, Judi exclaimed,

Amy Pike Bradshaw, in her fifties, competing and placing third in the 2017 Venice Ladies Skate Jam, by Jeff Greenwood

JEFF GREENWOOD / CONCRETE DISCIPLES

Judi Oyama racing slalom in her sixties as a member of Team USA at a World Cup event

Jean Rusen, in her late forties, blasts over a gap on the vert ramp in Malmo, Sweden, 2017, by Björn Handell

"I'm super stoked. I never thought I'd still be skating now. I thought Argentina [World Skate Games 2022] was going to be my last time. But I keep showing up, getting fourth and doing alright."[8] It has been so encouraging to witness Judi's perseverance, which is now receiving proper acknowledgment in the media. Her lifelong sponsor, Santa Cruz Skateboards, honored her in its fiftieth year celebration with a video that went viral. In it, Judi said, "An age doesn't mean you're done. If you love doing something, keep doing it."[9]

Judi began skateboarding at age thirteen and fell in love with it, entering her first slalom contest at Capitola two years later in 1975. The following year, at age sixteen, Judi became a sponsored amateur for Santa Cruz and Independent Trucks. Judi also rode for OJ Wheels, Park Riders, and Cellblock, brands owned by Jay Shuirman and Rich Novak, whom she ended up working for, using her talent in graphic design, which she studied at the San Jose State University.

Back in 1976, there was a fantastic photo shoot of the Santa Cruz team at Sierra Wave by Billing Golding, which included a group shot and a classic portrait of Judi. That shot was published in the book *Game Changers: The Unsung Heroines of Sports History* (2016) by Molly Schiot. Judi has also offered gratitude to her dad, a professional photographer, for "capturing decades of photos of my skating. He never told me I couldn't do something, and to this day is supportive (and unfazed) that I'm still skating. Thx, Dad."[10]

In the *National Skateboard Review*, Judi was represented with a photo in the "Special Women's Section"; the caption read,

> Skateboarding competitively for less than two years Judi Oyama has already become one of the top women slalom racers in the United States. In 1978 Judi has scored amateur competition victories in the Women's Slalom and Giant Slalom at Upland, CA and the Women's Slalom at SKATOPIA in Buena Park, CA. Judi looks forward to the professional races this year.[11]

In the 1970s and '80s, Judi recalled how, "You had to skate aggressive so you could get a run in at a park or a backyard pool. Respect from fellow riders had to be earned to find out where the secret spots were so you could skate them. Most of the time the guys you skated next to would barely speak to you."[12] And perhaps this is why Judi was always an advocate for her fellow female skateboarders, as expressed by Stephanie Person a few chapters earlier. Judi knew that that there "were few companies that truly supported women skaters,"[13] and that women had to elevate each other.

Judi was inducted into the Skateboarding Hall of Fame in 2018, and in her acceptance speech she said, "I've never been the best skater. Initially, I didn't skate for contest titles. I just skated for the fun of it — the mastery of shooting down a hill or reaching for a frontside grind in a 10-foot pool. It was always just me and my board."[14] Judi is a fountain of knowledge about skateboarding history and has experienced highs and lows over the decades, especially when it came to competitive skateboarding and the fickle world of contest judging, but the stopwatch doesn't lie, and Judi is flying. While she jokes about being mistaken for Peggy Oki, a fellow Japanese-American female skateboarder from the 1970s of Dogtown fame, it's appropriate that she is now recognized and validated for forging her own unique path, and it is a credit to Judi that she has consistently skated at such a high caliber for all these years.

Jean Rusen
Skateboarder (1990s-present)

Jean Rusen (aka Calamity Jean) is someone who has successfully ignored the assumption that skateboarding is purely a youthful pursuit, best taken up as a preteen before you have a chance to be deterred by pain and consumed by adult responsibilities. Jean is in her fifties, and she is a sponsored skater, surfer, musician, World Cup Skateboarding judge, and mother of two girls, Jada and Sadie.

Jean didn't start skateboarding until 1994 at age twenty-five, which might sound young but in the 1990s this decision was unusual. Jean had always been athletic, playing lacrosse and field hockey competitively in university and surfing in Ocean City, Maryland. And when she began spending winters in Tempe, Arizona, without access to the surf, skateboarding seemed like the best alternative.[15] There's even a tiny photo published in the mailbag section of the November 1994 issue of *Thrasher* showing Jean fearlessly bomb-diving a ditch called Hell Bank as a beginner.

From 1994 to 1997, Jean had access to a "beautiful, piece of shit ramp (and the crazy ass skaters who lived and sessioned there)"[16] in her backyard in Tempe. The ramp was a Frankenstein-like creation that evolved with added extensions, roll-in ramps, and bowled corners. Her new friends would take her to "huge ditches, burly pools, even hills and street spots." Jean's steady progression came with a series of "paying her dues" including "3 cracked teeth, one broken ankle, approximately 15 stitches, a mangled toe, bursitis of the knee, numerous sprained joints, extensive flesh loss, at least 2 concussions and more bumps, bruises and scrapes than I could ever keep track of. Oh yeah, not to forget, the dreaded staph [infection]"[17] over a fifteen-year period.

When a female-focused skateboarding pool and bowl contest series called Wicked Wahine was established at the Glendale skatepark, Jean made sure she was there. She placed second in the amateur division and competed at every Wicked Wahine event from 2004 to 2009, apart from one. And her efforts got noticed, resulting in Jean's first sponsorship at age thirty-five by the company Concrete Divas, based out of Idaho; she also got a cover shot and interview for the skate magazine *AZ Steez*, which is a major accomplishment at any age.

Jean loved entering contests, but she felt that being categorized with girls who were the same age as her daughters (because the female skaters were all lumped together) wasn't a healthy format. At the eleventh annual Tim Brauch Memorial Contest in 2009, Jean made the bold decision to compete in the grandmasters division against men her age, in their forties. The organizers said there was no rule against it, and she ended up placing twentieth out of twenty-four senior men. Jean was ranked in the World Cup men's masters division for three years in a row, with her best ranking in 2010, placing twenty-fourth out of seventy-nine men.

Contest organizers responded and began creating age divisions for female skaters, which further motivated women to compete. Jean's career highlight was at the Vans Girls Combi Pool Classic Contest in 2013. Jean was still competing against women barely closing in on thirty, but she felt proud to have placed third in the women's twenty-eight and over, receiving a cash prize. Jean's daughters waved handmade signs to encourage their "#1 MOM."

And then came the signature board. Hailey Villa, daughter of the legendary 1960s skater Patti McGee (who was on the May 1965 cover of *Life* magazine), had launched a company to honor her mom called Original Skate Betty. Hailey knew Jean because they were part of a skater girl gang in Arizona called Las ChicAZ, which was organized by Natalie Krishna Das. Jean was first invited to be on the Original Skate Betty team, and in 2015 they celebrated her with a "Calamity Jean" Masters signature board. The graphics were created by Shannon O'Connor from the animation department of *The Simpsons* and portrayed a cartoon purple octopus mom covered in tattoos, juggling beers, laundry, dishes, and baby octopi. It was a badass design for a badass mom.

In 2009, Jean explained that the accomplishments she was most proud of were related to being a mom. She had to be patient while pregnant, watching her friends skate, nursing her child in between runs at the skatepark, and then packing up her kids to travel to contests as a family.[18] Jean was a vocal advocate for finding ways for marginalized skaters to be positively recognized in skateboarding media and receive equal pay, and Jean extends this sentiment to all skateboarders, regardless of gender, sexuality, race, age, or ability. Jean shared with me how much she valued skateboarding's evolution to become more inclusive and welcoming, especially for nontraditional skaters.[19]

Jean proved that it's never too late to take up skateboarding, compete, get sponsored, and be part of a crew. Her vibrant presence has helped create space for older women to experience the festive energy of a skateboarding contest and feel appreciated. And when the beloved Vans Combi Pool Party Contest had their last-ever event in 2025, Don and Danielle Bostick of World Cup Skateboarding followed through on Kristy Van Doren's request for a female judge, and Jean was chosen to preside over the party, which was a true honor coming from the Vans family dynasty.

Amy Bradshaw
Skateboarder (1970s–present)

On Instagram, Amy Bradshaw has pegged herself @oldlady_skater, an identity which she celebrates. Over the years, Amy has documented her skateboarding progress in photos and videos, her wavy silver hair flowing, and has garnered a devoted following. She was born in Inglewood, California, in 1964 and started skating around age nine, thanks to one of her five older sisters who had a skateboard. "We all sort of shared everything. We were outside kids, riding bikes, skates, skateboards . . . I got pretty good on it. Then I guess in about 1976 I found urethane wheels and the San Gabriel River. It was a giant concrete banked riverbed and I became obsessed with it."[20]

Amy then became a regular at the Skatopia Skatepark after it opened in 1977. One day, Vans was having a tryout event for its amateur team at the park. "I really didn't want to try out but you could only skate if you were skating in the tryouts. So I tried out just so that I could skate for the day and I ended up making the Vans team."[21] Vans founder Paul Van Doren actively supported the community and described in his memoir how "each Vans store manager was encouraged to choose seven or eight skateboarders and supply them with shoes, and the skateboard companies donated their boards. Vans soon became an important partner and sponsor of the sport."[22] This meant that Amy, along with other amateur girls like Elaine Poirier, Heather Hall, Sunshine Lee, and Yvonne Cucci, were some of the earliest Vans riders, as well as more prominent competitors like Deanna Calkins, Edie Robertson, Ellen Oneal, Gale Webb, Jana Payne, and Terry Lawrence.

Amy enjoyed her time with Vans, performing demonstrations at Knott's Berry Farm and the Six Flags theme parks, and then joined the Sims Skateboards team. Amy had some solid contest results, but the events were more about catching up with friends and exploring an unfamiliar skatepark than achieving competitive success.[23] Amy stopped skating around age fifteen with all the skateparks closing and high school beginning, but in her thirty-year hiatus, she never stopped thinking about skateboarding. "During that time if I would see a freeway off-ramp, you know, like with the concrete in between or underpasses or overpasses, I'd always think, 'I could skate that.' . . . I thought about it all the time. Even when I wasn't skating, I was still a skater on the inside."[24]

In her early forties, Amy decided that she had done her time "adulting," and when her old Skatopia buddy Ken Hada invited her to skate, she went for it and discovered that the muscle memory was still there.[25] Amy became a regular with the Skateboard Moms and Sisters of Shred, initiated by Barb Odanaka in 2004, and began encouraging her peers to take up skateboarding. There's an awesome quote in a promo video for the group where Amy says skateboarding is "more fun than doing laundry or washing dishes."[26] And based on her Instagram activity, I would bet that she skates more today as a retired person than she did as a kid. In an interview for S1 Helmets, Amy said,

> I skate a lot lately. I went a couple weeks ago to the Orchid Ranch with a group of women. It's a wooden skatepark in a beautiful setting near Santa Barbara.

We were all different abilities, but we each had a goal. Everyone was pushing and laughing. We really enjoyed ourselves. There's a cool thing that happens in sessions where you really want to land your tricks and your friends help you believe it can happen. It comes out of nowhere. Kind of like magic![27]

Amy has even returned to contests on occasion. In 2017, she won the OG Jam Series for senior skaters at the Venice skatepark, grinding the pool coping with style and confidence, and followed it up with a third place finish in 2018. She was also acknowledged at the Third Annual Venice Ladies Jam in 2018, competing against sixteen riders in the twenty-five and over category. Amy has become an inspiration to many by simply doing what she loves and sharing her progress, without coming across like a marketing campaign, which is refreshing on social media. Amy is often seen skating with her best friend Julie Daniels (@jeezysk8s), blasting round a pump track, progressing in a mini-ramp or pool, jumping fences to access a stealthy spot, or cruising infinite lines on a snake-run. I turn to Amy's account in anticipation of a skateboard session to get me psyched.

Amy declared that skateboarding "saved me twice":[28] it was a positive way to occupy her time as a misfit teenager, and for the last fifteen years, it's been this incredible outlet for adventure and friendship. And now skateboarding is a bonding opportunity with her granddaughter who has recently taken it up, so long as a post-skate Slurpee is included in the day's agenda.

Beth Fishman and I settled into a Zoom interview in the early winter. I could see that she was camped out in her artist's studio, not unlike my mom's studio, with exposed wooden beams, pots of paintbrushes, canvases with bold abstract colors in varying stages of completion. I received a virtual tour that revealed rolls of paper and images pinned to the walls for inspiration and a mass of acrylic paints spread across her worktables. Originally, the space was designed to be Beth's glassblowing studio, but the need for a certain standard of ventilation meant that she was pursuing painting instead. In the background, on a worn lime-green couch I could see a small dog propped onto a pillow, passed out in a bundle of scruffy cuteness.

Beth was wearing a gray wool beanie and a black hooded puffy jacket to stay insulated, while I was layered in a vintage wool "Lady Pendleton" plaid shirt in shades of teal underneath a thick cardigan. We both felt the winter chill, but not for long. Our conversation started out in a predictable fashion because, like many skaters, Beth was fortunate to live in a beach town, although in New Jersey, not California. She had two older brothers, like me, and when Beth discovered one of their skateboards collecting dust in the basement, she began skateboarding in her driveway with a neighbor.

Beth noted that she had always been sporty, but skateboarding was an activity that she enjoyed immediately. "I loved it, and I just kept doing it and practicing tricks, and then they opened up the Paved Wave, which was in Oakhurst, New Jersey . . . it was the first skateboard park in New Jersey."[29] Beth's dad drove her to the park practically every day after school, happy to oblige his spirited daughter. There were no other girls in sight at the skatepark, but that was not a deterrent for Beth.

The New York skateboarding scene in the 1970s, unlike California, had harsh winters to contend with which meant that the activity wasn't quite as popular in comparison. In the 1978 article "Skating in the Big Apple" in *Skateboard World* magazine, the writer mentioned that there was a team called Performance Skateboard, which met up at Prospect Park and practiced on a collection of DIY wooden ramps. The subject of girls came up and it was declared,

> There are no girls in New York's only skateboard club — but none of the guys seem to miss them. "Girls around here are into disco. They're not into anything

good," says Sevino. "I can't blame them. You get kinda messed up riding around the city," responds his friend John. "Yeah, but in California girls are into it," Mick quickly points out, "Here, girls grow up too fast."[30]

And then turn the page, and voila! A photo of a girl kick-turning on the plywood ramp appeared with the caption "There are a few girls skating in the Big Apple." No shit.

Not far away, a team called the Islanders based out of a New Jersey surfing and skateboarding shop made a wise move and invited Beth to join them. "They had said to me, 'Hey, there's going to be a contest. And you can enter it skating for the team.' So, I was like, 'Okay, that's cool.'" Beth and I talked about the contest for some time and how she had to perform a five-minute choreographed freestyle routine and gain confidence skating on ramps. Beth admitted that she was competitive and became consumed by the challenge, rehearsing maneuvers in her driveway 24/7, even incorporating multiple boards into her routine for added difficulty.

"And so, the contest day comes, and I get there and it's like you saw in the article, five thousand people. It wasn't just Jersey; it was the East Coast championships. Tons of people . . . and I was really excited to do the routine I had practiced for weeks. I was thrilled to be there." Beth's family was also present, cheering for her as she performed her floor routine and tricks on a giant ramp. At some point, Beth's dad dashed away to bring Beth's grandma to the event, not wanting her to miss the action. And at the end of the day, the organizers called out the winners for her division. "The third place goes to John, second place goes Larry, and first place is Beth Fishman, and I'm like, 'Oh my god, I won,' It was an amazing feeling."

After Beth's win was announced, the treasured photo with her grandma Rose was taken by a journalist. Beth said it was rare for her to see a smile on her grandmother's face; she was a serious woman who had survived a harrowing journey as a Jewish immigrant fleeing to America. But what I didn't expect was for Beth to thank me. She had never seen the December 1977 article from the *National Skateboard Review* with her grandma's delightful quotes. I realized that the publication had been a California community newspaper, and an East Coast kid would have had no access to it. Beth said that the article's quotes were "literally like a message from the grave. That was like a gift for me." It felt good to be able to offer this fresh insight about Beth's grandma. And then she reciprocated with an epic story.

The day after the Eastern Skateboard Association championships, there was a phone call for Beth, which was strange because she rarely received a personal phone call as a kid. ABC wanted to feature her on television for a morning show in New York, and after getting her mom's permission, Beth found herself being interviewed alongside random people like the stylist Vidal Sassoon. Beth and her family were then featured on New Jersey public television (NJPTV) for a fifteen-minute segment, and newspaper and magazine articles interview requests followed. Every feature was clipped out and saved in a scrapbook, but this was all just a buildup to her big showcase.

While reviewing the recorded Zoom interview, I didn't even have to listen to the conversation to find the moment Beth dropped a bomb. I simply fast-forwarded to the point where I could see my eyes bugging out, my mouth hanging open, and a stunned expression on my face.

BETH: And then the big one was the *Kids Are People Too* [TV show].

NATALIE: Nice.

BETH: So, they were like, "We want you to be on this show." And the coolest thing, and this is another thing that I tear my hair out, the day I was on, Patti Smith . . .

NATALIE: Woah! Patti Smith.

BETH: . . . was on. With me!

NATALIE: That's so rad.

BETH: Dude.

NATALIE: [Speechless]

This opportunity to be on a children's variety show was pivotal for Beth. The episode was filmed in December 1978, and while waiting to perform on that long day of filming, Beth recalled how Patti Smith glided into the greenroom. "And she was amazing to me. I was a kid, and I was just like, 'Wow. Who is this woman? She's so powerful. She's so unusual. She's so cool.'" Beth spent the entire day with Patti because the filming began early morning and ran until late in the evening.

> Whenever there was a break or anything, she'd be like, "Hey kid, come with me." And we would hang out, and it was so cool. And we talked all day and then in the end of the day, she says to me — this is so funny — "What do you like to do besides skateboard?" And I said to Patti Smith, "Well, I like to write poetry."

The interview paused, and we looked at each other knowingly. Here was this innocent, oblivious child about to talk poetry with Patti Fucking Smith! The librarian in me was just dying with envy. I knew something magical was about to happen to Beth, and sure enough, Patti said, "Well, you know, I write poetry too. Come with me to my limo and I'll give you my new stuff." And that's exactly what happened. When they finished filming, Beth and Patti strolled out onto a wintery New York City street outside the recording studio. "Her limo pulls up and she gets out like this leather satchel, and she takes out all these papers and she hands them to me . . . She autographs it, *To Beth — the Champ*. And she says to me, 'You know, you're awesome. Such a cool kid.'" And then noticing that Beth was wearing braces, Patti said, "Take my advice, leave your braces on, because I tried to take mine off with a pair of pliers in my garage and it really fucked them up." At this point in the interview, we're both howling with laughter. Patti Smith rules.

I imagined that Patti, who was then in her early thirties, saw something of herself in young Beth. They both had roots in New Jersey, were fiercely independent, and lived a life that was true to themselves, which happened to be very cool — rock and roll music, skateboarding, and poetry. As Patti drove away, Beth shared how she thought to herself, *What a cool rocker lady*, but didn't clue in to Patti's identity until years later when the significance of their mutual appreciation for poetry hit home and felt like destiny.

The moment our interview was over, I tried to find the *Kids Are People Too* episode on YouTube. Instead of a singular video, I found Beth's performance on one clip and Patti's performance on an entirely different YouTube channel. You would have no idea that their paths had crossed, except for the fact that the host was wearing the same outfit — bell bottoms and a brown plaid shirt with flared collar. The stage was lit up like a Las Vegas showroom, and Patti sauntered out rocking some sweet cowboy boots and an oversized black smoking jacket in front of a cheering, youthful crowd. She perched on her tall chair and kicked out her heels, swinging her feet like a child. After a brief interview with the host, Patti launched into a raw and passionate rendition of "You Light Up My Life," accompanied by a pianist. A trippy light pattern, like a sun motif, was projected on the wall behind them.

For Beth's segment, the bulk of the footage was focused on child actor Adam Rich, who also liked skateboarding. He seemed to know that he was about to get schooled by the East Coast champion. The video is blurry, but Beth radiates confidence, wearing jeans and a sunshine-yellow long-sleeved shirt over a crisp white blouse and a matching yellow helmet. She brought out a ramp and easily performed a hippie jump over a measuring stick without any hesitation.

Beth would never forget her encounter with Patti. She continued writing poetry and kept up with her skateboarding. Beth has since had a prolific career as a multimedia artist, having studied at the Rhode Island School of Design and Pratt Institute. She became a glassblower and moved to Seattle to be part of the thriving glass-blowing community. Beth explained that glassblowing is also about movement and choreography, not unlike freestyle skateboarding, which she excelled at.

What I really wanted to know was if Beth ever reunited with Patti, and Beth confirmed that they came close decades later during one of Patti's book tours, which included a stop in Seattle. Beth purchased a ticket for the event, but Patti had injured her wrist, so she wasn't signing autographs for the public; the opportunity for a face-to-face encounter was lost. It was a packed house, so Beth sought out a stagehand and passed along a carefully wrapped, handblown vase, which she had made just for Patti and desperately hoped that it wouldn't be discarded.

If you've read anything by Patti Smith, you know that she cherishes the giving and receiving of simple gifts. Her publication *A Book of Days* (2022) is full of curated photographs and clusters of objects, which she describes as talismans. A seemingly insignificant item like a key ring, pair of reading glasses, or bandana becomes endowed with meaning when filtered through Patti's gaze and memory bank. And Beth reported that when Patti finally made an appearance, "She came out on stage, and she says, 'Hey, Seattle. It's so good to be here. I just got the most beautiful red glass vase. Whoever gave that to me, thank you so much. And somebody else gave me an apple pie.' And I was like, 'Oh my god, it made it!'"

I was relieved and delighted for Beth. If this conversation had happened ten or fifteen years ago, I may not have appreciated it as much, but now that I'm of a more mature age, I have a certain appreciation for Patti Smith. I'm inspired by how she's aged with grace, grit, and integrity, still living a creative and vibrant life despite fame. I also have a soft spot for acts of gratitude. It's important to find ways to say thank you to people who give you a piece of their time, right when you need it the most.

Beth's life trajectory had other significant events beyond this encounter with a rock legend. She had supportive parents who fostered her independence and competitive disposition, and a family that celebrated together in community, acknowledging their Jewish traditions. Even now, Beth continues to skateboard, and her experience, showing up as an older woman at a skatepark, has been consistently positive. She also has a group of friends in Seattle who meet up for a session of long-distance pumping, or LDP for short, and they cruise the streets en masse. Beth explained that "the thing with skateboarding is that it's all about consistency and just getting out there and doing it." It barely occurred to me that Beth was pushing sixty — she seemed so youthful. I felt like I was in my twenties again, chatting with a friend.

When you're in your teens and twenties, I think it's easy to take friendships for granted especially as a skateboarder. In the 1990s and early 2000s, there seemed to be a universal code of hospitality toward traveling skaters. In 1999, I had the opportunity to pursue a summer semester abroad in Prague, Czechia, at Charles University. My motives were not academic. I had heard of a derelict plaza covered in marble slabs where skateboarders gathered called Stalin, in reference to a monument that had been toppled, and I wanted to skate it. I had barely recuperated from jet lag and hadn't even visited the famous tourist spots, like Charles Bridge and the medieval astronomical clock in Old Town, before I bolted over to Stalin.

When I arrived at the skate spot, I instantly made friends with local skateboarders including two girls named Kate and Lucie

Kalinová. I remember feeling pleased that I had ventured out solo and had a means to connect with Czech youth. The girls I met were barely proficient in English, but we easily figured out a way to communicate and would meet up for skate sessions. At the end of my studies, I was invited to a family cottage in Bohemia and stayed at Kate's grandparents' home, experiencing a proper immersion. We might have had different backgrounds and upbringings, but because of this shared connection as female skateboarders, everything else was irrelevant.

In 2004, after living in Montréal, I returned to Vancouver and was excited but not surprised when I met Rhianon Bader at a Sunday soccer match in MacLean Park in Strathcona. This was not a sporting event but a weekly boozy gathering of skateboarders, art students, musicians, and other random dirtbag kids who occasionally chased a ball on the field and got some exercise. Rhianon was from Calgary and had produced an early skateboarding website called Skate of Mind in the 1990s. I had even quoted Rhianon in my thesis, particularly her interview with Jessie Van Roechoudt, the lone Canadian pro female skater in the 1990s who rode for Rookie, among many other sponsors, which made our meeting special.

My friendship with Rhianon would naturally evolve, especially after my apartment caught fire and we both ended up moving into the second floor of a heritage home, just blocks away from Antisocial Skateboard shop. We would learn to ride motorcycles together, purchasing beat-up 1970s Honda CB400s, and form a girl gang called the Majestic Unicorn Motorcycle Club with our fellow skater Erika Kinast. Our tea-drinking, bookish, skater nerd "gang" rocked denim vests, not unlike the Hags from Los Angeles, with a hand-stitched emblem of a purple unicorn and the letters MUMC. I liked the aesthetics of riding an old motorbike, even if it belched and backfired thanks to the DIY straight pipes my friend had welded on. A motorbike gave me freedom, access to distant skateparks, and a unique experience of being part of an inner circle of badass women.

We lived the dream as a skater-biker girl gang for a few glorious years before Rhianon and Erika left for Kabul to volunteer and work for Skateistan. The year they left, I was studying to become a librarian, and it was a harsh reminder that adulthood had descended. Making friends after being part of such a tight crew felt daunting. And the motivation to keep skating began to wane without friends my age.

This is why visibility and social media matters. I get excited when I see someone like Amy Bradshaw online, exploring new skateparks in the Californian sunshine with her buddy Julie Daniels, unconcerned with comments like, "Should you be doing that at your age?" It's important to see positive representations of senior women being adventurous, experiencing joy and friendship. Amy explained, "We just skate because it's freaking fun. We like to go somewhere new and then we'll kind of push each other like we're going to dial this in. We're gonna skate hard, learn new shit . . . it's just ridiculous, we're ridiculous!"[31] And if being ridiculous means going on road trips, signing yourself up for skate camp, exploring a different skatepark every day, and having a blast in your sixties, I am in. Bring on retirement.

And now I have a new friend to skate with. Did I manifest her into existence? How is it possible that an unknown female skater my age exists in a place that only a ferry boat or float plane can access? Just before we met at the skatepark, I was chatting with a little girl at the snake-run. She was so small, wearing coke-bottle glasses, and just a bundle of energy, marveling at how I could keep the momentum of my skateboard going without a push. And when my friend arrived and gave me a hug, this girl witnessed our bond: two women in their forties preparing for a skate session. I felt good, and with so many amazing matriarchs like Beth inspiring me, I'm no longer harboring my passion for skateboarding alone or with an ounce of embarrassment.

Jana Payne skating the Concrete Wave pool near Disneyland in Anaheim. The photo was published in the December 1977 issue of *Skateboarder* magazine

CHAPTER ELEVEN

ACCOUNTABILITY
(JANA PAYNE)

What gets me excited about researching and writing skateboarding history is finding threads that connect skateboarders across the decades, especially when I realize that a certain skateboarder inspired someone else to take it up, who motivated someone else to compete. I love seeing the domino effect of influence unfold. Jana Payne begat Terry Lawrence who begat Cara-Beth Burnside who begat an army. It's practically biblical. But when these threads are buried or severed and a legacy is ignored, it takes resolve to build that momentum again and reclaim history.

While it's important to have the facts in place, like contest results and a skater's sponsors, when there are gaps in the timeline and unexpected absences, I find that these blank spaces indicate a turning point and often contain a significant story. It could be a change in attitude toward women from the industry or something personal that occurred that altered the skater's path. I think of Denise Fleming who was sponsored by Pepsi and went pro for Powerflex in 1976. To see photos of Denise in her youth blowing bubble-gum while spinning 360s, wisps of blond hair streaming behind her as she rips around a pool, it's hard to envision that she would become a victim of a drive-by shooting incident in 2004 that left her wheelchair-bound for four years. If you saw her at a skatepark today, covered in tattoos and her hair streaked purple,

GIRL GANGS, ZINES, AND POWERSLIDES

you might sense she'd had a hard life, but the extent of adversity she has experienced is almost unimaginable.

I wouldn't be honoring people's stories if I skimmed over or ignored their struggles, especially when a person has explicitly sought me out to be their conduit for sharing and processing painful memories. Women in skateboarding have chosen a guaranteed portion of physical pain, but that doesn't mean they are so tough that they are unaffected by some of the more disdainful treatment of girls and women. And this is where you might want to pause; this chapter may be triggering as it deals with the sensitive topic of sexual violence. The #MeToo campaign has empowered women to speak out and demand accountability, but exploring trauma from one's past and deciding how to respond can take time and unfold differently for each individual.

Deep down I always knew that in doing this skate history project, I would become a keeper of secrets and confidences, entrusted with heartbreaking stories, because this was my experience back in 2002, interviewing my Skirtboarder friends for my thesis. I remember one evening when a group of us skaters came together for a potluck dinner at my friend's apartment, which was one of those classic Montréal walk-ups with a convenient fire escape, perfect for chain-smoking, swigging beer, and watching a summer sunset.

This gathering occurred midwinter, which meant that our skateboards were tucked away at home waiting for the ice to thaw. The indoor skatepark, the Taz Mahal, had ironically been shut down for a new library to be built in its stead, so we had to be patient. I never wrote about this night because I wasn't ready to position our conversation in an academic publication. I also didn't have the language to explore what we discussed with any theoretical distance, let alone a handy hashtag to allude to the topic without saying the word *rape*.

It was fun preparing food together. I had limited culinary skills and closely observed my friend create a basic oil and vinegar dressing with honey, lemon, balsamic, and Dijon mustard. This impressed me, and I was excited to replicate the simple recipe. Darkness came early, so we lit candles for the table, gathered round, and shared bottles of red wine. As we ate together, something shifted in our conversation. I don't know how it happened, but one of the girls asked our opinion of a date she had had. She knew what had happened was wrong. Her courage quickly gave the rest of the group permission to talk, and we all spoke of situations of sexual violence. It's tempting to offer up details, to name names of the perpetrators so that you can understand the scope and the gravity of what was revealed, but I know that would erode their trust. In summary, we cried, we felt angry, and we knew we were not alone.

Sometimes I wonder if we were drawn to skateboarding because we were broken, or if skateboarding was part of this breaking. A statistic was released by the World Health Organization stating that one in three women globally experience sexual violence across their lifetime, with one in four women aged fifteen to twenty-four years old experiencing violence by an intimate partner by the time they reach their mid-twenties.[1] And here we were confirming the stats like a focus group.

My friends and I never explored the significance of that evening's conversation, and maybe we should have, because certain destructive patterns in my life continued unchecked. At least we solidified as a crew. We skated with each other in the streets as a mob and felt invincible; we created videos, zines, and a website, and we made our presence known in the community. And after I moved away from Montréal, the Skirtboarders kept growing, with membership that can now boast an Olympian: Annie Guglia who represented Canada in women's street in Tokyo 2020 and is an LGBTQ2S+ icon. I am so proud to have played a small role in establishing a unique group of Canadian skaters.

I realize that my experience being part of girl gangs was a privileged one, as there are so many girls and women who have had to navigate violent situations without any support. I've also come to understand that sometimes the most courageous thing we can do to save ourselves from further harm is to disconnect and quit a path we're on until we're able to handle things in a healthy way and speak out from a position of strength. There's no shame in self-protection, and that's exactly how things evolved for Jana Payne.

Jana was raised in Anaheim, California, in a family with three brothers, and in the mid-1970s the Concrete Wave Skatepark opened right behind Disneyland, only five blocks from Jana's house. Jana said she was very enterprising at Concrete Wave and offered to help around the park, sweeping and picking up abandoned safety gear, to avoid paying an entry fee. After only three months skating the park, Jana was recruited for the Concrete Wave team, and other sponsors soon followed including Vans, Sims, and Gordon & Smith (G&S).[2] Becoming a skateboarder felt natural for Jana. "I found exactly the thing I wanted to do, and it was easy, and I had such a great time doing it. I was a gymnast before that and did other athletic things, but nothing that, you know, gave me the thrill [like skateboarding]."[3] Jana felt at home on a skateboard and in control.

In the November 1977 issue of *Skateboarder*, Jana received a "Who's Hot!" feature at age fourteen. Jana shared that technically she was "standing up and riding" a skateboard at age one, but that it was only years later when her big brother Bob took up freestyle that she received some instruction. Jana was highly praised in the article.

> However, more so than the sheer practice or exposure to hot riding, the basis for Jana's swift improvement has been a wide variety of good places to skate. She rode the popular Fruit Bowl a few times before it was destroyed, hitting tiles her second or third day. A number of trips to the Pipeline Skatepark has left her comfortable in the big bowls and hitting above vertical in the pipe. And, within a few days after the completion of the Wave's new pool, Jana was already one-wheeling the coping.[4]

Jana was considered a radical skater, and the photographer for the feature, James Cassimus, described her as the hottest female skater in the scene.

In a recent conversation about the "Who's Hot!" interview, Jana laughed at some of her youthful defiance and cluelessness, like being proud of accosting a boy for cutting her off and then calling the women's lib movement "dumb." Teenaged Jana decided that because she was going to do whatever she wanted no matter what, feminism had no bearing on her actions.[5] "I was kind of aggressive sometimes with other kids, and especially boys. You know they were not treating me right. I had two brothers that were older than me, so I didn't have any problems sticking up for myself . . . I had a big mouth."[6]

Jana loved skating the Fruit Bowl at the Concrete Wave, sneaking into empty pools during California droughts, as well as eighteen-foot steel pipes behind barbed wire at a manufacturing company where she got chased by a Doberman.[7] She then moved onto higher quality pools at skateparks like the Big O and Skatopia where she learned to progress in vert and started competing. Jana even had access to a team manager from one of her sponsors, who was expected to provide coaching and guidance to young skaters representing the brand and transport them to contests and demos in the team van. As a talented skateboarder and father, this man was a trusted mentor.

In July 1978, at the California State Championships held at Skatopia, Jana won the girls thirteen and over pipe-riding and slalom events, and with a combined effort of second in giant slalom and fourth in freestyle, she was declared the state champion for her age group. Based on Jana's competitive results and influence during the 1970s, she was an obvious candidate for a Skateboarding Hall of Fame award. In November 2022, at the Vans headquarters in Costa Mesa, Jana prepared herself to receive the award and simultaneously share why she disappeared from the skateboarding scene in 1979.

Jana's story was not the typical scenario: she did not choose to pursue higher education or discover that her local skatepark closed and opt for another sport. Jana boldly stood on stage in front of the crowd, full of industry leaders and skateboarding heroes, and declared,

> I want to stand up here for women in sports. I left skateboarding because I got molested by my coach. And I think that's something that we need to talk about, and people have been talking about it . . .
>
> I love the sport, but I left it in a sense to save myself from more harm. And I'm just so grateful — this is a very healing moment for me to honor that little girl inside of me that was so dishonored all those years ago. Thank you so much — it means so much to me.[8]

In a recording of the event, gasps are audible from the attendees followed by applause. Usually, the event is all about the glory of skateboarding with videos and speeches from peers honoring the recipients, and Jana interrupted the vibe. She knew that some of the audience members could connect the dots to her former team manager, and perhaps there was some discomfort, with people wondering what this public revelation would mean. Jana wasn't asking for people to take sides; she just wanted healing and to be known.

I was expecting a real shake-up after Jana's act of bravery, some kind of statement or acknowledgment among that generation of older skateboarders from the 1970s, and when nothing happened, I decided to reach out. My invitation to Jana was welcomed, and our conversation proved to be therapeutic for us both. I will say that Jana's story of being groomed and what occurred in that team van is seared in my memory, but I am honored that she spoke her truth to me.

The participants of the 2011 Annual Mighty Mama Skate-O-Rama, organized by Barb Odanaka from 2004 to the present

SAFE SPACES

Barb Odanaka
Skateboarder, author, founder of Mighty Mama Skate-O-Rama (2004–present)

Barbara Ludovise Odanaka's return to skateboarding as an adult in the early 2000s was the ultimate power move. Her decision resulted in a whole community of older women taking up skateboarding and defying expectations. But it was only after hearing Jana Payne speak out at the Skateboarding Hall of Fame that she came forward with her own #MeToo story. I was sought out to be the recipient of this story, and with Barb's permission, it was posted online to give others courage.

Barb was originally from Los Angeles before moving to Newport Beach, Orange County, in fourth grade. She looked up to her siblings, including a big brother thirteen years older than her who was obsessed with surfing. While surfing was never her calling, Barb was attracted to the culture, and skateboarding became her "in," which all began with a Hobie Super Surfer that she received for Christmas in 1972 at age ten.[9] In 1975, Barb was documented by her friend Dean Bradley while cruising a local ditch on her skateboard with the neighborhood kids. The black-and-white photos showcase a scene of boys and girls, all with long shaggy hair, some barefoot, enjoying their freedom. Barb recalled feeling completely accepted as an equal among this group. In fact, she was "always surprised to hear from other women when they would reminisce about being the only girl . . . or not being treated the same as the boys."[10]

Two years later, when Barb competed for Hobie Skateboards at the Oceanside Championships in August 1977, another photographer, Ed Economy, captured a critical moment: Barb had placed second in freestyle, and in the photo she's standing near a group of skaters, including Jana Payne. This would be Barb's one and only contest. Knowing what I know now, it's surreal to see Barb and Jana connected even way back then. When the photos were sent to Barb via Facebook, she burst into tears. "I was just so touched . . . I had a happy young childhood, and that was so special to get those pictures. It was so cool, just that slice of life . . . It's not like, oh, here's a picture of you with your teddy bear or climbing a tree, but oh my God, somebody has documentation that I actually was in that world, and it was really exciting."[11]

Our conversation then shifted to why Barb stopped skateboarding, and I was able to appreciate the impact of those cherished photos at a deeper level.

> It's actually a sad story. I had only been on the Hobie amateur team for six months or so when my high school cross-country coach said, "Well, you know you have to quit skateboarding." I remember just being like, "What?" But let's just say he was very persuasive.

I wish I could go back to that moment and shake my little self and say, "Don't let him do that to you!" And this is something I really haven't talked publicly about, but that same running coach, who was twice my age and married to our co-coach, began grooming me for what became a sexually abusive relationship. So not only did I lose skateboarding, I lost my innocence as well.

Barb's experience was traumatic, something she is still processing and healing from today, but in sharing her story, she was also relaying a message to Jana Payne: *I hear you.*

In 1995, Barb wrote an article on the 1970s skateboarding scene when she was working as a reporter and columnist for the *Los Angeles Times*. Barb wrote, "They soared like phantoms through the cool, night air. Gliding down smooth streets, unable to contain their Cheshire cat grins . . . You could hear them coming from a half-block away. *Clicketyclack, clicketyclack,* rolling down the sidewalks, riding that imaginary wave."[12] Barb's editor appreciated her poetic voice and encouraged her to launch a career as a children's picture book author, which naturally started with a book about skateboarding.

Barb was a new mom at age thirty-five with a colicky baby, and her therapist advised her to pursue a positive outlet, something that once made her happy, and she instantly thought, "Skateboarding!"[13] Barb said, "When I first got back on a board, I found one of my Hobie boards and stepped on it and I was suddenly ten years old again."[14] Barb felt liberated, and her reunion with skateboarding ended up impacting countless other women. In 2004, Barb launched her first children's book called *Skateboard Mom* at a local skateboard park, all about a mom who steals her son's skateboard and goes wild. At that inaugural event, nineteen skateboarding moms came out including Venice Beach legend Liz

Bevington, aged eighty, and "Calamity Jean" Rusen with her five-year old daughter, Jada.

The unique book event and title captured the imagination of newspapers including an *LA Times* article "Mothers Are Big Wheels" and a *New York Daily News* feature titled "Mom Is a Shredder." Barb was then motivated to establish a group of like-minded skateboarding women, which quickly expanded into a nonprofit organization called Skateboard Moms and the Sisters of Shred. Thanks to social media, members could reach out to each other, send encouragement, and organize workshops and skate sessions just for them. Reading through the blogs and posts, I can tell how important skateboarding and community is to them — that sense of accomplishment resonates no matter one's ability or age.

In time, the group was catapulted into the limelight because these badass senior women were annihilating stereotypes, and news agencies were fascinated. In the February–March 2016 issue of the *American Association of Retired Persons* (AARP) magazine, an article honored Barb and several participants, including Stevie Vanguard, Amy Bradshaw, Tamra Bowman, Claudia Hoag, Eva Armanto, Teresa McCabe, and Sandra Serna. There was also an accompanying video released called "Skateboarding in Her 50s and Killing It," which has racked up millions of views on various platforms. I remember watching it myself before returning to skateboarding in my early forties and feeling inspired.

Barb's book launch in 2004 became an annual event on Mother's Day called the Mighty Mama Skate-O-Rama, and it fundraises for children's organizations and victims of human trafficking. The event celebrated its twentieth anniversary in 2024. And while Barb's running coach convinced her to abandon skateboarding as a teen, "it's just that much more meaningful getting back on that board. It was like reclaiming my innocence . . . I'm sorry to bring that dark cloud over it, but I think it's important to start talking about it. Every time I hear another woman tell her story, I just feel like, 'It's time I start telling mine.'"[15]

Skate Like a Girl
Inclusive skateboarding program (2000–present)

Skate Like a Girl has developed over the last twenty-plus years from a simple concept in 2000, providing workshops and events for girls, to an inclusive community, actively extending support to trans and gender non-conforming skaters by offering safe spaces and clinics. Its vision is social equity, "promoting confidence, leadership, and social justice through skateboarding,"[16] as well as racial justice and trans rights, and its model has been replicated worldwide.

Skate Like a Girl began with Holly Sheehan who grew up in the North Bay region of San Francisco. She noticed a severe lack of representation of female skaters in the late 1980s. When Holly relocated to Olympia, Washington, to attend Evergreen College and met Fleur Larsen through the college snowboard team, something sparked between them. In August 2000, a six-day festival called Ladyfest was organized in response to the sexual assaults that happened at the 1999 Woodstock festival,[17] and "Holly and Fleur [were] committed to the coordination of a skateboard workshop and session to be held at Olympia's Yauger Skatepark."[18] The festival planning minutes record some trepidation — the organizers didn't have insurance to cover injuries — "but we're glad it is happening because it sounds cool."[19]

The response to the skateboard event was profound, and it was estimated that fifty participants came out to their follow-up event. "Fleur and Holly were inundated with requests, e-mails, and phone calls asking when another workshop and session would happen. The resulting thoughts, conversations, and organizing would lead to the official foundation of Skate Like a Girl."[20] One of their volunteers, Nancy Chang, helped turn the grassroots organization into a nonprofit back in 2009, always with the mission of striving for social justice.[21] And ever since those inaugural events, thousands of skateboarders have gained confidence and community because of Skate Like a Girl programs.

Hosting skate sessions exclusive to girls was not a new phenomenon. In the June 1978 issue of the *National Skateboard Review*, a feature called the "Special Women's Section" included a report on a successful meet-up for girls. Di Dootson Rose wrote,

> Girls' Night at the Runway Skatepark in Carson, Calif, has the best turn out of girls yet. They draw about 150 girls on their special Wednesday night programs . . . It is this kind of "hanging out" where skaters get the pointers from others that helps them improve.[22]

A photo accompanied the article: a group of girls at Runway huddling around professional skater Deanna Calkins, who represented Hobie skateboards and was providing some instruction. The difference with Skate Like a Girl, compared to these early gatherings, is that it's not only about learning new skate tricks; there's also a focus on leadership.

Skate Like a Girl offers mentorship, and the Skateboarding Inclusivity Program provides a unique curriculum designed to develop leaders who value inclusion and accountability to help make skateboarding accessible and safe for all. Skateboarding leaders who have emerged from these programs include Kim Woozy, the director of development for Skate Like a Girl, who produced the female-focused MAHFIA.TV network and advocated for the "Equal Pay for Equal Play" state bill in California; Alex White, the current chair of Skate Like a Girl, renowned for her history as a pro skater and roles as Krux brand manager and contest announcer; and Kristin Ebeling, executive director, pro skater for Meow, Krux team manager, and past creator of the *Skate Witches* zine. It's not uncommon for a Skate Like a Girl workshop participant to become a mentor and skateboard instructor, which helps maintain the vision and ensure the longevity of the program. The core locations for Skate Like a Girl are Seattle, Portland, and the San Francisco Bay Area, with activities in twenty other cities. These chapters host a skate session every week to suit a range of abilities and backgrounds, along with youth camps, outreach, adult, and trans sessions.

Skate Like a Girl also organizes the highly anticipated Wheels of Fortune contest in Seattle, which is a weekend festival including a hilarious scavenger hunt; it was highlighted in the documentary *Skate Dreams* (2022). The Witch Hunt is another nod to Danny Plotnick's cult classic film *Skate Witches* (1986); skaters are encouraged to take over the city streets and document their assigned tasks as a team. While the contest draws leading female and non-binary pros from around the world, Wheels of Fortune is more about being an inclusive celebration of community centered on having fun. You might come home with a bizarre new haircut or random tattoo after the event, but you'll also have a story to share and a ton of new friends.

Consent Is Rad
Safe and inclusive spaces campaign in skateboarding (2019–present)

The Consent Is Rad campaign — now under the umbrella of Respect Is Rad — was co-founded by Dr. Indigo Willing, Evie Ryder, Miljana Miljevic, and other female and non-binary skaters eager to educate their skateboarding communities. The campaign recognizes the need to normalize cultures of consent and respectful interactions at skateparks and online. At the 2019 Pushing Boarders conference in Malmö, Sweden, the campaign was propelled by Indigo Willing, who is a skateboarder, sociologist, mother, professor, war orphan, and coauthor of *Skateboarding, Power and Change* (2023) with Anthony Pappalardo.[23] Along with its international launch, the campaign's momentum has been bolstered through social media, skateboarding events, and a website full of resources, including services for survivors.[24] The powerful message that consent *is* rad has gained traction in the global skateboarding community.

Consent Is Rad takes pride in its collaborations with individuals and other skateboarding groups such as Break the Cycle in 2020, which was a community initiative where multiple organizations presented a series of questions and answers that explained why preventing sexual violence matters and how to enact change. There has also been positive support by mainstream magazines like *Thrasher* and nontraditional skateboard magazines like *Dolores*. Such wide coverage includes "audiences of young cis-men who are not often prompted to think about rape culture in skating and how to shift to cultures of consent."[25] The initiative also requires careful moderating, cyber safety, perseverance, and care planning for its volunteers. Willing stated that "any campaign focused on inclusion may need to navigate things like staff debriefing and practicing healthy boundaries and clear guidelines"[26] for everyone's safety.

Skateboarding projects like Consent Is Rad include people who have traversed a lifetime of adversity. To *Skateism* magazine, Indigo said,

> I've always wanted to skateboard. But it was also a hard time growing up in 1970s Australia. You need courage to skate and I had that, but it was being used up elsewhere in my teen years. As a war orphan from the Vietnam War, as a refugee and adoptee being the only Asian raised in an all white family, it was hard feeling at home in the world.[27]

Indigo, now in her fifties, only began skateboarding at age forty-one, and even when she felt like the "oldest person in the world at the skatepark," she found inspiration online, including a connection with Barb Odanaka's Skateboard Moms and Sisters of Shred.

In April 2023, the Consent Is Rad team was nominated by Skate Like a Girl in the best non-profit or social project category for the Get On Board Awards. The team won in a tie with the Canadian-based initiative Nations Skate Youth — led by Rose Archie who is sponsored by the Indigenous-owned brand Colonialism — which expands access to skateboarding for Indigenous youth through workshops and skate demos. It is evident that women are actively changing the skateboarding landscape for the better by proposing radical empathy as the alternative to toxic behavior while maintaining a no naming, shaming, or blaming mandate.

Dr. Willing's research aims to understand the broader social reasons for sexual violence that can sometimes go unacknowledged in skateboarding; her work includes an academic study of the cult classic film *Kids* (1995),[28] which included scenes of sexual assault and coercion within a New York skateboarding community. Her book also highlights the foundational work of organizations, individuals, and companies, including DIY publications like the zines *No Consent = Sexual Abuse* by Tessa Fox, *Smash the Skatriarchy* and *Times Up: No More Rape Culture in Our Skate Culture* by Amelia Bjesse-Puffin, among others. It was exciting to be reminded that tactile zines still have an impact today by discussing challenging topics and calling out inequity.

I love the vision of the team behind Respect Is Rad/Consent Is Rad. Dr. Willing sees that we each can have a role: "We all play a part in mapping the history and evolutions in skateboarding. As individuals or collectives, what we cannot help but bring to skateboarding are our various social, historical and cultural lenses, mosaics of differing experiences, and rich range of ways to construct and carry out our identities."[29] While there's still work to be done to ensure that skateboarding is welcoming for all, the Consent Is Rad campaign is dedicated to education, and it radiates hope and inspires courage for skateboarders to be agents of change and work together to prevent sexual violence.

As a fifteen-year-old in 1979, Jana Payne chose to quit skateboarding — the one thing that gave her joy — to protect herself. She said,

> There was really not a lot of women there to advocate for young girls and being in a male-dominated sport, and having coaches that were male, I ended up being molested and that totally scared me. I was supposed to go out of the country with my team, and I was scared. And so, I just decided to save myself — I would quit skateboarding even though it was a huge thing for me.[30]

Jana realized that the skatepark was no longer a safe place, and her skateboarding coach was not the mentor she needed; he was a predator.

The hardest part for Jana was the lack of curiosity from her friends and family over her decision to quit skateboarding, even though she had just become the California state champion and was invited to travel overseas with her sponsor's team. "I quit and left that industry, and nobody ever asked me like, 'Hey, what's going on,' you know? I just disappeared and I didn't have a safe place to tell anybody what happened to me ... Being traumatized and not understanding it — hiding it."[31] This was the turning point for Jana, a kind of benchmark of going downhill because she lost her friends, her sense of identity, and she couldn't explain what happened to herself, let alone to her parents, who weren't invested in her life.

Jana shared that her mother was not a fan of her daughter's skateboarding, or anything perceived as masculine. Jana's mom had been diagnosed with bipolar disorder and was raising Jana's brother who had cerebral palsy, and this intense home life left Jana feeling rejected, like she wasn't a cherished daughter.[32] As an adult, looking back on video footage of herself as a girl, Jana could see how she was trying to project a tough persona as a competitive skateboarder, but in truth, she was lonely, and her self-esteem was soon obliterated. Jana's team manager must have recognized her vulnerability. She was targeted, groomed, and convinced that, even though she was a teen, she was "having an affair" with a grown man. Jana referred to the HBO drama *The Tale* (2018), directed by Jennifer Fox and based on the sexual abuse she endured from a coach, as being particularly evocative of Jana's own experience.

Over the years, Jana experienced significant adversity, even going temporarily blind in 2015, but emphasized the impact of therapy, meditation, and being kind to yourself. She has also used making art as a "vehicle to connect with people," which led to a career in sculpture and commercial design.[33] But it was the #MeToo movement that prompted Jana to speak out, because it helped her overcome a fear of being demonized and called a liar. In sharing her story, Jana wanted to bring awareness to the skateboarding community that there are vulnerable children participating without a network of family support, and it's up to us to ensure that they are not grossly violated by adults in positions of trust and power. We would be deluding ourselves if we thought skateboarding was exempt from the sexual violence that's been exposed between coaches and young athletes in sports like gymnastics and hockey.

After her Skateboarding Hall of Fame speech, Jana was met mostly with silence. She was anticipating at least some words of comfort or affirmation from her old skateboarding community, but the lack of engagement left her feeling disoriented and hurt. "No one has contacted me since. It's just like I got my award and it's like, 'See you later.'"[34] It's possible that audience members had their own trauma to deal with, but it had been ten years since Jana first revealed her story on a podcast, and she was hoping to prompt some conversations. Despite the minimal response, Jana believes that "we're in this multigenerational healing [process] and people are tired of abuse, and people want to stand up to it."[35]

Whenever I've held onto hurtful memories with bitterness, I have ended up not liking myself. I know that bitterness can make me feel powerful for a moment, but ultimately it's destructive, especially when repetitive thoughts like *What if I had punched him in the face and screamed?* keep me tied to the past. It depletes me of energy. I think it's okay to be mad, especially when there's been injustice, but it's better to find a way to release the pain in a way that doesn't self-sabotage.

In my conversation with Jana, I shared how at age twenty-nine, in 2007, I phased out of skateboarding. It wasn't a hard stop, but I realized that skateboarding had become another identity I was using to mask personal pain. I needed a new outlet and to end a pattern of rejection from men that generated more acts of desperation, that made me stop loving myself. My #MeToo count had peaked. I had had several near misses, several encounters that crossed a line in consent and have thankfully been blurred by EMDR therapy, and then a situation that landed me at an organization called Rape Relief.

I was feeling empty, and as Barb Odanaka did, I tried to remember a time when I was happy and felt confident in my body. For me, that was being an eleven-year-old, when I loved running. I had an energetic golden Labrador, and we would take off from my house on a run and end up flying through the wooded trails of Harrison Park in Owen Sound in all seasons. I wanted to feel like a child again, so I chose to return to running, and I ran like a fiend.

I was pursuing my studies as a librarian at the time, and I likely appeared accomplished and self-assured, even though I was sitting in a lot of darkness. With running, I could clear my mind and focus solely on getting strong, perfecting my technique, repeating the lyrics of a song, and purging myself of nagging thoughts. It wasn't long before I could run for hours, looping around the seawall or out to the UBC campus and back. After six months of training, I entered the local marathon and completed it in 3:13, within the qualification range for the Boston Marathon.

The following summer, I was signed up to do a practicum at the San Francisco Public Library and entered the local marathon. I followed a schedule to build up mileage, but I only had one speed — as fast as I could go for every single run. The course was grueling with steep downhill sections at the exact moment your quads are ready to collapse, but I survived. Plus, my friends and girl gang members, Rhianon and Erika, rode their motorcycles down from Vancouver and cruised alongside me on their skateboards, powering me up to the finish line. I took off another minute, placing fifth out of 1,500 female runners. I was physically strong, but something still wasn't right.

Running was a great distraction, but the bubble burst when injuries debilitated me. Fortunately, this was around the time I began the real work to resolve feelings of disconnection and unhappiness. Prompted by a wise and compassionate person, I began working with a counselor. Each week we would go deeper into my past through prompts, and I would dismantle my judgmental thoughts that labeled me as ugly, unworthy, and undeserving of love.

And then fast-forward almost fifteen years later, and here I am listening to Jana talk about forgiveness and healing. I felt supported talking to her, but I had not been a child when this last negative encounter happened, and my sense of trust in adults had not been betrayed. I have only the deepest empathy for those who have been traumatized as children, someone like Jana who is bravely doing the work to renew herself and is now able to tell others that they are cherished. I know some might read this and find fault with such emotional sentiment in a book about skateboarding, but I genuinely want women, children, and non-binary people to feel safe. I'm tired of systems of power that infect mostly men's brains compelling them to prey on children, beat-up their girlfriends, or murder their partners. It's fucked up and infuriating.

I keep returning to Jana's words because they cause me to pause, breathe, and reflect, and she has more grace than I do. She told me,

> Underneath all of it, these predators have trauma as well, so I try not to condemn people . . . If we don't embrace each other, if we don't forgive each other, we are divided. I'm divided if I'm hating people and not trying to learn to understand what they've been through, why they think the way they do, and what they're missing. If they're pointing their finger out, it means they're divided within. And the work that we have to do is to unite within ourselves, our dark side in our light side.[36]

What Jana is proposing is restorative justice, but it's not just about individual accountability between a perpetrator and a victim; it's the broader skateboarding industry as well. If you own a skateboarding company or a magazine and you learn that there's been an act of violence by someone associated with your brand, even if it was a historical situation, there is still an opportunity to call it out, condemn the behavior, and demonstrate humility. I would love to see this kind of resolution for Jana because she is such a beautiful human being who has no interest in shaming an individual or her past skateboarding sponsor.

To those skaters who have been victimized and are grappling with violent incidents from the past, there is no obligation to go public, deliver a statement, or do anything that might trigger stress and fresh wounds. But if this is a path that could offer healing, just know that your voice contributes to a message of zero tolerance and that you're not alone. In fact, more women, particularly those who skated in the 1970s, have since reached out to share their #MeToo stories, and it is a privilege to connect with them. I think of Judith Cohen, who had a similar experience to Jana in the late 1970s when she decided to quit her skateboard sponsor, the Brewer Team, for her own protection; she's now been inducted into the Florida Skateboard Hall of Fame.[37] It's our time to rise up, project strength and courage, own our place in skateboarding history, and demand supportive environments for all skaters, especially children.

I look to skateboarding platforms like the Goodpush Alliance as a leader in our community that prioritizes safety. Rhianon Bader, my former Majestic Unicorn Motorcycle Club girl gang member, helped initiate it as an extension of the work of Skateistan. Rhianon explained,

> I don't think I ever consciously worked to build connection in the skate scene until I joined Skateistan. Up until that point I had been quite selfishly enjoying skateboarding and the many positives it had brought to my life. But when I first started to hear about organizations like Skate Like a Girl in Seattle, or Uganda Skateboard Union, I was really intrigued by this idea of sharing the gift of skateboarding with those who might not be able to easily access it, for whatever reason. Then I read an article about the opening of Skateistan's first skate school in Kabul that had photos of Afghan girls shredding and I felt so inspired. I went to their website and applied to volunteer immediately.[38]

The experience of working with Skateistan and then witnessing the demand for comparable programs around the world motivated Bader and her team to develop the Goodpush Alliance. This resource hub and knowledge-sharing network supports grassroots skateboarding initiatives in over one hundred countries, providing a forum, toolkits, program templates for skateboarding instruction, online training and webinars, and funding.[39] The Goodpush Alliance advocates for widespread change, such as the Commitment to Anti-Racism in Skateboarding project established in May 2021. This commitment has over one thousand signatories, including skateboard companies, governing bodies, nonprofits, and regular skaters.

The Goodpush is also dedicated to child protection because any "skateboarding project working with children has the responsibility to protect its participants from abuse, exploitation and/or neglect, within their programs and externally."[40] The Goodpush offers examples of codes of conduct, safe program partners, incident reporting, recruitment best practices, and even a template of a Child Protection Pledge for a team of instructors to sign. If a company is sponsoring underage skateboarders, they should use these methods on skateboard tours and in their training facilities. When skateboarders proactively commit to safety and accountability, the likelihood of sexual violence and exploitation is lessened, and that includes online activity.

Parental involvement is obviously at the heart of ensuring a child's safety, and it's evident through social media that there are parents heavily involved in celebrating their daughters' passion for skateboarding today. Most of these parent-run accounts simply celebrate their child's dedication and create memories, but sometimes things begin to blur. When a video goes viral, brands may approach these families, offering product endorsements and new followers. There is, of course, a dark cloud hovering over the intersection of internet fame and capitalism, like the extreme situation described in a *New York Times* article called "A Marketplace of Girl

Influencers Managed by Moms and Stalked by Men."[41] Validation and financial support can be game changers, but they can also be accompanied by the attention of toxic strangers, public scrutiny, or worse. Let's live and skate with compassion and integrity.

Canadian champion Pam Judge rocking a cast from a skiing accident while skating the Oasis skatepark, documented by Arne Ratermanis in May 1979

CONCLUSION
(PAM JUDGE)

I always thought that my fixation with the history of women in skateboarding would lead to a substantial book showcasing glorious photos from across the decades. It's still a project worth doing, but I believe it was for the best that I've been delayed in producing the "ultimate visual guide." I needed to grow, I needed confidence, and during the pandemic, I needed a research outlet. It would be inaccurate to suggest that I have COVID-19 to thank for motivating me to seek out connection because I am practically a hermit and forced isolation wasn't a burden. But those unusual times did encourage me to go online and explore social media. And it turns out that contributing historical context to an activity like skateboarding provided me with fulfillment, friendships, and opportunities that I never knew were possible.

I can see now how my early publication dream resulted in a hoarding mentality — waiting for that perfect moment to reveal my curated mother lode of facts and images in some monumental throw down. But hoarding information as a librarian is equivalent to a Mandalorian removing their helmet — that is *not* "the way." These aren't *my* stories; I've just been motivated enough to have recorded names, accumulated zines, and kept the content organized for the last twenty years.

GIRL GANGS, ZINES, AND POWERSLIDES

Knowing what I know now about the expanse of women's skateboarding history, I find my early writing attempts comical. A chapter in my 2003 thesis paper, an essay in a 2007 academic journal, a hand-written column for the Antisocial zine *Idlewood* (2009–2014), followed by a self-published ebook on the topic in 2014 — all of it now seems like a superficial scratch. And yet it makes sense that it has taken so long to gather substantial documentation. In the early 2000s, social media platforms were in a juvenile state. I had limited means to connect with the skaters themselves, let alone conduct interviews or source vintage photos.

The biggest challenge has been letting it all go, allowing whoever the internet leads to my website or Instagram account to comment, reinterpret, and poach if that's their heart's desire. I have no paywall or exclusive subscription, just open access because archival silence blows, and I want no part of it. Occasionally, I've experienced a twinge of irritation when I've worked hard at developing a full report, and then it's instantaneously regurgitated and uncredited on another venue. This has begun to happen more frequently thanks to AI. I've witnessed my content get stripped word for word and reposted without credit on a website that claims to support women, except for those who do the research apparently. But I remind myself that this project is about spreading awareness and validating the skaters themselves — that's the big picture goal. And at least the pleasure of unearthing someone's story and receiving some gratitude can never be taken away from me, which has been a real privilege.

I still struggle with bouts of frustration because even though I love doing it, why should it take an obsessive librarian an absurd number of hours, days, months, and now years to scour magazines and newspaper databases, sort through Facebook photo albums, cling to names and rumors of someone's sister being a skater, to dredge up and consolidate this history? I'm not content with seeing a small handful of women be tokenized, especially when there are skateboarders around the world who remain mostly unknown but whose stories could have an impact on their community. I just wish it wasn't such an ordeal, but then again, if it was easy, it wouldn't be as fulfilling. Kind of like skateboarding.

Consider PJ McKenzie, known as Pam Judge in her competitive years, who was the first female Canadian national skateboarding champion in 1977 and 1978. Her name should be revered among Canadian skateboarders and historians, but I had to tease this needle out of a haystack, and I only connected with her by luck. I had never heard of Pam before launching the archive, and there is no reason why I should have because she has never been properly celebrated outside a few Canadian newspaper clippings from the '70s and a skateboarding newsletter called *The Canadian Pipeline*.

I was fortunate to have found a profile on Facebook called Da Mad Taco Skates Again (whoever you are, I owe you a beer or perhaps a keg?) loaded with vintage magazines and random photos. During a deep dive of this account, I saw an unfamiliar girl grinding the coping of a pool at the Oasis Skatepark in Mission Valley, California, in 1979. Her left arm was bound by a cast from a skiing accident and the caption stated that "Pam" was a skier from Canada staying the summer in San Diego. My brain instantly sparked.

Being a diligent librarian, with an easy CTRL-F I cross-referenced my directory of every magazine issue I've consulted, the name of the skater, the page they appear, and a link when available, and I quickly found the article. Next to the entry for the July 1979 issue of *Skateboarder*, I had written "Pam Judge (Canada) has comments in contest article!" although I had yet to source a photo of her. The contest was the USASA Nationals in April 1979 at the Upland skatepark. Curtis Hesselgrave had wandered around, interviewing interesting new people in the scene including Pam. He wrote,

> Calgary is a ski town and naturally Pam is a skier, but Calgary also has a skatepark and Pam has been an active competitor there. She is the first skater from her area to come to the U.S. to compete. Although

she is somewhat behind U.S. women in her skate development, she doesn't feel that she or her fellow Canadians are that far behind. Given sufficient opportunity she feels that Canadian skaters can compete equally with those from the U.S. Pam says that SKATEBOARDER Magazine is the main source of inspiration to Canadian skaters. They learn maneuvers from the mag and it keeps their enthusiasm up.[1]

The contest results showed that Pam had placed first in the amateur women's sixteen to nineteen 2A category in freestyle, slalom, and bowl, representing her sponsor Gordon & Smith — a major U.S. skateboarding company. Now that I had her full name and city, I got to work pulling up newspaper clippings and found one from her ski racing years and several from her early days skateboarding in Alberta, but not a single lead regarding where she was today.

I hashed together a website bio for Pam followed by an Instagram post, waited for a bite from someone who recognized her, and then moved on. Seven months later, I received a message through the website contact form, and it was the kind of dream scenario I had always hoped for, a scenario which repeats itself today.

Hi Natalie,

Hope this finds you happy and healthy!!
I thought I might check google to see if I existed anywhere after 44 years, lo and behold, I found your article 3 days ago. So cool!! Please call me . . . Really would love to chat!! PJ

PJ would later tell me how she discovered the bio I'd written of her late one night, after she'd heard a whispering voice suggest that she Google herself. This was at a time when she was feeling down, having endured some health challenges and heartbreak. Our introduction felt miraculous, and it would only get better.

The interview didn't happen instantly. PJ's daughter reached out, informing me that her mom was readying herself to share and that she was living in a small picturesque mountain village called Kaslo, British Columbia, a place I had blasted through on my motorbike years ago on a camping trip. I had to wait a bit longer while PJ had a knee replacement, but when we finally connected over the phone, it was worth it. I was so inspired by our conversation that I traveled east to visit PJ over the Canada Day long weekend and had my first face-to-face interview with a stranger.

The Rosewood Restaurant, which PJ's husband ran for years as a chef, was easy to identify. It's a heritage house painted cotton-candy pink with mint-green trim, bordered by a white picket fence, and it overlooks the town's main drag. The restaurant had officially closed, prompted by a slowdown during the pandemic, but it remained PJ's residence. I was nervous approaching the door, not unlike during my first interview with KZ Zapata, feeling like a pseudo journalist, wondering who the heck I was to be investigating skateboarding history. But I had nothing to lose and a friend to gain.

I was greeted by PJ's dogs, including a cute Rottweiler and a scruffy pup named Charlotte on the veranda, before PJ beckoned me into the living room. Her home was packed with antiques and collectibles; it was as if I had been transported back to the gold rush era in small-town Canada. And then the grand reveal began. Visiting PJ offered me a whole new perspective of what this project could mean to someone ignored by the history books. We spent hours going through and admiring her photo albums, collection of skatepark ID badges, newspaper clippings, medals, trophies, skateboards, sticker books, vintage magazines, her original Vans shoes, team uniforms, and even a Tony Alva–style fedora.

I'm no photographer, but the soft afternoon light filtering through PJ's windows brought warmth to the scene, and when a friend popped by, we took some photos together that I'll always cherish. PJ was looking cool like a rocker chick with long blond hair and bangs, wearing a sporty black zip-up shirt and black shorts. And I was in summer mode, wearing a peach Antisocial T-shirt, jeans, and a denim cap, ready for a skate session. If the skateboarding paraphernalia surrounding us was erased, you would be hard pressed to figure out our connection, but our big smiles proved that something special had been shared.

Over a cup of tea and her husband's homemade coffee cake, PJ presented her journey to skateboarding: "I was a downhill ski racer, and I really needed a sport in the offseason, so I started [skateboarding] even before all the boys on my street."[2] PJ was racing in downhill and moguls, and performing freestyle at a highly competitive standard, as part of the Sunshine Ski Club in Alberta. And it made sense that PJ would come to dominate slalom skateboarding, as she had an athlete's mindset of what it took to be successful and practiced relentlessly.

PJ lived on a cul-de-sac, and when she placed cones on the street to perfect her skateboarding slalom technique, everyone was supportive, even her neighbor, the chief of police. "The neighbors were so great; I think they just got such a kick out of watching me." PJ alluded to a classic sibling rivalry with her brother, Peter, who would mark his skateboard wheels so that he could tell when his sister had come along and nabbed his board for a session and worn them out. Fortunately, PJ's dad picked up a Makaha skateboard as a gift for her during a trip to the States, which she still had in her collection.

During her ski racing career, PJ had a series of accidents and broken bones and was looking for a sporting environment that was encouraging, versus the fiercely competitive and political scene of skiing competitions. In skateboarding, "everybody wanted everybody to learn, to succeed, and we cheered each other on. If somebody broke [their board], we would give them ours." Skateboarding was fun and made PJ feel part of a community, while skiing had a completely different vibe and lost its appeal. PJ's decision to let go of the sport was delayed by her parents who expressed anger and disappointment, insisting on one more year of ski racing.

Meanwhile, PJ was having great success as a skateboarder winning events like the first-ever Canadian nationals in 1977, which led her to a coach in Toronto who wanted to work with her. This was a reasonable solution for PJ's parents, so at age seventeen with one hundred dollars in her pocket, PJ boarded a plane to Ontario and figured out how to catch a bus to the skatepark while being billeted by a local family. PJ was soon making friends, competing against the guys, and having a blast. "I just started skating with all the boys and tried to encourage the girls, as well." Even in the winter, she was able to skate because the Superbowl Skatepark in Scarborough was in a bubbled dome so the snake-runs, bowls, and obstacles were shielded from snow and harsh weather.

A highlight was when PJ moved into a university apartment on the corner of Spadina Avenue and Bloor Street with three students, including her friend Charlotte Rose. "We were so broke. I remember we all put in our quarters and dimes to get a turkey sub for Thanksgiving, and we cut it into seven pieces!" They were going to the *Rocky Horror Picture Show* on Friday nights, and PJ even performed a skateboarding demo at a university toga party, which she loved doing, although her parents were mortified when they heard about it.

Leading up to the 1978 nationals, contests were held in every province in Canada with the winners invited to the finals on the West Coast in Vancouver at the Pacific National Exhibition Fair. In the October 1978 issue of the *National Skateboard Review*, the results stated that PJ, at age eighteen, placed first in girls' slalom and fourth in girls' freestyle, making her the overall national champion again. PJ's success also meant that sponsors were taking notice, and that's when an owner of G&S Skateboards got in touch and flew her down to San Diego so that she could benefit from being part of the team. PJ recalled the many special friendships she made in

San Diego, like her partner at skateboarding demos, Leilani Kiyabu, who was inducted into the Skateboarding Hall of Fame in 2022. It made me think that if ever there was a Canadian Skateboarding Hall of Fame, PJ should be an inductee followed by skaters from across the country like Sophie Bourgeois, Denise Frohlick, and Margaret Winter, and an entourage of other female and non-binary competitors from the 1970s and onwards.

It was obvious that PJ's skateboarding years were a special time. Sadly, a skateboard contest broke her heart, because after winning a race, controversial judging resulted in a penalty and an unfair result, and the treatment felt personal. The combined wear and tear of skiing and skateboarding also meant ongoing surgeries, and PJ stepped away from competitions in the 1980s. Years later, in 2010, PJ helped support the construction of a skatepark in Kaslo, although no one in her village was remotely aware that they had a national champion in their mix. After two years of me petitioning Canadian news sources, PJ's local newspaper, *The Nelson Star*, finally featured her in August 2024, channeling some of the Olympic frenzy surrounding skateboarding and honoring someone who should at least be recognized as a local legend.

PJ's stories of learning to kickflip in a Calgary warehouse and performing demos at the Calgary Stampede and Loggers Sports events, where the loggers and skaters would switch disciplines and get up to all kinds of fun mischief, could fill a book. I'm convinced that many of the skateboarders I've come across are harboring a memoir just waiting for publication. And PJ shared that she has slowly begun to unpack her skateboarding memories, which she meticulously described in her diaries from the late 1970s.

Journals can be a Pandora's box. While reviewing my old diaries during the writing of this book, I came across an entry from when I was twenty-one. I was disheartened thinking about this vulnerable young person. She had formed strong values as a kid and stuck with them her entire life, but she didn't know her own worth.

> A few years ago my mom had met a young woman through her friends who was interested in women in sports. Mom had talked about my similar interests and participation in skateboarding, and criticism of the industry. Apparently, this woman wants to interview me for a book about "Unsung Sports Heroes," who happen to be women. I'm sort of worried because although I compete in skateboarding, I am far from being ranked among the top women skateboarders.
>
> Mom also told her about the letters I wrote for a school project intended for editors of various skateboard magazines. I have done research on women in sports, women's sports magazines, and I am adamant that women have a place in every sport — but I don't feel like a hero. I have not accomplished much.

I used to have boxes of journals, containing twenty-five tomes, but I destroyed all but ten, and even they are mangled and halved. If I could stop time in 1999 and give myself a pep talk about self-acceptance, perhaps the following decade wouldn't have been such a roller coaster of rejection. I wonder if others can relate to this false idea that we must accomplish something of significance before we can love ourselves. Even after writing my thesis in 2003, I never celebrated it. I never went to a single graduation ceremony, not for my high school or university degrees. I couldn't see the point of honoring myself and probably thought it was a wasteful spectacle. "I have not accomplished much." Why think like that? It's important to celebrate achievement or at least acknowledge one's privilege and feel grateful.

There were several times when I reached out to a skateboarder, someone I perceived as being a pivotal person in skateboarding history, who expressed doubt about their own significance. I would immediately refute this way of thinking. I'm willing to defend every single person that I've connected with in this project, and maybe it's time to include myself in the mix. Perhaps I'm ready now to consider myself a badass skateboarder, even if I am a verifiable nerd. But if Jana Payne was sitting next to me, she would remind me that *nerds make the world go round.*

I have been so fortunate to have been entrusted with personal stories (some of which will remain confidential) and for the opportunity to be equally vulnerable and honest by writing this book. I can't imagine ever finishing the archive, because there's a mountain of content to be explored, especially on a global scale, which means that the website as a living document will keep evolving. Taking a slower, more communal approach to growing an archive gives people the chance to share and reflect. Maybe I'll go to Japan and meet filmmaker Yuri Murai of the *Joy and Sorrow* videos, who propelled a revolution of female skaters in her country. Perhaps a tour of Brazil is in my cards, where I could meet the female skaters who were part of the original Anarquia! team in the 1980s. And I would love to banter with members of the French girl gang Les Poseuz Crew from the early 2000s to gain their perspective on the Paris Olympics.

I've also warmed to social media and am getting over my queasy gut reaction every time someone posts a comment or sends a DM. I love those extraordinary moments when a young person responds to a post with "That's my mom!" and I get to write, "Your mom is a badass!" which has happened more than once. Or the time that Terry Lawrence reached out looking for help. He had stumbled upon an awesome photo of himself online as a kid skating Marina Del Rey skatepark in the 1970s with an Alva skateboard deck in jaguar print and pink and yellow neon wheels. Terry wanted a print copy but had no recollection of the photographer. I posted to Instagram, and the followers did not disappoint. We were directed to William Sharp who'd included the image in his book *Back in the Day* (2020). The skater and photographer were successfully reunited, and it felt wonderful to give back to Terry — a person who means so much to nontraditional skaters.

I have found my unsung heroes. They have lived an existence that challenges both mainstream society and their own subculture by participating in something labeled as a delinquent activity, more appropriate for young men, whether they were conscious of it or not. And I love them all, especially those who have helped me heal and grow. There are many ways to overcome barriers, but it usually takes creativity, curiosity, community, and a mindset that is willing to take a risk, experience rejection, and keep rolling. And while I can't predict whose story might get picked up and promoted on a larger scale, I'm doing the legwork to get things moving; someone must initiate the process and dig up the content. Even if I'm not the most eloquent writer, it's still a contribution and I'm having a blast.

It's now obvious to me that part of my project has been about seeking wise and daring women to revere, emulate, and relate to as I move through middle age. I think about what qualities I want to cultivate as I get older, and I know that those qualities include love, wisdom, humility, and a sense of contentment, which I'm gaining now that I've put myself out there and elevated the stories of others. If I've learned anything, it's along the lines of what the Women's Skateboard Network encouraged, which was to embrace the power of collaboration and community and ignore the rest.

Channeling my skills as a librarian has aided this project. In library land, we conduct "reference interviews" with patrons: you decipher a person's research needs or interests through conversation, and the best results usually happen when there's trust and active listening. I have my library patrons from the Carnegie Branch to thank for developing this practice with me.

In 2014, I had the opportunity to thrive as a rogue librarian at the Carnegie — the cramped reading room inside the Carnegie Community Centre at Main and Hastings Streets in Vancouver's Downtown Eastside (DTES), and it was life-altering. The DTES is a neighborhood often cited as the poorest postal code in Canada, with a myriad of struggles such as addiction, mental health, lack of housing, and the residue of colonial oppression of Indigenous Peoples from residential "schools," the Sixties Scoop, and the foster care system. And yet to look at the Carnegie building, built in 1901 with its sandstone exterior and majestic stained-glass windows, you can sense something vibrant inside, and after you pass through its doors, you'll never be the same.

I was given advice early in my career by a senior librarian to climb the ladder and achieve managerial status. She felt that the quickest route was to secure a full-time children's librarian position; I refused to follow her advice. Children deserve librarians who are passionate about engaging with them, who love picture books, singing and playing the ukelele, and the latest fantasy series or Lego-themed program, and that's not me. And while I admire children's librarians, especially those advocating for diverse collections and combatting book bans, I knew I could do a better job working in the DTES, not out of pity or some belief I could save people, but because a lot of folks seemed to find me approachable.

I found the company of most of my DTES library patrons more enjoyable than that of the average patron anywhere else in Vancouver. The worst treatment I have ever had in a library was in the wealthiest neighborhoods. Witnessing entitled people blow up over a thirty-cent photocopy gone wrong or an accidental late fee and listening to rants about how their taxes pay my wage had left me feeling jaded. I wanted to feel useful, not shat on.

I began as a community librarian, bringing books and library cards to shelters, addiction centers, recovery houses, and to whomever wanted to partner on library programs. Then I became the Carnegie branch head for four years, and I sometimes wonder if I would still be there if Vancouver was an affordable place to live. The Carnegie was the only library where I felt like I could truly be myself. At the same time, if I hadn't left Vancouver, I might never have had the mental capacity to pursue my skateboard history project.

Every day at the Carnegie was a roller-coaster ride of beauty and tragedy that unfurled on an hourly basis. You could be enjoying the drama of Chinese seniors playing mahjong on your left, then turn to the right and see that the Memorial bulletin board had been updated and someone precious had passed away in the night. You could feel euphoria while taking down a poster of a missing Indigenous woman because she was found safe and unharmed thanks to a library patron's dedication. Then hours later, you could be waiting and hoping that naloxone would kick in and bring a patron back from the edge.

I am not a capital-R religious person, but I became a person of prayer because sometimes that's all you have when there's no control over an outcome. Nothing at library school could have ever prepared me for the Carnegie, but it was exactly where I wanted to be, and I never felt unsafe because I was known. Anytime I headed toward the entrance stairs, the cluster of drug dealers outside would clear space for "the library lady" to pass, and if I wandered past the black market on my break, it was a series of fist pumps and hugs. It just came down to smiling and acknowledging people. I suspect my experience as a skateboarder, interacting with people from all walks of life, instilled a different level of comfort with and empathy for those who are struggling. Mostly, I think skateboarding made me curious about people, especially those whom society stigmatizes.

The strangest thing was when people outside the community made assumptions that my role as a librarian was to deliver sage advice and fix people's problems. I think it would be pretty offensive if I was strutting around, doling out self-help books, telling people how to get a job, miraculously break free of addiction, and get over childhood sexual abuse. My role as a librarian was the exact opposite. I was there to listen. It didn't matter if the patron was requesting their favorite DVDs, extra photocopies of the daily sudoku, or wanted to banter about the latest John Grisham novel, because inevitably there would come a time when they needed something different — a person to hear them out, even if I didn't have a solution. And I'm grateful that I've been able to translate this experience and my own #MeToo situations into other arenas.

On a daily basis, I found time to sit with someone at the Carnegie and listen to their story, whether it was at the reference desk, during my coffee break in the senior's lounge, over a hot lunch in the cafeteria, or out on Hastings Street each Friday, giving away boxes of donated books. I learned quickly that you can never presume someone's reading tastes based on their appearance. I remember an intense conversation at the weekly giveaway with a young man about Russian literature, a topic he found comfort in as a youth in foster care, and being blown away. To look at him — the wounds on his skin, his lack of stability, and the state of his clothes — you could easily lump him under the dismissive label of "junkie," but he had a past, his own passions, and interests, if you were lucky enough to hear about them.

It's all about creating relationships of trust because no matter your background, we all have brokenness; some of us are just more buffered by privilege than others. While I can't compare these groups directly, I do see parallels in the way that a regular patron at Vancouver's Carnegie Centre can survive despite living in a bleak neighborhood by seeking out meaningful friendships and activities, and female skateboarders who faced harassment or dismissal forging on to generate collective change. Many of these women have had a profound effect on me, and I'm so glad I took the plunge. It's like I've returned to my youthful self, writing letters as a form of activism, but now I've replaced the letters with research and interviews with incredible women. I feel authentic.

Back in the introduction, I wrote about Liz Bevington modeling a life of contentment as a geriatric skater amongst the carnival of

Venice Beach. While her style wasn't defiant, she still demonstrated a level of confidence and stubbornness in her choices. I'm sure she came up against attitudes about "acting her age," but good things came naturally to Liz because she sought out positive interactions with others and stayed true to herself. I'll never be an extrovert on par with Liz, but I've found a route to engage with a community that gives me purpose and has provided healing. As Rebecca Solnit once wrote, "Sometimes it's not despite but because of something terrible that you become who you are meant to be and set to the work you're meant to do"[3] and instead of anger, it should be love that drives your activism (even when men like Skate Dad explain things to you).[4]

After a long day at work, I enjoy lounging on the couch, scrolling through my Instagram feed, reveling in the staggering momentum of today's champion skaters. We are witnessing new accomplishments daily, like Australia's vert skater Arisa Trew landing a monumental 900-degree spin in May 2024 at age fourteen — the same move that Tony Hawk first landed in June 1999 at age thirty-one that solidified his legendary status. While the mind-blowing progress and high caliber of women in skateboarding today feels profound, it hasn't happened overnight. It's undeniably fantastic when events like the Berrics, the X Games, and the Olympics reveal the talent of female skaters to a mainstream or male-dominated audience, but we need to pause and remember that this situation is a direct result of a long history of activism and perseverance by women skaters and organizers.

The talent has always been there, but the opportunities for girls and women have often been limited or denied. The internet and social media have certainly been a major contribution to our visibility because it took some of the control away from a small group of men publishing magazines and producing videos. Women and non-traditional skaters can now represent themselves, circulate footage, and connect as friends online much more easily despite geographical divides, and that fuels and motivates everyone to progress. And when there's evidence of excitement and a market that companies can tap, sponsorship and support follow. And I say, for the most part, bring it on.

One of the most impactful images of the 2020 Tokyo Games was when women's park skaters Poppy Starr Olsen and Bryce Wettstein hoisted fifteen-year-old Misugu Okamoto onto their shoulders after her soul-crushing fall that denied her a medal. It was an incredible moment of camaraderie, but as glorious as the scene appeared, it came with a cost. Misugu ended up being a casualty of Japan's media hype as the country's gold-medal favorite, disappearing from skateboarding altogether, and there was no acknowledgment of the former world champion with her soaring 540 spins at the Paris 2024 Games. This grated on me because it implied that a talented young skater was essentially disposable and irrelevant on this grand Olympic stage, which had moved on to the next best thing.

Instead, news reporters rhapsodized about the global trend of female skateboarders being their country's youngest athletes, which had typically been gymnasts before the age of eligibility was set at fourteen, then raised to sixteen in 1997. Zheng Haohao, an eleven-year-old street skater, was China's youngest Olympian ever and the youngest athlete in Paris. Vareeraya Sukasem at age twelve was Thailand's youngest, and Heili Sirviö was Finland's youngest at age thirteen. Among the fourteen-year-old skaters, Fay De Fazio Ebert was Canada's youngest, Lucie Schoonheere of France was the host country's youngest, alongside Australia's prodigies Arisa Trew and Chloe Covell. The average age of the six female Olympic medalists in Tokyo was fourteen; the Paris Games medalists came in slightly higher with an average age of fifteen.

This trend of very young female Olympian skaters will undoubtedly continue, although the World Skate federation is phasing in a minimum age for competitors of fourteen by 2028. I predict that Arisa Trew, the 2024 women's park gold medalist, will be on par with Nadia Comăneci, the fourteen-year-old Romanian gymnast who scored the perfect 10.0 at the 1976 Olympics and inspired thousands of young girls to pursue the sport. And thanks to keen parents investing time and money into their daughters' skateboarding aspirations, sometimes from the ages of three and four, as with bronze medalist Sky Brown, a whole new era of skateboarding talent will emerge.

The situation today is very different from previous decades when it was often young women, myself included, who chose to start skateboarding in their late teens as an act of rebellion without the advantage of learning the ropes as a toddler, supported by family and sponsors. This can be a good thing. I'm delighted that new possibilities are available so long as the path to Olympic glory doesn't make or break someone's love of skateboarding. If we value these contest skaters and want to see them thrive, we need to hammer home a reminder that there is ample room for them in skateboarding outside the Olympic bubble. Not everyone makes it onto their national team, especially in hypercompetitive countries, like Japan, loaded with talent, and it's inevitable that an Olympian will completely choke and bail during a contest run, at the exact time they wanted to be at their best, and that is okay.

Fortunately, we're seeing more skateboard companies stepping up, sponsoring multiple female and non-binary riders, including footage of them in team videos, and offering them pro board sponsorships, which result in epic celebrations shared online. And to showcase the range of opportunities available, it's also important to have women occupy meaningful leadership roles in the skateboarding industry and contest environment. In the qualifier contests and during both the Tokyo and Paris Olympics, skateboarders Vanessa Torres, Aimee Massie, Shari Lawson-Duffy, and Renata Paschini acted as judges. Mimi Knoop, Alexis Sablone, Miho Miyamoto, Melissa Williams, Lea Schairer, and Daniela Suárez provided

GIRL GANGS, ZINES, AND POWERSLIDES

coaching. And for contest commentary, we've been blessed with the wisdom and banter of announcers Amelia Brodka, Lucy Adams, Alex White, and Louise Hénault-Ethier. Just as the Paris Olympics boasted gender equity in the number of athletes participating, this approach needs to be expanded and extended to all positions of responsibility, otherwise a power imbalance will continue.

There are moments when I think that it may be better if girls today don't know the tumultuous history we've endured and instead remain blissfully convinced that skateboarding has always been 100 percent for teen girls as portrayed by the Olympics. It's a thought, but an unfair one, especially with my goal of validating senior women. It's also worth remembering that the Olympics is a spectacle, a singular moment every four years that is incapable of portraying the vast array of skateboarding experiences. Let's enjoy the magic and the accomplishments of our young Olympians, but let's not take for granted the literal blood, sweat, and tears of female and non-binary skaters who took up space, overcame barriers, demanded their own contest divisions and media coverage, and pursued sponsors and equal contest prizes for some sixty-odd years.

History and context matter, because when there are role models to revere and emulate, it ensures continuity and longevity rather than each new generation feeling disconnected from the past and forced to repeat previous struggles single-handedly. Only recently, I was reading a zine from 1999 by a skater named Zanna from Portland called *50-50 Skate Zine: Skateboarding and Gender*. Zanna described their ordeal challenging sexually explicit and fatphobic graffiti at their local park, Burnside, after a group of men drove her out of the park chanting, "No fat chicks." Zanna wrote, "I still heard them all the way up the hill as I rode away in fear, anger and disgust. I didn't go back for many days . . . not cuz I wanted him to win, but because I felt really violated . . . I'm tired of defending my own existence at the skatepark so I can simply exist."[5]

Zanna even provided a candid description of the 1999 All Girl Skate Jam, an event that was supposed to be a safe space but was sabotaged when an entitled Dogtown Z-Boy legend took on the duties of emcee, commenting on the female competitors' bodies and complaining about censorship when he was asked to stop. Zanna wondered,

> What will it take to mobilize girls to fight for a safe space? What will it take for skater boys to see that it's not ok . . . and that they need to deal with their internalized and blatant woman hating and sexism . . . They have so much power in this scene because they've always been on top.[6]

It was hard processing Zanna's words, feeling so alienated just twenty-five years ago, but I'm grateful that they were written. This is exactly why zines are important; they reveal stories of dissent and lived experience when the dominant community is unwilling to acknowledge them.

I did feel at peace when I read Zanna's hope for just a single chapter in a skateboard history book about women. Zanna wrote, "I guess I'm still waiting for something to be different, something to be accurate, something to tell my history as well as all the other girls who used to be and are now pros . . . where is all the documentation?"[7] On the following page, Zanna listed a small selection of heroes she was aware of from the 1970s, '80s and '90s that deserved celebration, and I can confidently say that I've got them covered on the Womxn Skate History archive, along with two hundred more and counting. I also believe that things have changed for the better and that Zanna's awful encounter at Burnside would be met with outrage and condemnation by the skateboarding community today.

In 2024, I had a profound experience while presenting at the Slow Impact skateboarding festival in Tempe, Arizona, which was organized by skateboarders Ryan Lay, Kyle Beachy, and Maurice Crandall. While the audience was still predominately made up of men, the response to my discussion on zines was mind-blowing.

I had never felt so seen as a skateboarding nerd, surrounded by attentive, thoughtful young skaters who posed interesting questions and reacted with enthusiasm and curiosity. The event began with an Indigenous welcome and performance by the Gila River Basket Dancers, and the agenda included sessions that discussed sobriety, mental health, healing from trauma, art, photography, architecture, as well as social issues like gentrification, poverty, and Palestinian skateboarders' views of necropolitics. The accumulation of wisdom and sense of accountability in that meeting room filled me with indescribable hope, as if I had finally found my crew.

The next generation will become stronger and more self-assured if they know their history and about those who have been fighting for inclusion and opportunity. And these young people should know that many of these skaters are standing alongside them now and even continue to skate. We all want to be seen, respected, and have our community acknowledged in the history books, and for this to happen, a communal effort is required. Not every skater gets to claim an Olympic medal or have footage and photos circulated by *Thrasher*, but there are still meaningful ways to contribute. Invite a friend out for a skate session, organize a workshop, film your crew progressing, start a book club, or create a zine. You can never predict the impact of a seemingly simple gesture when connecting with others. Just be present and keep skating.

Confederation skatepark crew, 1998

NATALIE PORTER

ACKNOWLEDGMENTS

The preparation for writing this book began in Owen Sound, Ontario, when my mom first encouraged me as a kid to dictate precious letters of feminist critique to magazines and my dad gave me an Aretha Franklin *Greatest Hits* cassette, so I would have a soundtrack to stay motivated. My parents' support has been foundational, alongside my big brothers who mostly tolerated their little sister when I trailed them into street hockey, running, skateboarding, snowboarding, even cutting class with me when a fresh snowfall was irresistible.

I've been fortunate to be part of several skateboarding girl gangs over the years, ripping up the streets of Vancouver and Montréal. A special thank you to Michelle Pezel of Antisocial Skateboard shop, who created *Idlewood* zine, and our Confederation Park crew, the Skirtboarders, for their contributions to my thesis, and Erika Kinast and Rhianon Bader of the Majestic Unicorn Motorcycle Club, who are the ultimate skater nerds and dearest friends.

I am eternally grateful for Jen Sookfong Lee of ECW Press, who validated the concept of this book and gave me new confidence that this was a worthy project. Thank you for your wise edits, feedback, and encouragement. I am delighted that I had the opportunity to work with the team at ECW Press, a true champion of Canadian content and creativity.

It's thanks to all the skateboarding collectors, photographers, zine creators, journalists, writers, magazine editors, Instagram followers, librarians, and archivists that I've been inspired to keep going with this skate history archive. Every day there's some new surprise waiting in the form of an Instagram message, photo, or historical tidbit, and I can't get enough. Keep the leads coming.

My husband, Scott Malin, deserves a shout-out . . . for everything. You know it.

Finally, it's because of all the skateboarders featured in this book and on the Womxn Skateboard History archive (and those whom I have yet to meet!) who have given me their time and entrusted me with their memories, heartaches, and celebrations that this book exists. Your integrity, defiance, perseverance, and love of skateboarding is my inspiration.

NOTES

Introduction

1. Tom Weinberg and Joel Cohen, "The 90's: Episode 402: Getting Older," Public Broadcasting Service, January 31, 1991, vimeo.com /224731118.
2. "Old Woman Rollerskating on Venice Beach, 1970s, 1980s, HD," Kinolibrary Archive Film Collections, April 12, 2019, youtube.com /watch?v=6afgV1mi_ZU.
3. Weinberg and Cohen, "The 90's."
4. Weinberg and Cohen, "The 90's."
5. "Naomi Klein Speaks on CUPE Picket Line," *Working TV*, YouTube, October 6, 2007, youtube.com/watch?v=6QWSj8Ha55o&t.
6. "Naomi Klein Speaks on CUPE Picket Line," *Working TV*.

Chapter 1

1. Jennifer Egan, "Girl Over Board," *Conde Nast: Sports for Women 2*, no. 4 (April 1998): 166.
2. Egan, "Girl Over Board," 166.
3. Clyde Singleton, "A Skate Legend Too Radical for the Industry," *Huck*, February 24, 2017, huckmag.com/article/clyde-singleton -black-skateboarder-legend-industry.
4. Clyde Singleton, host, *WCRP on Skateboarding*, podcast, season 6, episode 56, "Tony Hawk Pt. 2 — 900 Degrees," January 13, 2024, podcasts.apple.com/us/podcast/wcrp-tony-hawk-pt-2-900-degrees /id1565922132?i=1000641531310.

5. Thom Waite, "This Show Traces the Uncensored History of Underground Zines," *Dazed*, November 21, 2023, dazeddigital.com /art-photography/article/61380/1/underground-uncensored-history -zines-brooklyn-museum-copy-machine-manifestos.

6. Jane Doe, "Mail Drop: Who Are the Real Losers Here?" *Thrasher* 6, no. 1 (January 1986): 12.

7. KZ Zapata, personal interview, December 4, 2021.

8. Kurt Carlson, "Sacto: Blood, Sweat, and Cheers," *Thrasher* 6, no. 7 (July 1986): 57–67.

9. Billy Runaway, "Ocean Side," *Thrasher* 6, no. 9 (September 1986): 81.

10. Bonnie Blouin, "Sugar and Spice . . ?" *Thrasher* 6, no. 4 (April 1986): 56–61.

11. Lisa Whitaker, "Interview with Founder Mathilde Pigeon," *Girls Skate Network*, June 18, 2008, girlsskatenetwork.com/2008/06/18/movers -shakers-skirtboarders/.

12. Becky Beal, "The Subculture of Skateboarding: Beyond Social Resistance" (dissertation, University of Northern Colorado, 1992).

13. Natalie Porter, "Female Skateboarders and Their Negotiation of Space and Identity" (master's thesis, Concordia University, 2003), spectrum.library.concordia.ca/id/eprint/2270/.

14. Sounds Like Toronto, "Fifth Column: Queercore Movement Leaders Who Challenged the Cultural Landscape," Virtual Museum, 2020, soundsliketoronto.ca/en/stories/artists/fifth-column.

15. Billie Jean King, *All In: An Autobiography* (Knopf, 2021).

16. Susan Birrell and Nancy Theberge, "Ideological Control of Women in Sport," in *Women and Sport: Interdisciplinary Perspectives*, eds. Margaret D. Costa and Sharon R. Guthrie (Human Kinetics, 1994), 353.

17. Paul Willis, *Profane Culture* (Routledge and Kegan Paul, 1978).

18. Zapata, personal interview.

19. KZ Zapata, "Girls Scene," *Push, Push, Then Go!* 1 (1986): 6.

20. Zapata, personal interview.

21. Blouin, "Sugar and Spice . . ?" 61.

22. Jim O'Mahoney, "Skateboarding Makes the Big-Time TV Networks," *Wild World of Skateboarding*, August 1977, 63–66.

23. Patricia Kavanaugh, "Robin Logan: First Girl to Land a Kickflip Featured in Skateboarder in 1977," *Idlewood* 3 (2012): 9.

24. Di Dootson Rose, "SKAbo Directs CBS Challenge of the Sexes," *National Skateboard Review* 2, no. 10 (February 1978): 3.

NOTES

25. Elizabeth McNeil, "Kristy McNichol Is 'Overwhelmed with Love and Support,'" *People*, January 12, 2012.

26. Pete Pan, "The Third Strike," *Thrasher* 6, no. 6 (June 1986): 50–51.

27. Pan, "The Third Strike," 50–51.

28. Terry Trimble, "The Primo," *GTurn Freestyle Mag* 1, no. 2 (1987): 12–18.

29. Pan, "The Third Strike," 50.

30. Stone Monkey, "Etnies — Ollie King — Re-release," Monkeyboxing .com, September 27, 2008, monkeyboxing.com/etnies-ollie-king -re-release/.

31. Greg Sandoval, "The End of Kindness: Weev and the Cult of the Angry Young Man," *The Verge*, September 12, 2013, theverge.com /2013/9/12/4693710/the-end-of-kindness-weev-and-the-cult-of-the -angry-young-man.

32. Katherine Sierra, "Silicon Valley Could Learn a Lot from Skater Culture. Just Not How to Be a Meritocracy," *Wired*, February 23, 2015, wired.com/2015/02/silicon-valley-thinks-can-learn-skater -culture-terrible-idea/.

33. Sierra, "Silicon Valley Could Learn a Lot from Skater Culture."

34. Kilwag, "Mullen in Wired," *Skate and Annoy*, February 23, 2015, skateandannoy.com/blog/2015/02/mullen-in-wired/.

35. Kilwag, "Mullen in Wired."

36. Sierra, "Silicon Valley Could Learn a Lot from Skater Culture."

37. Zapata, personal interview.

38. Di Dootson Rose, "Long Beach Contest Greatest Ever," *National Skateboard Review* 1, no. 7 (November 1976): 4–5.

39. Cindy Whitehead, "Women's Skateboarding," in *Four Wheels and a Board*, eds. by Betsy Gordon and Jane Rogers (Smithsonian Books, 2022), 57.

40. Iain Borden, *Skateboarding and the City: A Complete History* (Bloomsbury, 2019), 134.

41. Borden, *Skateboarding and the City*, 134.

42. Peter Du Pre, "Freeskate L.A.," *Wild World of Skateboarding* 2, no. 5 (May 1978): 70–71.

43. "Last ASPO: Big O Wins!" *Skat'nNews* 3, no. 1 (January 19, 1981): 9.

44. KZ Zapata, "Jim Thiebaud," *Push, Push, Then Go!* 1, no. 1 (1986): 13.

45. Cory Johnson, "Mark 'Gator' Rogowski: Free Fallin'," *Village Voice*, December 8, 1992, villagevoice.com/mark-gator-rogowski-free -fallin/.

GIRL GANGS, ZINES, AND POWERSLIDES

46. Kilwag, "Old Legends Never Die, but Their Girlfriends Do," *Skate and Annoy*, June 1, 2009, skateandannoy.com/blog/2009/06/old -legends-never-die/.
47. Anthony Pappalardo, "Gator, Mark Oblow, and Apologies: There's a Thread and It's Narcissism," *Artless*, April 13, 2022, anthonypappalardo.substack.com/p/gator-mark-oblow-and -apologies/.
48. Borden, *Skateboarding and the City*, 33, 38.
49. Michelle Ticktin, personal email, October 28, 2024.
50. Tobi Haims, "Latinx Diversity Emphasized in KZ Zapata's BHS Classroom," *Berkley High Jacket*, October 10, 2021, berkeleyhighjacket .com/2021/features/latinx-diversity-emphasized-in-kz-zapatas-bhs -classroom/.
51. *Skategirl*, directed by Susanne Tabata (Bluebush Productions, 2006).
52. Zapata, personal interview.

Chapter 2

1. Lisa Jak Wietzke, Facebook conversation, March 30, 2022.
2. April Hoffman, Instagram conversation, September 25, 2023.
3. Michael Burnett, "Lest We Forget: Saecha Clarke," *Thrasher* 467 (June 2019): 58–59.
4. Myriam Gurba, "Betties on Boards," *Clamor Magazine* 19 (March– April 2003): 24–26.
5. Gurba, "Betties on Boards," 25.
6. Lynn Kramer, "Anita Tessensohn," *Equal Time* 1, no. 3 (1989): 13–15.
7. Natalie Porter, "Female Skateboarders and Their Negotiation of Space and Identity" (master's thesis, Concordia University, 2003), 106, spectrum.library.concordia.ca/id/eprint/2270/.
8. Porter, "Female Skateboarders and Their Negotiation of Space and Identity," 106.
9. Douglass Square, "Lisa Whitaker: Outtapocket and Underpaid," *Check It Out Skateboarding 4 Girls* 16 (2004): 41–43.
10. Ted Newsome, "This Is GOOD WORK: Episode 2: Lisa Whitaker and Meow Skateboards," Red Bull Media House, September 22, 2022, youtube.com/watch?v=rr3P20idkzw.
11. Suziie Wang, "An Interview with Lisa Whitaker," *Work in Skateboarding*, March 21, 2015, issuu.com/workinskateboarding/docs /lisawhitaker-v3.

NOTES

12. Maria Lima, "Creating an Archive of Womxn's Skateboarding History — A Conversation with Lisa Whitaker," *Skateism*, June 1, 2020, skateism.com/creating-an-archive-of-womxns-skateboarding -history-a-conversation-with-lisa-whitaker/.

13. Square, "Lisa Whitaker: Outtapocket and Underpaid," 41.

14. Wang, "An Interview with Lisa Whitaker."

15. Lisa Whitaker, email conversation, August 20, 2024.

16. *Skate Dreams*, directed by Jessica Edwards (Film First Co, Topiary Productions, 2022).

17. Newsome, "This Is GOOD WORK: Episode 2: Lisa Whitaker and Meow Skateboards."

18. Wang, "An Interview with Lisa Whitaker."

19. Newsome, "This Is GOOD WORK: Episode 2: Lisa Whitaker and Meow Skateboards."

20. Newsome, "This Is GOOD WORK: Episode 2: Lisa Whitaker and Meow Skateboards."

21. Newsome, "This Is GOOD WORK: Episode 2: Lisa Whitaker and Meow Skateboards."

22. Adam Abada, "The Skate Witches Are Giving Female Skateboarding a Voice," *Monster Children*, May 8, 2017, monsterchildren.com/articles/skate-witches-zine.

23. Abada, "The Skate Witches Are Giving Female Skateboarding a Voice."

24. Noah Remnick, "Sisterhood of the Skateboard," *The New York Times*, July 31, 2016, MB1.

25. Remnick, "Sisterhood of the Skateboard," MB1.

26. Leah Jasmine, "Skateboards: The Witch's New Broom," *After Dark*, July 16, 2018, jagermeisterafterdark.co.za/skateboards-the-witchs -new-broom/.

27. Ben Connor Barrie, "Interview with Skate Witches Director Danny Plotnick," *Damn Arbor*, October 31, 2018, damnarbor.com/2018/10 /interview-with-skate-witched-director.html.

28. Ethan Fox, personal interview, January 24, 2023.

29. JoAnn Gillespie, personal interview, December 17, 2022.

30. Fox, personal interview.

31. *Underexposed: A Women's Skateboarding Documentary*, directed by Amelia Brodka, produced by Brian Lynch (2012), ameliabrodka.com /underexposed-documentary/.

32. Samantha Reynolds, email conversation, March 28, 2022.

GIRL GANGS, ZINES, AND POWERSLIDES

33. Wietzke, Facebook conversation, March 30, 2022.
34. Scott Stump, "Aunty Skates Aims to Defy Stereotypes while Skateboarding in a Sari," Today.com, August 10, 2021, today.com /tmrw/aunty-skates-aims-defy-stereotypes-while-skateboarding-sari -t227848.

Chapter 3

1. Pete Gall, "'Surf' Skateboard: Bruising Along on PHS Craze," *Pasadena Independent*, May 29, 1959, 13.
2. Gall, "'Surf' Skateboard," 13.
3. Canadian Press, "Skurfing 'Out' for Teen-Agers: Doctors, Police Happy," *The Ottawa Citizen*, August 6, 1965, 25.
4. Pete Gall, "Scraped Skin and Broken Bones: Skateboard Casualties Mount," *Pasadena Independent*, June 3, 1959, 11.
5. Bay Area News Group, "Pleasanton Grandmother Honored for Skateboard Pioneering," *East Bay Times*, August 15, 2014, eastbaytimes.com/2014/08/05/pleasanton-grandmother-honored -for-skateboard-pioneering/.
6. Bay Area News Group, "Pleasanton Grandmother Honored for Skateboard Pioneering."
7. Glenn Sakamoto, "Linda Benson," *Liquid Salt,* January 2010, liquidsaltmag.com/2010/01/linda-benson-something-special.
8. Sakamoto, "Linda Benson."
9. Patty Segovia and Rebecca Heller, *Skater Girl* (Ulysses Press, 2007), 117.
10. Segovia and Heller, *Skater Girl*, 117.
11. Joe Hammeke, "Classic Covers: Patti McGee," *Thrasher* 376 (November 2011): 48.
12. Steve Olson, "Patti McGee," *Juice Magazine*, November 13, 2018, juicemagazine.com/home/patti-mcgee/.
13. Olson, "Patti McGee."
14. Olson, "Patti McGee."
15. "84 Compete in Skateboard Tournament," *Los Angeles Times*, January 13, 1965, 265.
16. Olson, "Patti McGee."
17. Susan Adams, "Profile: The Lady Is a Champ," *Skateboarder* 1, no. 4 (October 1965): 11.
18. Claude Queyrel, "Jim Fitzpatrick," *Endless Lines*, 2011, endlesslines .free.fr/ghost/ghostpages/ghostfitzpatrick1vo.htm.

NOTES

19. "Hossegor: 27 candidats au 1er championnat de France de roll'surf," *Sud-Ouest de Landes*, August 18, 1965.

20. "Le Skate au Feminin," *Skate France International* 5 (1978): 24–27.

21. Claude Queyrel, "Nicole Boronat: Exclusive Interview," *Endless Lines*, 2004, endlesslines.free.fr/ghost/ghostpages/ghostboronat.htm.

22. Editor, "Editorial: Sidewalk Surfing?" *The Quarterly Skateboarder* 1, no. 1 (Winter 1964): 7.

23. Editor, "International Skateboard Championships," *Skateboarder* 1, no. 3 (August 1965): 13–37.

24. Editor, "International Skateboard Championships."

25. Megan MF Kelleher, Instagram conversation, September 28, 2022.

26. Megan MF Kelleher, Instagram conversation, October 20, 2024.

27. *Skate Dreams*, directed by Jessica Edwards (Film First Co, Topiary Productions, 2022).

28. Trina Calderón, "Female Skateboarders Still Striving for Even Footing with Male Peers," *Vice*, April 5, 2017, vice.com/en/article/4xz44d/female-skateboarders-still-striving-for-even-footing-with-male-peers.

29. Alyssa Roenigk, "Girls Spotted on Vert Ramp," EXPN.com, August 17, 2003, expn.go.com/expn/summerx/2003/story?pageName=030817_women_vert.

30. Alyssa Roenigk, "Torres Takes Gold," EXPN.com, August 15, 2003, expn.go.com/expn/summerx/2003/story?pageName=030815_womens_jam.

31. Ian Browning, "How a Group of Women Fought for Equal Pay in Contest Skating," *Jenkem Magazine*, January 8, 2020, jenkemmag.com/home/2020/01/08/group-women-fought-equal-pay-contest-skating/.

32. "The Beginning," Women's Skateboarding Alliance, womensskateboardingalliance.com/asa/.

33. Browning, "How a Group of Women Fought for Equal Pay in Contest Skating."

34. Browning, "How a Group of Women Fought for Equal Pay in Contest Skating."

35. Matt Higgins, "Skateboarding: On a Mission, and Rolling," *The New York Times*, July 26, 2006, D5.

36. Lisa Whitaker, "X-Games Women's Street Skateboarding 2007," The Side Project, YouTube video, August 26, 2007, youtube.com/watch?v=3WjraoYiITw.

37. Cathy Jetter, "All-Time Rider: Tri-Valley Woman Inducted into Skateboarding Hall of Fame," *Pleasanton Weekly*, June 20, 2014, danvillesanramon.com/news/2014/06/20/all-time-rider.

38. Editor, "Editorial: Sidewalk Surfing?"

39. Di Dootson Rose, "AESA Backs Olympic Effort," *National Skateboard Review* 2, no. 1 (April 1977): 7.

40. Rose, "AESA Backs Olympic Effort," 7.

41. Vicki Charlton, "Skateboard! Interviews Two of America's Hottest Female Stars," *Skateboard!* 70, no. 2 (October 1977): 26–27.

42. "Olympic Skateboarding Uniforms?" *Thrasher*, August 19, 2016, thrashermagazine.com/articles/olympic-skateboarding-uniforms/.

43. Nat Kassel, "We Asked Skaters How They Feel About Skateboarding Making the 2020 Olympics," *Vice*, August 17, 2016, vice.com/en/article/nny3nm/we-asked-skaters-how-they-feel-about-skateboarding-making-the-2020-olympics.

44. Nick Butler, "Petition Unveiled Campaigning Against Skateboarding Being Added to Olympic Programme," *Inside the Games*, October 12, 2015, insidethegames.biz/articles/1030894/petition-unveiled-campaigning-against-skateboarding-being-added-to-olympic-programme.

45. "Skating in the Olympics: The Skaters' Perspective," *Thrasher*, December 21, 2016, thrashermagazine.com/articles/skateboarding-in-the-olympics/.

46. "Skating in the Olympics."

47. Porter, "Female Skateboarders and Their Negotiation of Space and Identity," 110–133.

48. *Stay on Board: The Leo Baker Story*, directed by Giovanni Reda and Nicola Marsh (Netflix, 2022).

49. Rachel Joyner, "Skateboarding does not need Games validation, says Hawk," *Reuters*, August 10, 2019, https://www.reuters.com/article/sports/-skateboarding-does-not-need-games-validation-says-hawk-idUSKCN1V00OY/.

50. Bay Area News Group, "Pleasanton Grandmother Honored for Skateboard Pioneering."

Chapter 4

1. Gloria Steinem, "The Ins and Outs of Pop Culture," *Life*, August 20, 1965, 72–89.

NOTES

2. Lily Rothman and Liz Ronk, "When a Young Gloria Steinem Played the Pop-Culture Pundit," *Life*, March 1, 2017, life.com/history/gloria-steinem-pop-culture-1965/.

3. Rothman and Ronk, "When a Young Gloria Steinem Played the Pop-Culture Pundit."

4. Steinem, "The Ins and Outs of Pop Culture, 80.

5. Lauri Kuulei Wong, "Note from the Editor," *Ladies Skateworld* 1, no. 1 (April 15, 1986): 1.

6. Wong, *Ladies Skateworld* (1986), 5.

7. Lauri Kuulei Wong, "Note from the Editor," *Ladies Skateboard* 1, no. 2 (1987): 5.

8. Wong, *Ladies Skateboard* (1987), 12.

9. Lora Lyons, email conversation, July 31, 2022.

10. Lyons, email conversation.

11. Hillary Carlip, *Girl Power: Young Women Speak Out!* (Grand Central Publishing, 1995), 481.

12. Gabby Bess, "Alternatives to Alternatives: The Black Grrrls Riot Ignored," *Vice*, August 3, 2015, vice.com/en/article/9k99a7/alternatives-to-alternatives-the-black-grrrls-riot-ignored.

13. Carlip, *Girl Power*, 481.

14. Ramdasha Bikceem, "Mail Drop: Real Roll Models," *Thrasher* 11, no. 11 (November 1991): 8.

15. Ramdasha Bikceem, *Gunk* 1 (1991): 1.

16. Carlip, *Girl Power*, 494.

17. Carlip, *Girl Power*, 482.

18. Maria Lima, "Creating an Archive of Womxn's Skateboarding History — A Conversation with Lisa Whitaker," *Skateism*, June 1, 2020, skateism.com/creating-an-archive-of-womxns-skateboarding-history-a-conversation-with-lisa-whitaker/.

19. Lori Damiano, "Villa Villa Cola," 2023, loridamiano.com/community/vvc-community.

20. Sharon Harrison, "Villa Villa Cola: Working Together to Support Female Skateboarding, *Skateboarder* 14, no. 6 (February 2005): 34–35.

21. Shanti Sosienski, "Getting Somewhere Fast," *TransWorld Business* (April 2005): 38, 41.

22. Sosienski, "Getting Somewhere Fast."

23. Lima, "Creating an Archive of Womxn's Skateboarding History."

24. Douglass Square, "Lisa Whitaker: Outtapocket and Underpaid," *Check It Out Skateboarding 4 Girls* 16 (2004): 41–43.

25. Meghan McGuire, "Revisiting Villa Villa Cola's 'Getting Nowhere Faster' — The Words of Tiffany Campbell," *Bigfoot Skateboarding Magazine* 1, no. 1 (May 26, 2022), bigfootskatemag.com/getting -nowhere-faster/.
26. Damiano, "Villa Villa Cola."
27. Alex White and Nic Dobija-Nootens, "Remembering the First Women's Skate Mag, 'Check It Out,'" *Jenkem Magazine*, June 7, 2019, jenkemmag.com/home/2019/06/07/remembering-first-womens -skate-mag-check/.
28. White and Dobija-Nootens, "Remembering the First Women's Skate Mag."
29. White and Dobija-Nootens, "Remembering the First Women's Skate Mag."
30. Monica Polistchuk, personal interview, October 3, 2024.
31. Tiffany Steffens, "Girls Kicking Ass," *TransWorld Skateboarding* 16, no. 2 (February 1998): 160–161.
32. White and Dobija-Nootens, "Remembering the First Women's Skate Mag."
33. White and Dobija-Nootens, "Remembering the First Women's Skate Mag."
34. Norma Ibarra, "Women Who Skateboard Shred Expectations," *Globe and Mail*, June 7, 2024, theglobeandmail.com/opinion/article -in-the-world-of-skateboarding-women-are-shredding-expectations/.
35. Hannah Bailey, "We Mind the Gap," *Glorious Sport*, August 30, 2024, glorioussport.com/articles/hannah-bailey-olympics-gender-balance -sports-photographers/.
36. Lauri Wong, "About a hundred birthdays ago (1980's) I was riding my motorcycle (Katana) home from Los Angeles back to Long Beach on the 405 in rush hour traffic," Facebook post, January 27, 2020, 3:27 p.m.
37. Lauri Wong, "7 years ago today I get this post on my page referring to a period of time when I was renting a room from #Tony Hawk," Facebook post, October 5, 2016, 8:55 a.m.
38. Tony Hawk, "Keynote," The Stoke Sessions Conference, San Diego State University, April 20, 2023.
39. Diane DeMatteis, "I was just watching KPBS Skate SD, featuring the Del Mar Skate Ranch, and I always felt a heart connection to this place," Facebook post, Del Mar Skate Ranch, February 9, 2023, 9:34 p.m. https://www.facebook.com/groups/38306074095

NOTES

/?hoisted_section_header_type=recently_seen&multi_permalinks
=10160358401224096.

Chapter 5

1. Rodger Mallison, "Freewheelin' Fun," *Fort Worth Star-Telegram*, May 12, 1977, 23.
2. David Read, "Georgina Matthews: Folklore," *Manual Magazine* 68 (April 2022): 68–69.
3. Merryn Anderson, "Surely Girls Can Skate," *Newsroom NZ*, February 10, 2022, newsroom.co.nz/lockerroom/surely-girls -can-skate.
4. Stacey Roper, personal interview, June 4, 2024.
5. Read, "Georgina Matthews," 69.
6. Joske Films, "Skullz Bitch," YouTube, January 12, 2010, youtube .com/watch?v=06IGTvD9KcU.
7. Stacey Bodger, "Meet a Natural-Born Skateboarding Ace," *New Zealand Herald*, June 29, 2000, nzherald.co.nz/nz/meet-a-natural -born-skateboarding-ace/NMVMJO4SR2D63HDRNASMX7RGG4/.
8. Bodger, "Meet a Natural-Born Skateboarding Ace."
9. Dave Carnie, "Gallaz in Australia: An All-Female Skate Tour," *Big Brother* 85 (June 2002): 68–83.
10. Steve Rocco, "Back Issues," *Big Brother* 1, no. 1 (1992).
11. *AKA: Girl Skater*, directed by Mike Hill (White Knuckle Action Sports, 2003).
12. Chelsea Woody, "Do You Know Mary Mills? Well You Should," Textured Waves, August 13, 2019, texturedwaves.com/roots/mary -mills.
13. Mary Mills, "Mother/Son Skate Date!" *Surf and the Fury*, August 27, 2011, surfandthefury.blogspot.com/search?q=mother%2Fson+skate.
14. Building the Revolution, "Interview with Surf Icon and Mold Breaker, Mary Mills," *Building the Revolution*, November 13, 2020, buildingtherevolution.com/2020/11/13/interview-with-surf-icon -and-mold-breaker-mary-mills/.
15. Andrew Kahrl, "America's Segregated Shores: Beaches' Long History as a Racial Battleground," *The Guardian*, June 12, 2018, theguardian. com/world/2018/jun/12/americas-segregated-shores-beaches-long -history-as-a-racial-battleground.
16. Woody, "Do You Know Mary Mills."

GIRL GANGS, ZINES, AND POWERSLIDES

17. Mary Mills, "My New Life as a Surfer Who Skates," *Surf and the Fury*, October 12, 2011, surfandthefury.blogspot.com/search?q=my +new+life+as+a+surfer+who.

18. Woody, "Do You Know Mary Mills."

19. Chris Pastras, "Lest We Forget: Person," *Thrasher* 482 (September 2020): 86–87.

20. Cindy Whitehead, "'80s Skateboarder Stephanie Person: What You Didn't Read in Thrasher!" Girl Is Not a 4 Letter Word, February 22, 2021, https://www.girlisnota4letterword.com/blog//2021/02/80s -skateboarder-stephanie-person-what.html.

21. Whitehead, "'80s skateboarder Stephanie Person."

22. Whitehead, "'80s skateboarder Stephanie Person."

23. Pastras, "Lest We Forget," 96.

24. Stephanie Person, "Equal Time," *Poweredge* 2, no. 2 (March 1989): 38–39.

25. Whitehead, "'80s skateboarder Stephanie Person."

26. Pastras, "Lest We Forget," 97.

27. Bamber Shaw, "Stephanie Person," *Skateboard!* 6 (November 1989): 16–19.

28. Shaw, "Stephanie Person," 19.

29. Alexis Castro, "Briana King on Teaching the Next Generation of Skaters," *Jenkem*, June 30, 2020, jenkemmag.com/home/2020/06/30 /briana-king-teaching-next-generation-skaters/.

30. Jen Valenzuela, Instagram conversation, April 12, 2022.

31. Valenzuela, Instagram conversation.

32. Read, "Georgina Matthews," 68.

33. Anderson, "Surely Girls Can Skate."

34. Anderson, "Surely Girls Can Skate."

Chapter 6

1. Iain Borden, *Skateboarding, Space and the City: Architecture and the Body* (Berg, 2001), 147.

2. Denise Williams, "The Lady of Dogtown," *Push* 1, no. 1 (Summer 2002): 2–3.

3. Williams, "The Lady of Dogtown," 3.

4. Ben Marcus, *The Skateboard: The Good, the Rad, the Gnarly: An Illustrated History* (MVP Books, 2011).

5. Iain Borden, *Skateboarding and the City: A Complete History* (Bloomsbury, 2019), 113.

NOTES

6. John Smythe, "Interview: Tony Alva," *Skateboarder* 3, no. 3 (February 1977): 34–41.

7. Smythe, "Interview: Tony Alva," 39.

8. James O'Mahoney, "Laura Thornhill," *Juice Magazine*, December 1, 2008, juicemagazine.com/home/laura-thornhill-caswell/.

9. Jack Smith, "Girl Dropping In: Cindy Whitehead," *Lives on Board: The Skateboarder's Journal* (Morro Skateboard Group, 2009), 303–304.

10. Canon Price, personal interview, June 30, 2022.

11. Richard Taylor, "Skatelady: Marilyn Latta," *Wild World of Skateboarding* 2, no. 6 (June 1978): 33–34.

12. Yvonne Cucci, personal interview, September 2, 2022.

13. Brian Gillogly, "Who's Hot! Jana Payne," *Skateboarder* 4, no. 4 (November 1977): 108–109.

14. Denise Williams, "A Scene Within a Scene," *Concrete Wave* 1, no. 1 (Winter 2002): 15.

15. Bonnie Blouin, "Poetry in Motion," *Thrasher* 6 no. 3 (March 1986): 51.

16. Bonnie Blouin, "Mail Drop: Thirst Quencher," *Thrasher* 6, no. 3 (March 1986): 12.

17. Bonnie Blouin, "Sugar and Spice . . ?" *Thrasher* 6, no. 4 (April 1986): 56.

18. Robin Pailler, "In Conversation with Magdalena Wosinska," *Wasted Talent*, May 4, 2024, wastedtalentmag.com/blog/2024/05/04/in -conversation-with-magdalena-wosinska/.

19. Sean Mortimer, "About a Girl," *Skateboarder* 9, no. 3 (January– February 2000): 46–50.

20. Blouin, "Sugar and Spice . . ?" 61.

21. Blouin, "Sugar and Spice . . ?" 60.

22. Bonnie Blouin, "Skater's Edge," *Thrasher* 8, no. 2 (February 1988): 41.

23. Blouin, "Skater's Edge."

24. Blouin, "Skater's Edge."

25. Deborah Stoll, *Drop In: The Gender Rebels Who Changed the Face of Skateboarding* (HarperCollins Publishers, 2024), 116.

26. Blouin, "Skater's Edge."

27. Blouin, "Skater's Edge."

28. Kim M., "Mail Drop: Unstoppable," *Thrasher* 8, no. 5 (May 1988): 14.

29. John O'Malley, *Urethane Revolution: The Birth of Skate — San Diego 1975* (History Press Library Editions, 2019), 88.

30. Ellen Berryman, "From Recluse to Footloose, and Back," in *Lives on Board*, ed. Jack Smith (The Skateboarder's Journal, 2009), 308–310.

31. Cindy Berryman, "Let's Hear It for the Ladies," *Skateboarder* (August 1976): 58–63.
32. Berryman, "Let's Hear It for the Ladies," 58.
33. Berryman, "Let's Hear It for the Ladies," 60.
34. Berryman, "Let's Hear It for the Ladies," 61–62.
35. Berryman, "Let's Hear It for the Ladies," 62.
36. Berryman, "From Recluse to Footloose, and Back," 308.
37. Tunnel Skateboards, "Leslie Jo Ritzma," 2006, tunnelskateboards.com/team/leslie_jo_ritzma.html.
38. Mike Horelick, "Board out of Their Minds," *Los Angeles Times*, November 18, 2007, 77.
39. Tunnel Skateboards, "Leslie Jo Ritzma."
40. Mike Horelick and Jon Carnoy, "Signal Hill Speed Run 1975–1978," Longboardlabs.com, November 15, 2014, longboarderlabs.com/15/signal-hill-speed-run-1975-1978/2014/11/blog/re-issue/.
41. Leslie Jo Ritzma, "Letters to the Editor," *National Skateboard Review* 2, no. 3 (June 1977): 7.
42. Tunnel Skateboards, "Leslie Jo Ritzma."
43. Jim Goodrich, "Who's Hot! Vicki Vickers," *Skateboarder* 5, no. 5 (December 1978): 112–113.
44. Goodrich, "Who's Hot! Vicki Vickers," 113.
45. Goodrich, "Who's Hot! Vicki Vickers," 113.
46. Jim Goodrich, "Vicki Vickers," *Skateboarder* 6, no. 5 (December 1979): 46–51.
47. Goodrich, "Vicki Vickers," 48.
48. Goodrich, "Vicki Vickers," 48.
49. Goodrich, "Vicki Vickers," 51.
50. Skip Towne, "Bonnie Blouin: A Trailblazing Skater and Writer," *Thrasher* 493 (August 2021): 40.
51. Towne, "Bonnie Blouin."
52. Natalie Porter, "Bonnie Blouin," Womxn Skateboard History, June 2, 2022, womxnskatehistory.ca/2022/06/02/bonnie-blouin/.
53. Bonnie Blouin, "Skater's Edge: True Devotion," *Thrasher* 8, no. 11 (November 1988): 39.

Chapter 7

1. Patty Segovia and Rebecca Heller, *Skater Girl* (Ulysses Press, 2007), 121.

NOTES

2. Lynn Kramer, personal interview, August 23, 2022.
3. Kramer, personal interview.
4. Kramer, personal interview.
5. Lynn Kramer and Geth Noble, "UCSD Ramp," *Thrasher* 9, no. 8 (August 1989): 42–43.
6. Kramer, personal interview.
7. Kramer, personal interview.
8. Lynn Kramer, "Street Life," *Girls Who Grind* 1, no. 1 (December 1988): 2–3.
9. Kramer, "Street Life," 2.
10. Liza Araujo, "Saecha Clarke," *Check It Out Magazine* 16 (2004): 54–57.
11. Lynn Kramer, "Contacts," *Poweredge Magazine* 2, no. 2 (March 1989): 18.
12. Jennifer Sells, "We Are Progressing Aren't We?" *Equal Time* 1, no. 2 (April 1989): 11–12.
13. Sells, "We Are Progressing Aren't We?" 12.
14. Sells, "We Are Progressing Aren't We?" 12.
15. Kramer, personal interview.
16. Stacey Roper, Instagram comment, September 13, 2022.
17. Kramer, personal interview.
18. Sells, "We Are Progressing Aren't We?" 12.
19. Karen Billing, "1960s Skateboard Pioneer Colleen Turner Inducted into Skateboarding Hall of Fame," *Encinitas Advocate*, November 3, 2021, encinitasadvocate.com/news/story/2021-11-04/1960s-skate board-pioneer-colleen-turner-inducted-into-skateboarding-hall-of -fame.
20. Billing, "1960s Skateboard Pioneer Colleen Turner."
21. Todd Huber, "Colleen Boyd Turner — 2021," Skateboarding Hall of Fame, September 2021, skateboardinghalloffame.org/2021/09 /colleen-boyd-turner-2021/.
22. Billing, "1960s Skateboard Pioneer Colleen Turner."
23. Billing, "1960s Skateboard Pioneer Colleen Turner."
24. Emily Savage, "Hell on Wheels: In the 1980s, This All-Girl Skateboard Gang Took over the Streets of L.A.," *Bust* (December– January 2017), bust.com/living/18944-hell-on-wheels.html.
25. Savage, "Hell on Wheels."
26. Savage, "Hell on Wheels."
27. Ann Japenga, "Head over Heels in Love with Skateboarding," *Los Angeles Times*, August 10, 1984, 55, 62.

28. Savage, "Hell on Wheels."

29. Japenga, "Head over Heels in Love with Skateboarding," 62.

30. Eric Ducker, "From Thrashin' to Kids and Beyond: A History of Skateboarding Movies," *The Ringer*, August 16, 2018, theringer.com /movies/2018/8/16/17693288/minding-the-gap-skate-kitchen-skateboarding-movies.

31. Bread and Cinemas, "'Thrashin' Revisited: The Daggers Unlikely Origins," YouTube, October 29, 2022, youtube.com/watch?v=re Ft8YB3aYc.

32. Lauraine Leblanc, *Pretty in Punk: Girls' Gender Resistance in a Boys' Subculture* (Rutgers University Press, 1999), 226.

33. Jessie Van Roechoudt, "How Rookie Skateboards Shaped Women's Skateboarding," *Quell / Jenkem*, July 2, 2021, jenkemmag.com/home /2021/07/02/rookie-skateboards-shaped-womens-skateboarding/.

34. Tristan Patterson, "Getting Radical," *Salon*, August 28, 2000, salon .com/2000/08/28/skater/.

35. Hillel Slovik, "Up Front: Under the Bridge," *Thrasher* 177 (November 1995): 22.

36. Catharine Lyons, "Rookie Skateboards," in *Four Wheels and a Board*, eds. Betsy Gordon and Jane Rogers (The Smithsonian, 2022), 128.

37. Patterson, "Getting Radical."

38. Mimi and Sushi Girl, "Interview with Maura Sheehan," *Mimi's Revenge* 1 (1996), 4.

39. Patterson, "Getting Radical."

40. Lyons, "Rookie Skateboards," 130.

41. Dan Sinker, "Not Just Boys' Fun Anymore: The Growing Girls' Revolution in Skateboarding," *Punk Planet* 25 (May–June 1998): 85–87.

42. Patterson, "Getting Radical."

43. Jesse McKinley, "Neighborhood Report: Chinatown; Skirting the Skateboarders," *The New York Times*, September 28, 1997, section 13, 7.

44. Van Roechoudt, "How Rookie Skateboards Shaped Women's Skateboarding."

45. Brindle Pit, "Mail Drop: Hot Date," *Thrasher* 223 (August 1999): 12.

46. Ally, "Mail Drop: Point Being," *Thrasher* 225 (October 1999): 10.

47. Ron Barbagallo, "In Her Own Words: Lynn Kramer," *Everything Skateboarding Magazine*, January 2012, everythingskateboarding magazine.blogspot.com/.

48. Barbagallo, "In Her Own Words: Lynn Kramer."

NOTES

Chapter 8

1. Warren, "80's Research Lab: Sue Hazel," *Sidewalk* magazine 58 (July 2001): 92–95.
2. Neftalie Williams, "Colour in the Lines: The Racial Politics and Possibilities of US Skateboarding Culture" (PhD thesis, University of Waikato, 2020), researchcommons.waikato.ac.nz/handle/10289/13741.
3. Williams, "Colour in the Lines," 178.
4. Brian Gillogly, "Who's Hot! Kim Cespedes," *Skateboarder* 3, no. 3 (February 1977): 80–81.
5. Warren, "80's Research Lab: Sue Hazel," 93.
6. Claudine Cauble, "UK Icon and Our Heroine, Sue Hazel," *Rock Rip Roll Girl*, April 24, 2010, rockriprollgirl.com/2010/04/sue-hazel-sk8-to-send/.
7. Sue Hazel, personal interview, September 21, 2022.
8. Kate Mahony, "Kate the Skate," *Skateboard Scene* 3 (January 1978): 8.
9. "Reports on the First National Championships," *Skateboard Special* 1 (September 1977).
10. Kate Mahony, "Kate the Skate," *Skateboard Scene* 4 (February 1978): 65.
11. "Who's Hot: Minh Duc Tran," *Skateboard!*, August 1977, 18.
12. Di Dootson Rose, "National Skateboard Review Was There," in *Lives on Board*, ed. Jack Smith (The Skateboarder's Journal, 2009), 306.
13. Di Dootson Rose, "NSR Founder Di Dootson Rose — Skateboard Biography," *National Skateboard Review*, January 1, 2019, nationalskateboardreview.com/SlalomRacing/nsr-founder-di-dootson-rose-skateboard-biography/.
14. "Girls Who Skate," *Thrasher* 168 (February 1995): 66–71.
15. Anonymous, "Mail Drop: Lady Finger," *Thrasher* 168 (February 1995): 10.
16. Cauble, "UK Icon and Our Heroine, Sue Hazel."
17. Cauble, "UK Icon and Our Heroine, Sue Hazel."
18. Cauble, "UK Icon and Our Heroine, Sue Hazel."
19. Warren, "80's Research Lab: Sue Hazel," 95.
20. *Radical Moves*, directed by Larry Dean (Transworld Skateboarding, 1986), VHS.
21. John Lucero, "Ten Days in a Zoo," *Thrasher* 6, no. 6 (December 1986): 53–59, 94, 95.
22. Warren, "80's Research Lab: Sue Hazel," 93.

GIRL GANGS, ZINES, AND POWERSLIDES

23. Hazel, personal interview.
24. Hazel, personal interview.
25. Mark Lawer, "Sue Hazel: Interview," *Skateboard!* 6 (November 1989): 21.
26. Lawer, "Sue Hazel: Interview."
27. Patterson, "Getting Radical."
28. *Skategirl*, directed by Susanne Tabata (Bluebush Productions, 2006).
29. Tabata, *Skategirl*.
30. Holly Lyons, "Bio," 2014, hollylyons.net/pages/bio.html.
31. Jean Zimmerman, *Raising Our Athletic Daughters: How Sports Can Build Self-Esteem and Save Girls' Lives* (Doubleday, 1998).
32. John Moore, "All Girl Skate Jam — Level Red," YouTube, November 9, 2010, youtube.com/watch?v=Q_E8xfrBNIA.
33. Jenna Selby, "England: Tea, Crumpets and Backside Boardslides," *Check It Out Magazine* 15 (2003): 43.
34. Hazel, personal interview.
35. Warren, "80's Research Lab: Sue Hazel," 93.
36. Warren, "80's Research Lab: Sue Hazel," 93.
37. Warren, "80's Research Lab: Sue Hazel," 95.
38. Sue Hazel, personal email, July 24, 2023.
39. Warren, "80's Research Lab: Sue Hazel," 94.

Chapter 9

1. Lauraine Leblanc, *Pretty in Punk: Girls' Gender Resistance in a Boys' Subculture* (Rutgers University Press, 1999), 110.
2. Leblanc, *Pretty in Punk*, 108–109.
3. Kate Mahony, "Kate the Skate Meets Robin Logan," *Skateboard Scene* 6 (1978): 74.
4. Iain Borden, *Skateboarding and the City: A Complete History* (Bloomsbury, 2019), 33.
5. *The Devil's Toy*, directed by Claude Jutra (National Film Board of Canada, 1966).
6. Ray Miller, "Salina 'Surfers' Soar and Suffer," *The Salina Journal*, April 9, 1965, 1.
7. Sheila Rule, "Oslo Journal: In Ibsen's Land, Skateboard Is a Social Problem," *The New York Times*, October 17, 1989, A4.
8. JoAnn Gillespie, "Letter to the Editor," *Equal Time* 2, no. 1 (1990): 3.
9. JoAnn Gillespie, personal interview, December 17, 2022.

NOTES

10. Gillespie, personal interview.
11. Lynn Kramer, "Santa Barbara," *Equal Time* 2, no. 1 (January 1990): 8.
12. Editor, "Tea Bowls," *The Skateboarding Crucible*, July 3, 2023, skateboardingcrucible.com/post/tea-bowls-california.
13. Patty Segovia and Rebecca Heller, *Skater Girl* (Ulysses Press, 2007), 121.
14. *SK8HERS*, directed by Ethan Fox (Burnt Toast Productions, 1992).
15. Segovia and Heller, *Skater Girl*, 121.
16. Beth Jones, "Michelle Ticktin," *Brighton Argus*, August 1994.
17. Michelle Ticktin, personal email, October 28, 2024.
18. Jones, "Michelle Ticktin."
19. Tristan Kennedy, "Tas Pappas on Drugs, Death and the Dark Side of Skateboarding," *The Guardian*, August 17, 2014, theguardian.com/lifeandstyle/shortcuts/2014/aug/17/tas-pappas-interview-drugs-death-dark-side-skateboarding.
20. Kennedy, "Tas Pappas."
21. Jean Edwards and Alison Caldwell, "Coroner Blames Champion for Ex-Girlfriend's Death," *ABC News*, December 9, 2012, abc.net.au/news/2012-12-10/coroner-blames-champion-for-ex-girlfriend27s-murder/4419580.
22. Editor, "Ben Pappas Burns," *Slam Skateboarding Australia* 29 (April–June 1995).
23. Vans, "Loveletter to LGBTQ+ | Jeff Grosso's Loveletters to Skateboarding," YouTube, June 11, 2020, youtube.com/watch?v=kqD4xfNwd6k.
24. Todd Huber, "Terry Lawrence," Skateboarding Hall of Fame, April 2020, skateboardinghalloffame.org/2020/04/teri-lawrence-2020/.
25. Marlene Medford, "Cara-Beth Burnside: Skateboard Pioneer Shaping the Next Generation of Female Pros," *Patch*, July 31, 2012, patch.com/california/encinitas/cara-beth-burnside-skateboard-pioneer-continues-to-tr8957ca4861.
26. King James, "Who's Hot: Teri Lawrence," *Skateboarder* 5, no. 11 (June 1979): 76–77.
27. James, "Who's Hot: Teri Lawrence," 77.
28. Emanuele Barbier, "Blazing the Trail in the '70s," *Skateism*, July 4, 2020, skateism.com/blazing-the-trail-in-the-70s/.
29. Barbier, "Blazing the Trail in the 70s."
30. Barbier, "Blazing the Trail in the 70s."
31. Grosso, "Loveletter to LGBTQ+."

GIRL GANGS, ZINES, AND POWERSLIDES

32. Kim Adrian, personal interview, March 12, 2023.
33. Marla Rainey, "Letter to the Editor," *EDO* (1986): 4.
34. Cyndy Pendergast, personal interview, March 22, 2023.
35. Pendergast, personal interview.
36. Cyndy Pendergast, personal email, October 27, 2024.
37. MTV News Staff, "Bad Religion, NOFX Join 'Ladies Lounge' on Warped Tour," MTV.com, January 29, 1988, mtv.com/news/80kegi /bad-religion-nofx-join-ladies-lounge-on-warped-tour.
38. Leblanc, *Pretty in Punk*, 112.
39. Leblanc, *Pretty in Punk*, 119.
40. Savage, "Hell on Wheels."
41. Frank Harlan, "The SkateBettys Interview," *Warning* 11 (July 1984): 11, 30.
42. Harlan, "The SkateBetty's Interview," 30.
43. Thalia Zelnik, personal interview, November 27, 2023.
44. Tobi Vail, "Addendum to the Nu Skate Movement," *Grand Royal* 2 (1996): 124.
45. Tammy Watson, "The Frumpies," *Thrasher* 161 (July 1994): 63.
46. Vail, "Addendum to the Nu Skate Movement."
47. Eben Benson, "Jeffrey Cheung: Unity and Community, One Board at a Time," *Juxtapoz: Art and Culture*, August 13, 2018, juxtapoz.com /news/magazine/features/jeffrey-cheung-unity-and-community -one-board-at-a-time/.
48. Leblanc, *Pretty in Punk*, 231.
49. Lydia Jupp, "LGBT Books Disproportionately Affected as Florida Schools Ban More Than 700 Books," *Star Observer*, November 15, 2024, starobserver.com.au/news/lgbt-books-florida-schools-ban- 700-books/233867.

Chapter 10

1. Robin Logan and Brian Logan, "First Family in Skateboarding," *Backside Magazine* 12 (June 2022), backsideskatemag.com/logan -earth-ski-first-skateboard-family/.
2. Gale Webb, "About Gale," March 2001, galewebb.com/About_Gale /about_gale.htm.
3. Editor, "Mrs. Skateboard Gale Webb: Can Your Mom Skateboard as well as She Does?" *Wild World of Skateboarding* (October 1977): 20, 21, 68–70.

NOTES

4. Melissa Guerrero, "Pack Lunch, Drop Kids Off, Skate, Work," *The New York Times*, August 24, 2024, D1.

5. Di Dootson Rose, "SKAbo Championships," *National Skateboard Review* 2, no. 8 (December 1977): 5.

6. Beth Fishman, Facebook comment, June 18, 2016. https://www.facebook.com/photo.php?fbid=10153531024645723&set=pb.625075722.-2207520000&type=3

7. Neil Britt, "She's a Small-Fry: But on the East Coast, Beth Fishman Is a Whale of a Skater," *Wild World of Skateboarding* 2, no. 4 (April 1978): 22–25.

8. Jim Seimas, "Santa Cruz's Judi Oyama, 63, Named to 2024 USA Slalom Skateboarding Team," *Santa Cruz Sentinel*, November 19, 2023, santacruzsentinel.com/2023/10/17/santa-cruzs-judi-oyama-64-named-to-2024-usa-slalom-skateboarding-team-local-roundup/.

9. Santa Cruz Skateboards, "63-Year-Old Female Skateboarding Pioneer Breaking Barriers & Going Fast! | Judi Oyama," YouTube, March 8, 2023, youtube.com/watch?v=fcHpec4qy4k.

10. Judi Oyama, "My Skateboard Hall of Fame Induction 2018 Speech," May 6, 2018, judioyama.blogspot.com/2018/05/my-skateboard-hall-of-fame-induction.html.

11. Di Dootson Rose, "Judi Oyama," *National Skateboard Review* 3, no. 3 (June 1978): 13.

12. Malakye, "Judi Oyama — Arist, Art Director, Skater," Malakye, June 1, 2006, malakye.com/news/1400/judi-oyama-artist-art-director-skater.

13. Malakye, "Judi Oyama."

14. Oyama, "My Skateboard Hall of Fame Induction 2018 Speech."

15. Kim Cook, "Bang! Bang! Make Room for Calamity Jean," *AZ Steez: Arizona's Skate Culture Magazine* 5 (May–June 2009): 31–34.

16. Cook, "Bang! Bang!," 33.

17. Cook, "Bang! Bang!," 33.

18. Cook, "Bang! Bang!," 33.

19. Jean Rusen Keyser, Instagram conversation, May 29, 2023.

20. "Interview w/Amy Bradshaw @oldlady_skater," S1 Helmets Blog, May 5, 2023, shop.s1helmets.com/s1-helmet-blog/interview-w-amy-bradshaw-oldlady_skater-/.

21. Ken Hada, "The History of Women's Skateboarding," Facebook, June 21, 2020, facebook.com/watch/?extid=CL-UNK-UNK-UNK-IOS_GK0T-GK1C&mibextid=2Rb1fB&v=2682815825324627.

22. Paul Van Doren, *Authentic: A Memoir by the Founder of Vans* (Vertel Publishing, 2021), 153.
23. Hada, "The History of Women's Skateboarding."
24. Hada, "The History of Women's Skateboarding."
25. "Interview w/ Amy Bradshaw @oldlady_skater."
26. Barbara Odanaka, "Mighty Mama Skate-O-Rama promo," YouTube, April 19, 2014, youtube.com/watch?v=btujS4FJjyM&t.
27. "Interview w/ Amy Bradshaw @oldlady_skater."
28. Hada, "The History of Women's Skateboarding."
29. Beth Fishman, personal interview, February 23, 2023.
30. Mark Diamond and Charles Feldman, "Skating in the Big Apple," *Skateboard World* 2, no. 12 (December 1978): 32–33.
31. Hada, "The History of Women's Skateboarding."

Chapter 11

1. Joint News Release, "Devastatingly Pervasive: 1 in 3 Women Globally Experience Violence," World Health Organization, March 9, 2021, who.int/news/item/09-03-2021-devastatingly-pervasive-1-in-3 -women-globally-experience-violence.
2. Ken Hada, "The History of Women's Skateboarding," Facebook post, June 21, 2020, facebook.com/watch/?extid=CL-UNK-UNK -UNK-IOS_GK0T-GK1C&mibextid=2Rb1fB&v=2682815825324627.
3. Hada, "The History of Women's Skateboarding."
4. Brian Gillogly, "Who's Hot! Jana Payne," *Skateboarder* 4, no. 4 (November 1977): 108–109.
5. Jana Payne, personal interview, June 18, 2023.
6. Hada, "The History of Women's Skateboarding."
7. Hada, "The History of Women's Skateboarding."
8. Jana Payne, "Acceptance Speech," Skateboard Hall of Fame, November 10, 2022.
9. Barb Odanaka, "From Skateboard Girl to Skateboard Mom," in *Lives on Board*, ed. Jack Smith (The Skateboarder's Journal, 2009), 296–298.
10. Barb Odanaka, personal interview, June 22, 2023.
11. Odanaka, personal interview.
12. Barbie Ludovise, "Behind the Wheels: In the '70s, Skateboarding Was About Big Hills and Simple Thrills. A New Appreciation for Those Early Days Is Emerging," *Los Angeles Times*, September 8, 1995, latimes.com/archives/la-xpm-1995-09-08-ls-43422-story.html.

NOTES

13. Dani Abulhawa, "'Crack on Wheels': Barbara Odanaka — 'Skateboard Moms & Sisters of Shred,'" GirlSkateUK.com, December 27, 2015, girlskateuk.com/2016/01/04/crack-on-wheels -barbara-odanaka-skateboard-moms-sisters-of-shred/.

14. Odanaka, personal interview.

15. Odanaka, personal interview.

16. "About," Skate Like a Girl, skatelikeagirl.com/about.html.

17. Beth Stinson, Kanako Wynkoop, Tina Herschelman, "Guide to the Ladyfest 2000 Collection, 2000-2001," *New York University Libraries*, August 20, 2023, findingaids.library.nyu.edu/fales/mss_360/.

18. Skate Like a Girl, "Folks Say You Have to Know Where You Came from to Know Where You're Going," Facebook post, April 2, 2020, facebook.com/skatelikeagirl/posts/pfbid02XPv1T1ZoiZadivrPBF zyvD5BNSzguEgTzLW wsXdWxk8CeiR2pyDi79LzxM3MeDxyl.

19. Ladyfest 2000, "Planning," Ladyfest.org, ladyfest.org/planning/.

20. Skate Like a Girl, "Folks Say You Have to Know."

21. Taylor Moore, "Dynamic Seattleites: Skate Savvy, Nancy Chang," *Seattleite*, August 30, 2011, seattleite.com/2011/08/30/dynamic -seattleites-skate-savvy-nancy-chang/.

22. Di Dootson Rose, "Special Women's Section," *National Skateboard Review* 3, no. 3 (June 1978): 13.

23. Indigo Willing and Anthony Pappalardo, *Skateboarding, Power and Change* (Palgrave MacMillan, 2023).

24. Indigo Willing, "Our History," Consent Is Rad, consentisrad .wordpress.com/our-history/.

25. Willing and Pappalardo, *Skateboarding, Power and Change*, 208.

26. Indigo Willing, personal email, September 17, 2024.

27. Sander Hölsgens, "University of Skate: 'Community Before Cliques' — An Interview with Indigo Willing," *Skateism*, June 20, 2019, skateism.com/university-of-skate-community-before-cliques -an-interview-with-indigo-willing/.

28. Indigo Willing, "The Film *Kids* 25 Years On: A Qualitative Study of Rape Culture and Representations of Sexual Violence in Skateboarding," *YOUNG* 30 no. 2 (April 2022): 149–164.

29. Hölsgens, 'University of Skate."

30. Ken Hada, host, *I Had a Conversation*, podcast, "Artist/skateboarding pioneer, Jana Payne-Booker," April 9, 2020, podcasts.apple.com/si /podcast/artist-skateboarding-pioneer-jana-payne-booker/id 1370265820?i=1000471028885.

31. Payne, personal interview.
32. Payne, personal interview.
33. Hada, "Artist/skateboarding pioneer, Jana Payne-Booker."
34. Payne, personal interview.
35. Payne, personal interview.
36. Payne, personal interview.
37. Judith Cohen, personal interview, January 20, 2024.
38. Rhianon Bader, personal interview, June 27, 2021.
39. Bader, personal interview.
40. "Child Protection," The Goodpush Alliance, goodpush.org/behind-the-scenes/child-protection.
41. Jennifer Valentino-DeVries and Michael H. Keller, "A Marketplace of Girl Influencers Managed by Moms and Stalked by Men," *The New York Times*, February 22, 2024, A1.

Conclusion

1. Curtis Hesselgrave, "Observations on the USASA Nationals," *Skateboarder* 5, no. 12 (July 1979): 56.
2. PJ McKenzie, personal interview, July 4, 2023.
3. Rebecca Solnit, *Recollections of My Nonexistence* (Viking, 2020), 237.
4. Solnit, *Recollections of My Nonexistence*, 225.
5. Zanna, *50-50 Skate Zine: Skateboarding and Gender* (1999).
6. Zanna, *50-50 Skate Zine*, 26.
7. Zanna, *50-50 Skate Zine*, 5.

INDEX

17th Avenue Skatepark, 125
41st Ave Skateboards, 160
411 Video Magazine, 46, 54, 108
5boro Skateboards, 47
50-50 Skate Zine (zine), 314
90's, The (television), 2-3

'A'ala Park, 126
Abal, Raisa, 113
Abruzzini, Bibbi, 6-7
Action Sports Alliance. *See* Women's
   Skateboarding Alliance
Action Sports Retailer, 185
Adams, Janet, 201
Adams, Lucy, 314
Adrian, Kim, 36, 44, *233*, 235-38
Affleck, Sally, 126, 204
Agresti, Kym, 42, 106
Aguilar, Olga, 113
Airwalk, 99
AKA: Girl Skater (film), 56, *121*, 127, 129, 140
Alaway, Robin, 159
Alfred Cox Skatepark, 141
All Girl Skate Jam (AGSJ), 56, 107, 111, 126,
   176, 212-14, 229, 244, 314
All Saints, 21
All Systems Go! (film), 47
All This Mayhem (film), 231
Allen, Jane, 139-40
Allen, Sophie, 126
Alter, Hobart "Hobie," 80
Alva Skates, 306
Alva, Tony, 145-46, 182, 301

American Association of Retired Persons
   (magazine), 282
Anarquia!, 306
Angry Amputees, 245
Antisocial Skateboard Shop, 63, 109, 247,
   270, 298, 302
Aotearoa Skate (television), 125, 129, 137, 139
Apramian, Lisa Rose, 106
Arataki Skatepark, 122
Araujo, Liza, 110-12
Archie, Rose, 215, 287
Arguelles, Zhenya, 197
Armanto, Eva, 282
Armanto, Lizzie, 115
Armpit (zine), 20, 149
Armstrong, Danielle, *94*
Arquie, Jackie, 81
Art Linkletter's House Party (television),
   78-79
Artificial Intelligence (AI), 298
As If, And What? (film), 214
Association of Skatepark Owners (ASPO),
   37, 173
Australian Girls' Street Skate Jam, 126
AZ Steez (magazine), 258

Back to the Future (film), 30
Bader, Rhianon, 62, 270-71 291, 293-94, 319
Bahne, 143
Bailey, Hannah, 113
Baker Bootleg (film), 47
Baker, Leo, 91
Ball Hitch Ramps, 135

345

GIRL GANGS, ZINES, AND POWERSLIDES

Barbagallo, Ron, 189-90
Barter, Denise, 163
Bates, Sevie, 180-81
Beach Boys, The, 131
Beach Party (film), 78
Beachy, Kyle, 315
Bearer, Wendy, 83
Beastie Boys, 171, 212, 244
Bedell, Wendy, 238
Belmont Park Freestyle Contest, 158
Ben Raemers Foundation, 165
Bennett, Debbi, 36
Benson, Linda, 78-79
Bergsten, Jessica, 37
Berrics, The, 5, 311
Berryman, Cindy, 156-59
Berryman, Ellen, 34, 35, 59, 158, 202
Béton Hurlant Skatepark, 82
Betty (television), 45
Bevington, Liz, *viii*, 1-3, 11, 281-82
Bianco, Marie-Pierre, 81
Big Brother (magazine), 10, 127-29, 148, 230
Big O Skatepark, 36, 102, 234, 277
Bikceem, Ramdasha, 104-06, 123
Bikini Kill, 244
Billabong, 133
Bjesse-Puffin, Amelia, 287
Black Flag, 32
@black_girls_skate, 124
Black, Noel, 44
Blackett, Kim, 208-09
Blender, Neil, 210, 239
Blouin, Bonnie, 17, 19, 25, 98, 121, *142*, 148, 150-56, *157*, 164-67, 172, 198
Bolster, Warren, 156, 195
Bomeisler, Kathy, 203
Bond, James, 95
Bones Brigade, 132
Bootleg Skateboards, 47
Borden, Iain, 36, 145, 195
Boronat, Nicole, 82
Bostick, Danielle, 14, 260
Bostick, Don, 14, 260
Bourgeois, Sophie, 34, 54, 209, 304
Bowman, Tamra, 282
Boy (film), 51
Boyd, Colleen, 83, 178-80
Bradley, Dean, 280
Bradshaw, Amy, 260-62, 271, 282
Brand X, 210

Brandenburg, Liz, 213
Break the Cycle, 286
Breakers Surf Shop, 99
Brevard, Samarria, 134
Brewer Skateboards, 293
Brittain, J. Grant, 134
Brodka, Amelia, 60-61, 215, 314
Brolin, Josh, 45
Bronx Girls Skate (girl gang), 135
Brooke, Michael, 195
Brookhurst Park, 236
Brooklyn Bridge Anchorage (vert ramp), 184
Brooklyn Skate Moms (girl gang), 250
Brotherhood Board Shop, 84
Brown, Debra, 201
Brown, Sky, 313
Brown, Terry, 34, 203
Brujas (girl gang), 58, 135
Bufoni, Leticia, 110, 111
Building the Revolution (website), 130
Bun Buster, 79
Burdell, Sheenagh, 200
Burnett, Michael, 148
Burnquist, Rebecca, 107
Burnside Skatepark, 314
Burnside, Cara-Beth, 14, 36, 37, 44, 47, 53, 56, 60, 64-65, 85, *105*, 115, 126, 129, 132, 173, 187, 189, 1*95*, 199, 210, 212-13, 228-29, 234, 242, 273
Bust (magazine), 180

C&D Skateshop, 236
Caballero, Steve, 18
Calgary Stampede, The, 304
California Amateur Skateboard League (CASL), 24, 99-100, 103, 114
California State Championships, 35
Calkins, Deanna, 203, 261, 284
Canadian Pipeline, The (newsletter), 299
Capitola Classic, 256
Cardiel, John, 48
Carlsbad Skatepark, The, 203
Carnie, Dave, 127-128
Caron, Amy, 56, 86, 109, 111, 127-28, 186
Carter, Clarissa, 222-23
Carter, Lynda, 44
Cash, Donna, 178-79
Cassimus, James, 233, 277
Catalano, Sonja, 99
Cathey, Steve, 175

INDEX

CBS Sports Spectacular (television), 160
Cell Block, 156
Cespedes, Kim, 158, 163, 196, 203, 220
Chadbourn, Sandy, 147, 238
Challenge of the Sexes (television), 28
Chang, Nancy, 284
Check It Out (magazine), 110-13, 174, 214
Cherries Wheels, 187
Cherry Skateboards, 135, 187
Cheung, Jeffrey, 246
Child Protection Pledge, 294
Circle A Boardshop, 135
Claire, Mimi, 180, 182
Clark, Sal, 126
Clarke, Saecha, 27, 38, 47, 60, 105, 174-75, 177
Clash, The, 224
Clifford, Graeme, 45
Cobb, Dee Jay, 69, 73
Cohen, Judith, 203, 293
Cohen, Lesli, 215
Colonialism Skateboards, 287
Comăneci, Nadia, 313
Commitment to Anti-Racism in Skateboarding, 294
Concrete Divas, 258
Concrete Queenz, 135
Concrete Wave Skatepark, The, 234, 236, 272, 276-77
Confederation Skatepark, 63, 317
Consent Is Rad, 285-88
Converse, 49
Cooper, Tara, 60
Coppa, Jennifer. *See* Dimon, Jennifer
Cosgrove, Ben, 221
Covell, Chloe, 312
COVID-19, 21, 66-67, 91, 297
Crandall, Maurice, 315
Credits (film), 58
Crigar, Elise, 113
Crystal Palace, 201-02
Cucci, Yvonne, 147, 261
Cutts, Thea, 201

Da Mad Taco Skates Again, 299
Dal Santo, Marisa, 86, 111
Dalmacio, Airra, 205
Damiano, Lori, 107-08, 109
Daniels, Julie, 262, 271
Danielson, Denise, 36

Daughters of Ally, 140
Days Like These (film), 214
De Fazio Ebert, Fay, 312
Dean, Larry, 208
Defeating Projections (film), 108
Del Mar Nationals, 144
Del Mar Skate Ranch, 98, 103, 114-17, 144
Delfino, Fabiana, 58
Derby Park, 132-33
Descendents, The, 225
Desiderio, Diane, 2, 27, 30-32, 60
Desiderio, Primo, 27, 30, 32
Devera, Ed, 135
Devil's Toy, The (film), 221, 223
Devine, Brenda, 163
Devine, Deirdre "Dee Dee," 152
Devries, Elizabeth, 180
Different Kind of Winning, A (television), 44
Dimon, Jennifer, 44, 158
Dine, Keva Marie, 186
Dittrich, Scott, 44
Dogtown Z-Boys, 144, 161, 229, 245, 257, 315
Dolores (magazine), 286
Dominy, Dave, 202
Domond, Beatrice, 134, 215
Don't Need You: The Herstory of Riot Grrrl (film), 104
Double Down (zine), 68
Douglass, Barbara, 45
Doyle, Rhonda, 60, 204, 229
Dressen, Eric, 147
Dubé, Erika, 20, 112
Duffy, Kyla, 186, 213
Dunn, Chuck, 236
Dupin, Corinne, 82
Duran, Mariah, 252
Duran, Martina, 131
Dynamite 8, 245
Dysinger, Carol, 62

East Bay Punk Rock Riders, 245
Eastern Skateboard Association Championships, 248, 251, 253, 265
Ebeling, Kristin, 56-57, 284
Economy, Ed, 280
EDO (zine), 238
Edwards, Jessica, 60-61
Eilbacher, Cindy, 44
Eldredge, Debi, 44

347

GIRL GANGS, ZINES, AND POWERSLIDES

Element Skateboards, 108
Equal Credit Opportunity Act (ECOA), 35
Equal Time (zine), 27, 53, 59, 134, 172-78, 179, 190, 197, 210-11, 224, 227-228
Equal Time Ramp, 210, 218, 227
Engblom, Skip, 23
Engel, Laura, 203
English Skateboard Association (ESA), 207, 210
Epic Skatepark, 214
Eppridge, Bill, 79, 221
Erickson, Kit, 226
Escalante, Danny, 83
ESPN, 85, 92
Etnies, 32
Everything Skateboarding (website), 189
EXPN (website), 85
Expo 86, 64, 208-09, 211
Exposure, 61, 81, 215

Faction, The, 57
Fahrney, Babs, 153
Family (television), 28-29
Farnborough (vert ramp), 207
Farrar, Una, 58
Faulkner, George, 50, 63
Faulkner, Gordon, 50, 63
Fawcett, Farrah, 164
Feitosa, Karen, 85
Fernández, Stephanie, 162
Ferreira, Maria Elaigne, 110
Ferrero, Antonella, 197
Field, Joanna, 36
Fifth Column, 21
Fire It Up (film), 47
Fishman, Beth, 238, 248, 251, 253-54, 262-69, 271
Fishman, Rose, 248, 253-54, 265
Fitzgerald, Heidi, 60
Fitzpatrick, Jim, 81
Fleming, Denise, 273-74
Florida Skateboard Hall of Fame, 147, 293
Flynt, Larry, 127
Föche, Mörizen, 121
Forman, Lisa, 36, 173
For Our Daughters (film), 7
Footloose (film), 26
Foundation Skateboards, 186
Fox, Ethan, 27, 32, 53, 59-61, 227
Fox, Gardia, 180-81, 243

Fox, Jennifer, 289
Fox, Tessa, 287
Free Former World Freestyle Championships, 159
Freeman, Jim, 44
Freestyle Hall of Fame, 32
Freewheelin' (film), 44
Friedberg, Josh, 108
Frohlick, Denise, 304
Frontside Betty (website), 149, 152
froSkate, 135
Frumpies, The, 244
Funicello, Annette, 78
Future First Responders of America, 101
Future Primitive (film), 132

Gage, George, 44
Gale Webb Action Sports Park, 250
Gall, Pete, 73-74
Gallaz, 56, 121, 126-29, 139, 213
Gallaz Skate Jam, 213
Gardner, Suzi, 243
Geering, Breana, 58
Gérard, Isolde, 81
Getting Nowhere Faster (film), 56, 108-09
Ghetto Fabulous (film), 137
Gidget Goes Hawaiian (film), 78
Gil, Arianna, 58
Gila River Basket Dancers, 316
Gillespie, Doug, 225
Gillespie, Frank, 225
Gillespie, JoAnn "Rawkmom," 59-60, 176, 210, 218, 220, 224-30, 241, 245-46
Gillogly, Brian, 147
Girl Is NOT A 4 Letter Word, 115
Girls Skate Network (website), 55-56, 112, 213
Girls Skate Out, 214
Girls Who Grind (zine), 172, 174-75
Gits, Gigi, 98, 150, 152
Gleaming the Cube (film), 45
Glendale Skatepark, 258
Globe Industries, 126-27
Globe World Cup, 126
Go-Go's, The, 49
Godoy, Esther, 126
Golding, Billing, 256
Gonçalves, Gini, 197
Gonzales, Mark, 18
Goodpush Alliance, The, 293-94

INDEX

Goodrich, Jim, 161, 164
Gordon & Smith (G&S), 143, 175, 203, 276, 300, 303
Gordon, Kim, 105
Grand Royal (magazine), 212, 244
Grandmaster Flash, 243
Greater New York Safety Council, 223
Green Day, 226
Greenwood, Jeff, 255
Grinding to Win (film), 43, 49-50, 63-66
Grisham, John, 310
Grosso, Jeff, 18, 235
Guerrero, Tommy, 18
Guglia, Annie, 275
Gullwing Trucks, 132
Gunk (girl gang), 103
Gunk (zine), 104

Hackemack, Dodie, 44
Hada, Ken, 261
Haggerty, Dan, 28
Hags, The (girl gang), 180-83, 243, 270
Hall, Heather, 261
Handell, Björn, 255
Hang Ten Olympics, 88
Hansen Surfboards, 78-79
Hansen, Don, 78
Haohao, Zheng, 312
Hardskate (zine), 111
Harmon, Koji, 54
Harris, Naomi, 82
Harrison, Jo, 126
Hart, Lulu, 283
Hawk, Frank, 99, 229
Hawk, Steve, 116
Hawk, Tony, 14, 37, 91, 97, 99, 114-17, 120, 213, 231, 245, 311
Hawkins, Lyn-Z Adams, 86, 111
Hazel, Nicky, 198
Hazel, Sue, 134, 177, *192*, 194, 197-200, 206-11, 214-17, 220, 227
Heads (film), 47
Hectic Times (zine), 106
Heller, Rebecca, 100
Hénault-Ethier, Louise, 20, 314
Hesselgrave, Curtis, 299
Hester Pro Bowl, 234
Hester, Henry, 175
Hill, Francine, 158
Hill, Frankie, 226, 228

Hill, Mike, 56
Hoag, Claudia, 282
Hobie Skateboards, 74, 80, 83, 143, 161, 178, 203, 280-81, 284
Hobie Surf Shop, 80
Hoffman, April, 2, 46, 88, 153, 209
Hoffman, Jeanne, 46, 99
Hoffman, Pattie, 36, 60, 146, 154-55, 240
Hogtown Skateboard Shop, 176
Hollywood Teen-Age Fair, 79
Hoopla Skateboards, 187
Hosoi, Christian, 18
Howard, Rick, 206
Howell, Russ, 195
Hubba Wheels, 34
Hunter, Charmaine, 213
Hurtado, Gerry, 36
Hurting Crew, 245
Huston, Sarah, 113

Ibarra, Norma, 113
Iceland Skatepark, 214
Idlewood (zine), 298
Idol, Billy, 45
Independent Trucks, 76, 99, 234, 256
Inside the Games (magazine), 89
International Olympic Committee (IOC), 87-88, 91
International Skateboard Championships, 70, 83, 86, 179
Into the Mirror: Fragmentos (film), 110
ISA Northern California Pro Championship, 234

J.D.'s (Juvenile Delinquents) (zine), 29
Jackass (television), 128, 166
Jaime, Faye, 107
Jaks, The, 181
Japenga, Ann, 181
@jeezysk8s, 262
Jenkem (magazine), 110
Jethro Tull, 159
Jodie Foster's Army (JFA), 243-44
Johnson, Sara, 180
Jones, Colleen, 79
Jones, G. B., 29
Jordahl, Christy, 174-75
Joy and Sorrow (films), 306
Judge, Pam, 299-304
Jump Off a Building (film), 47

GIRL GANGS, ZINES, AND POWERSLIDES

Jutra, Claude, 221

Kalinová, Lucie, 269-70
Karlsen, Liz, 201-02
Karren, Billy, 244
Kaupas, Natas, 18
Kelleher, Megan, 84
Kenney, Michelle, 238
Kibler, Karen, 57
Kids (film), 287
Kids Are People Too (television), 265
Kinast, Erika, 62, 270-71, 291, 319
King, Billie Jean, 21, 28, 163
King, Briana, 136, 215
Kinsley, Kim, 238
Kiyabu, Leilani, 163, 234, 304
Klein, Naomi, 7-9
Knoop, Mimi, 85-86, 187, 313
Kobes Du Mez, Kristin, 7
Koch, Kerri, 104
Kohner, Kathy, 81
Kramer, Lynn, 60, 134, 168, 170-77, 187, 189-91, 197-98, 210-11, 224, 227-28
Krause, Jessica, 48-49
Krishna Das, Natalie, 259
Krux Trucks, 284-85
Kryptonics Wheels, 161
Kwan, Jung, 183

L7, 242-43
La Costa, 44, 158, 202-03
La Costa Racing Team, 187
La Femme (girl gang), 178-80
Labor Day Skate Jam, 177
LaBruce, Bruce, 29
Ladies Skateworld (zine), 24, 94, 98-103, 113, 115-18, 133
Ladyfest, 283
Lafonte, Morgan, 242
Lagwagon, 226
Lakewood Skatepark, 233, 237-38
Lakewood World Pro Halfpipe Contest, 234
Lannes, Laurence, 82
Lapper (zine), 150
Larsen, Fleur, 283
Las ChicAZ (girl gang), 259
Late Bloomers Skate Club, 250
Later Skaters Gang, 250
Latta, Marilyn, 147
Lavigne, Avril, 140

Lawing, Jessica, 60
Lawrence, Terry, 146, 163, 232-35, 233, 246, 261, 273, 306-07
Lawson-Duffy, Shari, 313
Lay, Ryan, 315
Lazerwolf, 245
Leal, Rayssa, 110
Learning to Skateboard in a Warzone (film), 62
Leblanc, Lauraine, 183, 219, 242, 246
Lee, Michelle, 201
Lee, Sunshine, 261
Leighton-Boyce, Tim, 210
Les Poseuz Crew (girl gang), 306
Lessler, Andria, 107
Lethal Arms, 182
Lévesque, Julie, 171
Levy, Debra Ann, 7-8
Life (magazine), 79-80, 95, 124, 221, 259
Limbaugh, Rush, 149
Lindgren, Astrid, 107
Lindsay, Susie, 147
Live and Let Ride (film), 60
Logan Earth Ski, 143, 155, 203, 249
Logan, Barbara, 249
Logan, Brad, 249
Logan, Brian, 249
Logan, Bruce, 249
Logan, Robin, 28-29, 59, 158, 203, 220, 249
Loges, Crystal, 238
Look Back Library, 197
Loveletters to Skateboarding (television), 235
Lucero, John, 209, 239
Lyon, Shodie, 135
Lyons, Catharine, 183-86
Lyons, Danielle Black, 131
Lyons, Holly, 213
Lyons, Lora, 99-103, 173

MacGillivray, Greg, 44
MacKillop, Traci, 50
Maclean's (magazine), 118
Madrid Skateboards, 30, 133
Mae, Michelle, 244
Magic Rolling Board, The (film), 44
MAHFIA TV (website), 56
Mahony, Kate "Kate the Skate," 200-02, 220
Majestic Unicorn Motorcycle Club (girl gang), 225, 270, 293
Makaha Skateboards, 81, 83, 302
Malczewski, Andra, 44

INDEX

Mallison, Rodger, 121, 123
Manual (magazine), 126
Marina Del Rey Skatepark, 195, 306
Marks, Kevin, 197
Marsh, Kelly, 238
Martin, Ernie, 28
Massey, Stephanie, 60
Massie, Aimee, 313
Matthews, Georgina, *122*, 124-27, 129, 137, 139-41, 176
McCabe, Teresa, 282
McClelland, Shirley, 36
McDonald, Jodi, 38-39
McDonald, John, 44
McGee, Patti, *69*, 79-81, 124, 221, 259
McGhee, "Bootsey", 83
McKenzie, PJ. *See* Judge, Pam
McNichol, Kristy, 28-29, 34, 45
McQueen, Steve, 225
McRad, 32
#MeToo, 274, 279, 289-90, 293, 310
Mearns, Drew, 86
Medlock, George, 134
Melling, Lizzie, 201
Mendelssohn, Dana, 57-59
Mendonça, Vitória, 215
Meow Skateboards, 52, 56-57, 85, 187, 252, 285
Meyen, Janna, 118
Meyers, Elisabeth "Eli," 197
Midwest Amateur Ramp Series (M.A.R.S.), 239
Mighty Mama Skate-O-Rama, 2, 81, *279*, 282
Mike Douglas Show, The (television), 80
Miljevic, Miljana, 285
Miller, Leslie Anne, 88
Miller, Michel, 180
Mills, Mary, 129-31
Mimi's Revenge (zine), 184
Miyamoto, Miho, 187, 313
Miyoda, Glenn, 157
Moberly, Sofia Lauren, 206
Mollica, Lauren, 127, 186
Monthly Shredder, The (zine), 241
Moon Spinners, The (film), 80
Morgan, Nicole, 106-09
Morgan, Perri, 47
Morgan, Tiffany, 106-09
Moselle, Crystal, 45
Mountain, Lance, 53, 210

Ms. (magazine), 96
MTV, 144, 242
Muir, Lisa, 283
Mullen, Rodney, 31-34
Mundy, Liza, 193
Murai, Yuri, 306

Narducci, Jeannie, 147, 238
National Film Board of Canada, 221-22
National Skateboard Association (NSA), 88, 229
National Skateboard Review (magazine), 87, 157, 161, 202-03, 249, 251, 256, 265, 284, 303
Nations Skate Youth, 287
Negrão, Ana Paula, 111-12
Neuman, Molly, 244
Nevada State Fair, 229
Newton-John, Olivia, 30
Nguyen, Van, 107
Nine Club, The (podcast), 38
No Comply (film), 6
No Comply Coven (girl gang), 58
No Consent = Sexual Abuse (zine), 287
No Fear, 96
NOFX, 242
Non Fiction (film), 47
Not Bad for a Girl (film), 106
Novak, Rich, 256
Nu Skate Movement, 244

O'Brien, Allison, 205
O'Brien, Jen, 85-86, 204, 242
O'Connor, Shannon, 259
O'Connor, Sinéad, 224
O'Malley, John, 157
O'Toole, Monique, 56
Oasis Skatepark, *296*, 299
Ocean Pacific Girls Learn to Ride, 109
Oceanside Championships, 280
Oceanside Pro-Am Freestyle Contest, 35
Odanaka, Barb, 2, 261, 279-83, 287, 290
Offspring, The, 226
OG Jam Series, 262
OJ Wheels, 156
Okamoto, Misugu, 312
Oki, Peggy, 144, 257
@oldlady_skater, 260
Oliver, Aina Maria, 197
Oliver, Emily, 135, 187

GIRL GANGS, ZINES, AND POWERSLIDES

Olivia, Zorah, 113
Olsen, Poppy Starr, 312
Olympic Games, 28, 49, 67, 82, 87-92, 113, 208-09, 223, 242, 245, 304, 306, 311-14, 316
On Any Sunday (film), 225
Oneal, Ellen, 34-35, 44, 162, 203, 261
Orchid Ranch Skatepark, 261
Original Betty Skate Company (OG Betty), 80, 152
Osiris (shoes), 135
Ostos, Isa, 246
Ové, Horace, 44
Oyama, Judi, 133, 203, 254-57, *255*

Pacific National Exhibition, 303
Palisades Team, 83, 178
Palmero, Romina, 246
Pappalardo, Anthony, 38, 286
Pappas, Ben, 230
Pappas, Tas, 230
Park Riders, 156
Parker, Jenny, 57
Parkin, Leigh, 36
Pascal, Athena, 206
Paschini, Renata, 197, 313
Pastras, Chris, 134
Paul, Amy, 25, 153
Paved Wave Skatepark, The, 263
Payne, Jana, 88, 147-48, 162, 234, 261, *272*, 273, 275-81, 288-92, 306
Pearce, Hilary, 126
Pendergast, Cyndy, *233*, 238-41
Pennywise, 171, 242
People (magazine), 28
Pepsi Team, 161, 197, 234, 273
Peralta, Stacy, 50
Perez, Valerie, 80
Person, Stephanie, 19, 25, 99, *121*, 132-35, 153, 175, *179*, 209-11, 257
Peters, Duane, 145
Pezel, Michelle, *63*, 107, 109
Phillips, Lynette, 231
Piasta, Laura, 195
Pickett, Billy, 157
Pig Wheels, 47
Pigeon, Mathilde, 20, 51-52,
Pipeline Skatepark, 46, *256*, 299
P. J. Ladd's Wonderful, Horrible, Life (film), 47
Place du Trocadéro, 82
Plotnick, Danny, 57-58, 285

Plourde, Derrick, 227
PMS, 17, 19, 227
Poirier, Elaine, 261
Polistchuk, Monica, 11, 197
Poot!, 186
Powell Peralta, 34, 47, 50, 53-54, 99, 173, 177, 224
Powell Skate Zone, *53*, 59, 61, 228-29
Powell, Sharon, 238
Poweredge (magazine), 133, 175
Powerflex Skateboards, 143, 234, 250, 273
Pratt, Nathan, 161
Price, Canon "Bunny," 147, 163
Progressive Skateboards, 147
Propaganda (film), 47
Prospect Park, 263
Public Domain (film), 54
Push (magazine), 112, 149
Push, Push, Then Go! (zine), 17, 23-25, 27, 40
Pushing Boarders, 285

Quarterley Skateboarder, The (magazine), 82, 87
Queyrel, Claude, 81
Quit Your Day Job (film), 56

R.A.D. (magazine), 209-10
Radical Moves (film), 208-09
Raemers, Ben, 165
Ragged Edge Zine Collection, 238
Rainbow Skatepark, 239
Rainey, Marla, 239
Rancid, 226
Rape Relief, 290
Rarey, Lori, 44, 162-63
Ratermanis, Arne, 296
Rattray, John, 165
Ray, Miller, 222
Razaq, Shamsia, 205
Ready to Shred, 173
Real Hot Skate Moms, The (girl gang), 250
Real Skate (website), 135
Real Skateboards, 47
Rector Pads, 133
Red Hot Chili Peppers, 46
Reis, Chris, 177
Repas, Erich "Shreddi," 236
Respect Is Rad. *See* Consent Is Rad
Reyes, Jaime, 47, 111, 126-27, 129, 186, 204
Reynolds, Samantha, 50, 64-65

INDEX

Rich, Adam, 267
Rich Kids on LSD (RKL), 225
Richmond Skate Ranch, 64
Richter, Nathalie, 134
Ride Like a Girl, 213-14
Riggs, Bobby, 28
Rigsbee, Lori, 38, 47, 54, 94, 98-99, 105, 117, 206
Riot Grrrls, 21, 42, 104, 106, 140, 204, 206, 231, 243-44
Risk It (film), 47, 64
Ritzma, Leslie Jo, 159-61
Robertson, Edie, 34, 44, 261
Rocco, Steve, 127
Rocky Horror Picture Show (film), 303
Rogowski, Mark "Gator," 37-38, 230-31
Rogue Skateboards, 187
Roller (magazine), 161
Rookie Skateboards, 54, 183-87, 213, 270
Roper, Jax, 176
Roper, Stacey "Stace the Ace," 125-26, 176-77
Rose, Di Dootson, 202-04, 284
Roskopp, Rob, 76
Rowland, Suzie, 178-79
Roy, Oorbee "Aunty Skates," 67
Rubbish Heap (film), 47
Rusen, Jean "Calamity Jean," 255, 257-60, 282
Runway Skatepark, The, 284
Ryder, Evie, 285

S1 Helmets, 261
Sablone, Alexis, 47, 111, 128, 313
Sack, Julie, 60
Sacks, Alan, 182
Sacks, Keren, 180, 182
Sacto Streetstyle, 18, 27, 34
Sampson, Jenny, 113
Sanderson, Gary, 209
Sanderson, Michelle, 88, 153, 209
Sandor, Elska, 183-86,
Sandoval, Erik, 56
Santa Cruz Skateboards, 33, 76, 130, 133, 179, 203, 210, 257
Santa Cruz Speed Wheels, 47, 210
Santa Monica Airlines (SMA), 23, 174
São Bernardo do Campo Skatepark, 111
Sassoon, Vidal, 265
Saturday Night Fever (film), 2
Savage, Emily, 180-81
Saye, Alicia, 126

Schairer, Lea, 313
Schillereff, Johnny,
Schiot, Molly, 256
Schoonheere, Lucie, 312
Schulz, Joachim "YoYo," 199
Screamin' Sirens, 182
Sefton, Nancy, 180-82
Segovia, Patty, 60, 100, 111-12, 172, 176, 212, 229, 244
Selby, Jenna, 187, 214
Sells, Jennifer, 175-76, 178
SERISA, 162
Serna, Sandra, 282
Seylynn Bowl, 43, 64, 209
Sharp, William, 306
Shaw, Monica, 126
Sheehan, Holly, 283
Sheehan, Maura, 184
Shetterly, Margot Lee, 193
Shillingford, Lynne, 201
Shuirman, Jay, 256
Siciliano, Giola, 80
Side Project, The (website), 56, 86
Sidewalk (magazine), 192, 199, 210, 217
Sierra Wave Skatepark, 256
Sierra, Kathy, 32-34
Signal Hill Downhill, 159-160
Silly Girl Skateboards, 80
Simpsons, The (television), 259
Sims Skateboards, 19, 44, 161, 163, 236, 261, 276
Singleton, Clyde, 14, 148
Sinift, Jaime, 107
Sirviö, Heili, 312
Sixties Scoop, 308
SK8HERS (film), 32, 38, 53, 59-61, 155, 211, 227-28, 232
Sk8Kings, 32, 170
Skat'nNews (newsletter), 36
Skate and Annoy (blog), 34, 38, 96
Skate Bunneys (girl gang), 244
Skate City Girls (girl gang), 201
Skate Dreams (film), 60-61, 285
Skate Kitchen (film), 45
Skate Like a Girl, 32, 57, 215, 283-85, 287, 293
Skate of Mind (website), 270
Skate Rider (magazine), 147
Skate Witches (film), 57-59, 285
Skate Witches, The (zine), 57, 285

GIRL GANGS, ZINES, AND POWERSLIDES

SkateBettys (girl gang), 243
Skateboard! (magazine), 88, 134, 200, 202, 211
Skateboard: The Movie (film), 44
Skateboard Kings (film), 44
Skateboard Mag (magazine), 210
Skateboard Moms and Sisters of Shred (girl gang), 261, 282, 287
Skateboard Safety (film), 44
Skateboard Scene (magazine), 200, 202
Skateboard Special (magazine), 200
Skateboard World (magazine), 263
Skateboarder (magazine), 59, 80, 145, 147, 156, 158-59, 161-64, 179, 195-96, 234, 272, 276-77, 299-300
Skateboarding Hall of Fame, 44, 47, 81, 83, 87, 92, 159, 164, 179, 204, 217, 239, 249, 257, 277, 279, 289, 304
Skategirl (film), 40, 56, 60
Skateism (magazine), 134, 234, 286
Skateistan, 34, 62-63, 271, 293-94
@skatemaniabrasil, 197
SkaterCross Skatepark, 173
Skaterdater (film), 44, 80
@skatersofcolor, 137
Skatopia, 44, 233, 256, 260-61, 277
Skirtboarders (girl gang), 20, 41, 51, 66, 91, 213, 274, 275
Skoundrelz, The, 182
Skullz, The (girl gang), 126, 149
Slade, Sue, 201
Slam City Jam, 20, 56, 84-85, 211, 214
Slap (magazine), 32, 186
Slater, Christian, 45
Slime Balls Wheels, 76
Sloboh, Adrianne, 134
Slow Impact, 315
Smash the Skatriarchy (zine), 287
Smith, Christy, 60
Smith, Patti, 265-69
Smith, Sue, 36
Solnit, Rebecca, 311
SOLO (magazine), 113
Solomon, Crystal, 135-37
Sonic Youth, 105
Southsea Skate Contest, 209
Southsea Skatepark, 207
Southsea Skateshop, 210
Souza, Emilie "Pipa," 110
Sparks, Donita, 243

Spice Girls, 21
Spreiter, Corina "GoGo," 208-09
Springer, Gale, 36
SRSLY (film), 58
Stalin Plaza, 269
Starr, Scott, 126, 218
Stay on Board: The Leo Baker Story (film), 91
Steamer, Elissa, 47-48, 84, 86, 111, 128, 148-49, 152, 189
Steenhoudt, Maité "Club Maiteee," 215
Steinem, Gloria, 95-96
Stiepock, Chris, 86
Stop, Drop, and Roll, 215
STP Zoomer Toomer, 201
Street Life, 174
Striking Fear into the Hearts of Teenage Girls (film), 107-08
Suárez, Daniela, 313
Suicidal Tendencies, 32, 77, 242
Sukasem, Vareeraya, 312
Sung, Jess, 113
Sunny Skateboard, 187
Super Surfers, 74, 83
Superbowl Skatepark, 303
Supreme, 135
Surely Skate, 141
Surf and the Fury, The (website), 130
Surf Flyer, 199
Surf Guide (magazine), 78
Surfer (magazine), 78
Swank, Tod, 186
Swatch, 133
Swenson, Krishna, 226

Tabata, Susanne, 40, 50
Tale, The (film), 289
Tamez, Cat, 187
Tantillo, Renee "Ne," 106
Taz Mahal Skatepark, 274
Tea Gardens, The, 228
Templeton, Ed, 48, 84
Tessensohn, Anita, 50, 53, 54, 177
Textured Waves (website), 130-31
There Skateboards, 246
Thiebaud, Jim, 37
Think Skateboards, 48
Thomas, Helen, 201
Thomas, Stefanie, 186
Thornhill, Laura, 35, 59, 88, 146, 154, 158, 189, 195, 203

INDEX

Thornton, Cheryl, *121*, 123-24
Thrasher (magazine), 2, *12*, 16, 18-19, 25, 27, 30-31, 54, 60-61, 89-90, 105, *121*, 123, 126, 132, 134-35, 148, 150-57, *157*, 164, 166-67, *168*, 173, 175, 186, 203-07, 209-10, 212, 229-30, 240, 243-44, 258, 286, 316
Thrashin' (film), 45-46, 182
THX (film), 58
Ticktin, Michelle, 39, 211, 230
Tim Brauch Memorial Contest, 258
Time (magazine), 118
Times Up: No More Rape Culture in Our Skate Culture (zine), 287
Title IX, 34
Toland, Amanda Brix, 180
Toledo, Luciana, 111-12
Topsiders, 74
Torres, Vanessa, 52, *55*-56, 86, 109, 111, 127-28, 313
Toy Machine, 47-48, 84, 148
Tracker Trucks, 30, 143, 174, 203
Tran, Minh Duc, 202
TransWorld (magazine), 32, 38, 64, 109, 115, 119, 127-29, 132, 134, 148, 175, 190, 208
Treinen, Leaf, 50
Trew, Arisa, 311-13
Tribo (magazine), 110
True Devotion (zine), 98, 150, 167
Tunnel Wheels, 160
Turf Skatepark, The, *233*, 239-41
Turner, Laurie, *70*, 74-75, 82-83, 87, 92 179
Turner, Peggy, 238
Tutifruti, 246

U.K. Ladies Skate Series, 141
U.S. Open Snowboarding Championships, 118
Ueno, Chihiro, 187
Uganda Skateboard Union, 293
Underexposed (film), 60-61
Underworld Skateshop, 171
United States Skateboard Association, 87
Unity Skateboarding, 246
USASA Nationals, 299
Uyemura, MaryAnne, 197

Vail, Tobi, 244
Valenzuela, Jen, *135*, 137
Van, Nam-Chi, 113

Van Doren, Kristy, 260
Van Doren, Paul, 260
Van Roechoudt, Jessie, 129, 183, 186, 270
van Zyl, Alicia, 58
Vanguard, Stevie, 282
Vans, 151, 199, 210, 234, 250, 259-61, 276-77, 301
Vans Combi Pool Contest, 260
Vans Girls Combi Pool Classic, 259
Vans Warped Tour, 213, 242-43
Variflex Skateboards, 146, 155
Vasconcellos, Nora, 90, 215
Veerman, Diane. *See* Desiderio, Diane
Venice Ladies Jam, 255, 262
Venice Skatepark, 262
Venture Trucks, 133
Verge, The (website), 33
Vice (magazine), 89
Vickers, Vicki, 154, *157*, 161-64, 195, 203
Villa, Hailey, 80, 259
Villa Villa Cola (girl gang), 56, 106-09
Villa Villa Cola (zine), 106-09
Vision Sims Street Attack, 19
Vision Skateboards, 37-38
Vita-Pakt Juice Company, 74
Vogue Philippines (magazine), 249
Von Essen, Desiree, 34, 158

Walden, Peggy, 60
Walley, Deborah, 78
Warning (zine), 243
. Washington, Nika, 134
Watson, Ericka, *94*, 117-18
Watson, Rhonda, 117
WCRP on Skateboarding (podcast), 14
Webb, Gale, 36, 203, 249-50, 261
Welcome to Hell (film), 47, 84
West Side Story (film), 182
Wettstein, Bryce, 81, 312
Whang-Od, Apo, 249
What's My Line? (television), 80
Wheels of Fortune, 215, 285
Wheldrake, Joyce, 176
Whitaker, Lisa, 52-56, 85-86, 107-08, 127, 186-87, 213
White, Alex, 108, 111, 284, 314
White, Shari, 57-58
Whitehead, Cindy, *35*-36, 115, 132, 134, 146
Whittier Skatepark, 37, 237
Why So Sad?, 165

GIRL GANGS, ZINES, AND POWERSLIDES

Wicked Wahine, 213, 258
Wide World of Sports (television), 83, 131, 180
Wietzke, Lisa Jak, *42*, 45-46, *63-65*
Wilcox, Kathi, 244
Wild World of Skateboarding (magazine), 28, 159, 249, 254
Willamette Dammit Skate Contest, 50
Williams, Denise, 112, 149
Williams, Melissa, 313
Williams, Neftalie, 196
Williams, Tammy "Bam Bam," 213
Willing, Indigo, 285-88
Wilmot, Janie, 201
Winchester Skatepark, 234
Winter, Margaret, 304
Winters, David, 45
Wired (magazine), 32-34
Wodecki, Patricia, 206
Women's Equal Action League, 160
Women's Battle at the Berrics, 5
Women's Skateboarding Alliance, 86
Women's Skateboarding Club, *94*, 99-100, 153, 173, 175
Women's Skateboard Network (WSN), 59, 100-01, 134-35, 172-73, 177, 189-90, 232,
Womxn Skateboard History (archive), 3, 6, 10-11, 102, 112, 117, 119-20, 124, 139-40, 148, 165, 167, 198, 203, 245, 251, 253, 298-300, 306, 315
@womxnsk8history, 197, 232
Wong, Lauri Kuulei, *95*, 98-103, 113-17, 123, 133, 173

Woodstock '99, 283
Woody, Chelsea, 130-31
Woolf, Virginia, 227
Woozy, Kim, 56, 284
Worland, Wig, 192, 199
World Cup Skateboarding, 14, 85, 126, 255, 257, 259-60
World Health Organization, 275
World Industries, 47, 127, 175
World Skate Games, 256
World Skateboarding Association, 146, 174
World Slalom Championships, 170
Wosinska, Magdalena, 112-13, 152
Wright, Trish, 152

X Games, 1, 85-86, 213, 311
XSTV Productions Limited, 139

YAKK (zine), 150
Yarbrough, Gail, 80
Yauger Skatepark, 283

Zanna, 314-15
Zapata, KZ, *12*, 17-26, *27*, 34-35, 37, 39-41, 68, 98, 101, 123, 132, 153, 164, 226, 301
Zaremba, Leigh, *69*, 73-74, 91, 123
Zelnik, Thalia, 243-44
Zephyr Skateboards, 143
Zephyr Skate Team, 144
Zilda Natel Skatepark, 110
Zoo York, 47

NATALIE PORTER is the founder of @womxnsk8history on Instagram and the online archive Womxn Skateboard History. She began skateboarding in 1995, wrote the thesis paper "Female Skateboarders and Their Negotiation of Space and Identity" in 2003, and became a librarian with the Vancouver Public Library in 2009. Natalie is a subject expert for the Smithsonian Museum's skateboarding advisory board and writes a column for *Closer Skateboarding* magazine. She lives in Powell River with her husband on the traditional territory of the Tla'amin Nation and works for the British Columbia Library Association.

Entertainment. Writing. Culture. ─────────

ECW is a proudly independent, Canadian-owned book publisher. We know great writing can improve people's lives, and we're passionate about sharing original, exciting, and insightful writing across genres.

─────────────────── **Thanks for reading along!**

We want our books not just to sustain our imaginations, but to help construct a healthier, more just world, and so we've become a certified B Corporation, meaning we meet a high standard of social and environmental responsibility — and we're going to keep aiming higher. We believe books can drive change, but the way we make them can too.

Being a B Corp means that the act of publishing this book should be a force for good — for the planet, for our communities, and for the people that worked to make this book. For example, everyone who worked on this book was paid at least a living wage. You can learn more at the Ontario Living Wage Network.

This book is also available as a Global Certified Accessible™ (GCA) ebook. ECW Press's ebooks are screen reader friendly and are built to meet the needs of those who are unable to read standard print due to blindness, low vision, dyslexia, or a physical disability.

This book is printed on FSC®-certified paper. It contains recycled materials, and other controlled sources, is processed chlorine free, and is manufactured using biogas energy.

ECW's office is situated on land that was the traditional territory of many nations, including the Wendat, the Anishinaabeg, Haudenosaunee, Chippewa, Métis, and current treaty holders the Mississaugas of the Credit. In the 1880s, the land was developed as part of a growing community around St. Matthew's Anglican and other churches. Starting in the 1950s, our neighbourhood was transformed by immigrants fleeing the Vietnam War and Chinese Canadians dispossessed by the building of Nathan Phillips Square and the subsequent rise in real estate value in other Chinatowns. We are grateful to those who cared for the land before us and are proud to be working amidst this mix of cultures.

ecwpress.com